Imagination
and
Innovation

The Story of
Weston Woods

All rights reserved. Published by Scholastic Press, an imprint of Scholastic Inc., *Publishers since 1920*. SCHOLASTIC, SCHOLASTIC PRESS, and associated logos are trademarks and/or registered trademarks of Scholastic Inc.

A Sideshow Media Book
Editorial director: Dan Tucker
Project editor: Elizabeth B. Zechella
Book design by Language Arts

Library of Congress Cataloging-in-Publication Data

Cech, John.
 Imagination and innovation : the story of Weston Woods / John Cech ; with a foreword by Maurice Sendak.
— 1st ed.
   p. cm.
 ISBN-13: 978-0-545-08922-7/ ISBN-10: 0-545-08922-0
 1. Weston Woods Studios—History. 2. Schindel, Morton. 3. Motion picture producers and directors—United States—Biography. 4. Children's literature, American—Film and video adaptations. 5. Animated films—United States—History and criticism. 6. Children's films—United States—History and criticism. I. Title.
 NC1766.U52W473 2009
 791.4302'32092—dc22
 [B]
                          2009014207

10 9 8 7 6 5 4 3 2 1   09 10 11 12 13

Printed in China
First edition, December 2009
Scholastic editor: Andrea Davis Pinkney
Scholastic art director: Elizabeth B. Parisi

Imagination and Innovation

The Story of Weston Woods

by John Cech

Foreword by Maurice Sendak

Scholastic Press / New York

For Francelia Butler,
An invaluable mentor, bold innovator, creative spirit, and dear friend,
who introduced me to Mort Schindel and Weston Woods,
and to the domains of childhood
as a field of study, a state of mind,
and a way of life
—JC

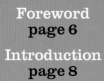

Foreword
Into the Woods

For me, Mort Schindel represents a part of the children's book world that we've lost now—with his unique kind of homemade collaboration that involved a team of writers, artists, and filmmakers working closely together. Mort was inventing something that hadn't existed before, carefully putting picture books on film, and he was of a particular time of exhilarating, bold publishing that was the beginning of the golden age of children's books in America right after, or soon after, World War II. Literally going into the woods at Weston Woods and making movies and talking about books was great fun, and it seemed like the most natural thing to do. The assumption was that it would always be this way—and it was that way for three decades.

I can't remember the actual event of meeting Mort—but I do remember liking him right away. And that was also true for the people I published with, the artists growing up around me and the editors with whom we worked. Weston Woods was a thriving world that had nothing to do with the bottom line. In fact, we never even thought of such things. And Mort was emblematic of the energy, excitement, and spirit of that period—a great contributor and a great man.

Where the Wild Things Are was my first animated film with Weston Woods and with Mort and Gene Deitch. That project was difficult because resources were limited. I also gave Mort and Gene a book that is unmovable. The big problem was that the animals in the book are crosshatched, and to make a work like that move on film and keep the integrity of the crosshatching is impossible.

But Gene came up with a good idea: a montage effect of the animals moving. It's not the way I would have imagined the wild things moving if we could have done

Maurice Sendak (left), Morton Schindel, and friends, ca. late 1960s.

it, technically, but we couldn't. Despite these impossibilities, Weston Woods did an exceptional job and I know just how hard and long they labored to make a film that was true to the book.

From the beginning, Weston Woods was an amazingly ingenious idea for bringing together the isolated world of children's books with the more mainstream media of television and movies. Not only were you able to have your book and see it on the screen at the same time, but the films, in fact, brought you back to the book. More important, the films provided a whole new way of seeing while still preserving the integrity of the printed page. In the end, it was an exploration and an emancipation of the picture book itself, done so beautifully that the result wasn't ever hokey or compromised. Mort was as serious as everybody else in those days about how this should be done and about being sure to truly honor the book. He bowed to the book. And as his work proves, he felt that way whether it was a filmstrip or an animated film.

It was nirvana in Weston Woods—there was such great freedom. Looking back on it, you can hardly believe it existed. We did books and films just the way we wanted to do them, and nobody said, "Oh, who's going to buy that?" or "Where is that going to go on the shelf in the bookstore?" Weston Woods was a flourishing, happy world, and I was one of the lucky ones who was there.

Maurice Sendak

Whose Woods These Are...

Morton Schindel, ca. 1960s

Conversations with Mort Schindel, the founder and guiding spirit of Weston Woods, are like a proverbial walk in the forest; one never quite knows where the walk or the talk will lead. This element of surprise is part of the pleasure of gathering information about the man and the studio. Schindel generally likes to meet his visitors midmorning in his office on the twenty-two-acre grounds of the former Weston Woods Studios complex. (The studio itself was moved in 1996 from Weston, Connecticut, to neighboring Westport, and then again in 2001 to Norwalk.) Visitors turn in from the rural Newtown Turnpike into an idyllic, secluded grove, with timber houses and a pond set in a gentle indentation of land surrounded by birches, maples, and oaks. Just visible beyond the pond is the former main office of the studio, a modern split-level building that looks like it could be at home in a suburban setting. Behind the office and a little up the hill sits an older, shingled house called the library. This building had once been a private residence and has been used for years to store many of Weston Woods' archives and to provide guest accommodations for visitors to the studio. During the 1990s, for example, Robert McCloskey—the author and illustrator of such classics as *Lentil* (1940), *Make Way for Ducklings* (1941), the Homer Price stories (1943), and *Blueberries for Sal* (1948)—was often in residence here.

On the opposite side of this peaceful property stands the studio, where many of the Weston Woods films were made, and the gallery, in which visiting groups of schoolchildren and librarians would receive short but engrossing talks about the animation process and view examples of these techniques drawn from Weston Woods films. Nestled next to the pond is the main house, where Schindel lives, and across the gravel driveway from this is the lodge, which houses Schindel's office. This log cabin

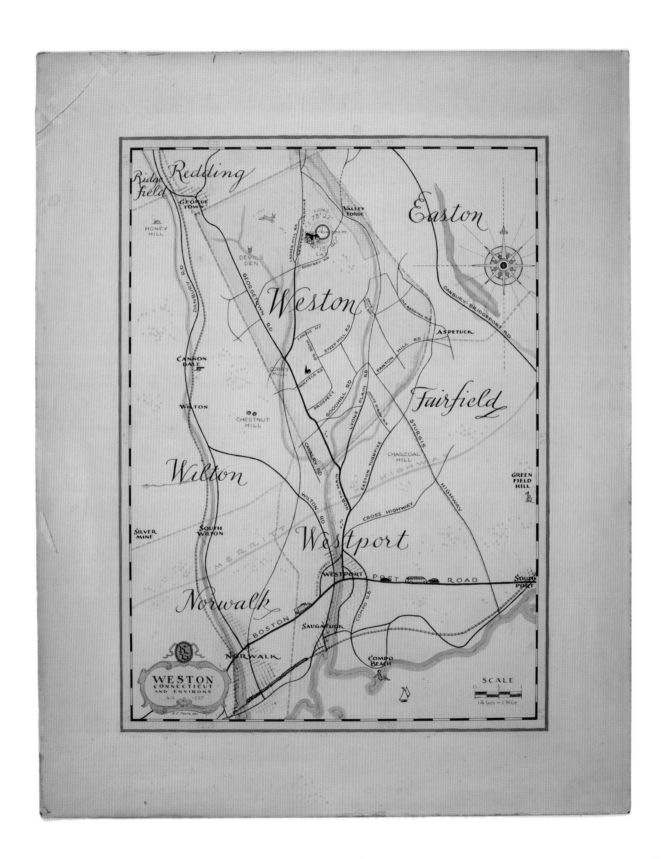

Top: Schindel in the garden behind the main house, ca. 1980s.

Right: Entrance to the main house.

Opposite: In 1950, when artist Karl Godwin sold Schindel the land that gave Weston Woods Studios its name, he presented this 1937 map of the area, demarcating the site of the property in red.

structure—with its mammoth stone fireplace, vaulted ceiling, and chinked, chestnut timbers—would fit in perfectly in the Montana mountains or the Swiss Alps. Like the rustic rooms of the main house, which for over four decades served as a central meeting place for Weston Woods functions, the lodge is overflowing with mementos of the studio's film projects and reflects Schindel's collecting passions. In both places, one finds unusual antique photographic and musical devices, rescued props and objects from Weston Woods films (like a genuine red metal toy steam shovel from the pages of *Mike Mulligan and His Steam Shovel* [1939, 1956 film]), numerous framed commendations and awards, and original art from the authors and illustrators whose works have been transformed into films. Inside the lodge, a cinnamon-colored bear with a missing overall button, a costume for the actor who played the main character in the live-action film *Corduroy* (1968, 1984 film), relaxes in an easy chair, opposite a glass-covered model of Peter, Ezra Jack Keats's little boy, from the film *Whistle for Willie* (1964, 1965 film). Nearby sits a large, blue, stuffed Wild Thing from Maurice Sendak's *Where the Wild Things Are* (1963, 1975 and 1988 film), which Weston Woods made into one of the studio's most ambitious and successful fully animated films. An antique wooden box—a viewer for stereographic photos from the end of the nineteenth

One of the galleries at Weston Woods used for workshops and school visits. Displays include video-viewing stations and examples of animation cels, props, and other artwork from the studio's films.

century—stands in the bay window, shedding a rainbow of light from its crystal turning knob. And in another corner, one's eye is drawn to the enormous sound horn of an Edison wax cylinder phonograph, still in good working order.

On a typical day, Schindel may have just received a new copy of *Voyage to the Bunny Planet* by Rosemary Wells (1992, 2008 film) or a reformatted version of *Diary of a Worm* (2003, 2004 film) by Doreen Cronin. "Did I ever tell you about the time that I met Einstein?" he might ask. And then for an hour, in softly pitched, perfectly shaped, and articulated sentences—with long ellipses while he answers the phone or speaks with a delivery person, or the general handyman for the Weston Woods property, and then resumes his narrative at exactly the place where he left off—he tells the story about his encounters with the renowned physicist.

"But it actually wasn't the first time I met Einstein," Schindel may well continue, as the morning moves into the afternoon, with more deliveries arriving and more directorial decisions needing to be made. Schindel again returns seamlessly to his recollection. "I first saw Einstein on Saranac Lake in New York years before. We met at the dock where we kept our boats. He had a sailboat that he used to go out on alone, and I had a little motorboat. We never actually talked, just nodded to each other."

The mutual presence of Schindel and Einstein at Saranac Lake at this time—not long before the atomic bombs were dropped on Japan—is woven into the larger biographical fabric of Schindel's life. In his twenties, he had been recovering from tuberculosis at the lake, a well-known resort in the mountains of upstate New York. This period of convalescence turned out to be a formative time in his life, when he remembers experiencing literature and language, powerfully, for the first time. And the experience would turn the course of his life in a new direction.

Schindel leads the listener on synchronistic rambles through biography and history that have crossed his life—like the songlines of ancient Aboriginal culture in Australia that Bruce Chatwin has described in his book *The Songlines*—those intersections of forces and movements, myths and facts, migrations and rituals that delineate the life of a tribe as well as those of its individual members. Chance meetings would be of enormous consequence later in Schindel's life. A distant cousin, Arthur Kleiner, whom Schindel's father helped to relocate to America before the Holocaust, would become one of the first composers of music for the films that Schindel would make when he launched Weston Woods in the mid-1950s. Even the location where Schindel chose to set down roots as an artist—Weston, Connecticut—was not, in his story of things, a pure accident. Weston had long been, and continues to be, a refuge for artists, eccentrics, and free spirits who still are following their own impromptu bliss in the woods above pricey and more densely settled Westport. Some of these "outlivers" ran cottage industries like Weston Woods, which, at its peak, had more than forty full- and part-time employees.

Schindel has often maintained that his success in life was largely attributable to what he calls "tough luck."[1] Like the young man in "The Magic Horse," a famous Chinese fable that tells the story of a young man who falls while riding a wild horse and, thus, is spared from the carnage of war because of a broken leg, Schindel, too, was absolved from going to war (and from following in his father's ill-fated footsteps in the department store business) because of a sudden change of fortune. Right out of college, Schindel contracted tuberculosis. In hindsight, he claims to have been in the right place at the right time. His illness led him to pick up a camera to make films, and this, in turn, led him to become the first person to pursue a graduate degree from Columbia University's Teachers College with the view to becoming a producer of educational films. Partly as a result of his degree, the State Department of the United States offered Schindel a position in postwar Turkey to make educational films for distribution in rural regions of that country. Schindel returned home, and following numerous intuitive hunches and considerable experimentation, he had a group of seven of his own

Schindel in one of the galleries at Weston Woods, surrounded by the "stars" of his studio's films.

movies ready and waiting for distribution in 1956 when, as fate would have it, the producer of the new *Captain Kangaroo* television show came to call. Its programming executives were in a pinch for films because the *Tom Terrific* cartoons they were planning to run were late in arriving. Though Schindel thought he might have reached an impasse with his films, another door was in the process of opening.

But as the Oscar-winning animator Gene Deitch, Schindel's longtime friend and collaborator, would observe in his online book, *How to Succeed in Animation* (2001), "Everyone, at one time or another, happens upon an opportunity. The vital difference occurs in how a person perceives the opportunity, and how he or she reacts to it, grabs it, and runs with it. Many things seem to come out of the blue, a pure chance of being in the right place just as a door opens. But without preparation for that chance event, you will not be the one who will be beckoned inside."[2]

Yet having gone through the door doesn't mean that every problem is solved or every difficulty overcome. Other factors distinctly come into play, including the ability of the imagination to find vital, innovative ways to transform problems into potential solutions. In his book *The Power of Form: A Psychoanalytic Approach to Aesthetic Form* (1980), Gilbert J. Rose, Schindel's psychoanalyst in the 1950s, gives a brief case study of a certain artist whom Schindel, in conversation, has identified as himself. Through Rose's analysis, Schindel recognized that "his pattern in life had always been to get into trouble and work his way out."[3] The Romantic poet John Keats saw this kind of creative and psychological turmoil as a state of "negative capability," in which the artist finds himself struggling through periods of intense uncertainty and doubt, coping with the mysteries and vagaries of his work without needing to explain away or rationalize his creative process or the results that it was achieving.[4] He simply gave himself over to the work.

In conversations with Schindel, certain themes emerge, threads of personal narrative that are in keeping with this sense of crisis and resolution, and these themes have become hallmarks, undercurrents in so much of Schindel's own life and the life of the studio he built. The first of these has to do with the imagination and its ability to envision possibilities where none had existed before. The second is to find the innovative means to bring these visions and new, unproven ideas into reality. Woven into both of these are elements of timing, luck, preparation, and, of course, hard work.

For Weston Woods, the result of this process has led to a truly remarkable, increasingly rare, and unexpected thing—a film studio devoted to making quality films for children through a process that is not driven primarily by profit or wholly by commercial motives. Rather, the motivating factors and values have been aesthetic, intellectual, and cultural. As the evolving media for children, especially film, television, and recordings, were becoming more mainstream and commercial (see, for example, the growth of Disney or Nickelodeon), Weston Woods worked from very different starting premises, took smaller steps, moved at a slower pace, and ultimately reached its own conclusions. While Disney was building an increasingly global and widely diversified entertainment empire, Weston Woods was quietly creating a body of work for young people that would use the emerging media of film and television for one specific purpose: to bring great literature into the lives of millions of children around the world. As the Disney studios and other entertainment conglomerates built mass-market audiences through highly visible advertising campaigns that successfully branded their products, Weston Woods, on the other hand, worked personally, without a sales force and, initially, without even a catalog of its products, to build a customer base of librarians and educators who were dedicated advocates of introducing children to quality, book-based experiences.

But most important, when large corporate entertainment giants were intent on producing films and spin-offs that they could tailor to their purposes, and essentially own, Weston Woods' goal from the outset was to make works based on well-known children's books that would preserve the character of the original stories and, ultimately, send its audiences back, or for the first time, to the books themselves. Disney, by contrast, was interested in ownership and thus in the strict control and exploitation of its entertainment properties. In the Winnie the Pooh series, for example, Disney felt free to change these works to suit the studio's ends, to make a distinctly Disney version of an already well-loved story. The chief concern of Weston Woods lay in enriching and complementing the experience of the original picture books that provided the films with their stories, but the films did not fundamentally change these narratives.

Weston Woods was, and remains unique, for its purposeful intention to work small rather than large; to preserve the artistic integrity of the originals rather than to appropriate and alter the works; and, essentially, to create a space in the cultural landscape in which one could find the closest equivalent that we have to an "art film" studio for children. This is a quirky, unexpected, improbable occurrence—a refreshingly innovative result of Weston Woods' equally quirky, unexpected, improbable history. As Paul Gagne, one of the guiding artistic presences at the studio for more than thirty years, explains, it's a "miracle" that Weston Woods has survived and continues to thrive.[5] This miracle was helped, as we shall see, by a steady willingness to imagine possibilities where none existed and to rely, often unknowingly, on innovation to open the doors for the miracles to enter.

Chapter 1

Snapshot of a Studio

Do good work and people will beat a path to your door. —Louis Bamberger

The Weston Woods Studios in Norwalk, Connecticut, are located in a nondescript industrial building. Only a small awning over the main door announces the presence of America's first studio devoted entirely to films for children. But once inside the building, it opens into an attractive, welcoming space, with bright offices, generous meeting and work areas, and state-of-the-art sound and editing studios. And what is created inside this modest building by its friendly, talented production team is anything but ordinary. The walls are a gallery of posters, pictures, and other visual reminders of Weston Woods' efforts and of the awards the company has received. On any given day, the small, permanent staff of Weston Woods are at work on a handful of the studio's signature short films based on outstanding picture books for children. Each year the company releases more than a dozen new films, according to its vice president and general manager, Linda Lee, along with fresh productions in more current media. An example is a music compilation like *Books Sing!*—a CD music sampler from the company's film soundtracks that includes traditional songs like "The Fox Went Out on a Chilly Night" alongside contemporary works like Mary Chapin Carpenter's interpretation of Rosemary Wells's lyrics for "Gonna Read to My Bunny."

Maurice Sendak's monsters watch over the entrance to the Weston Woods Studios in Norwalk.

The subjects of Weston Woods films are as wide-ranging, unusual, and diverse as any year's harvest of picture books. The studio has produced Jean Fritz's *Where Do You Think You Are Going, Christopher Columbus?* (1980, 1991 film), a biography of the renowned explorer; *I Lost My Bear* (1998, 2004 film) by Jules Feiffer, a touching story concerning the search for a beloved stuffed animal; and also Mordicai Gerstein's Caldecott Award–winning book, *The Man Who Walked Between the Towers* (2003, 2005 film), about the high-wire performer who undertook the spectacular feat of walking

Top: Actor James Earl Jones (left), with Paul Gagne, director of production, rehearses the narration of Verna Aardema's *Who's in Rabbit's House*, 1994. Jones also narrated Lane Smith's *John, Paul, George, and Ben.*

Bottom: Sound designer Steve Syarto prepares the mix for a new production in one of the studio's digital sound rooms.

between New York City's Twin Towers. In the fall of 2007 the studio was putting the finishing touches on *My Senator and Me: A Dog's-Eye View of Washington, D.C.,* by Edward M. Kennedy, about the legislative process told through the eyes of the senator's Portuguese water dog, Splash; and Lane Smith's take on the childhoods of four of America's founding fathers, *John, Paul, George, and Ben* (2006, 2007 film), narrated by James Earl Jones, which gives a whole new, Beatlesesque spin to these exemplary young lives. The studio was fine-tuning for future release the final version of Wells's collection of interlinked stories, *Voyage to the Bunny Planet* (1992, 2008 film) and also working on the sound for the adaptation of Doreen Cronin's *Dooby Dooby Moo* (2006, 2007 film), one of her recent stories about an immensely talented, over-the-top barnyard of animals. The singer Randy Travis provided the narration for this film, but if you happened to have been in the studio on the day that they were looking for other voices to add to the crowd sounds, you might have been enlisted in the project to cheer and mumble, as this author was. You might be strolling down Main Street in Norwalk and swear that you just saw Meryl Streep, Cyndi Lauper, Billy Dee Williams, Zach Braff, Nikki Giovanni, or John Lithgow in the Weston Woods parking lot; all of their voice talents have been heard on Weston Woods films.

Weston Woods has adapted many works by modern masters of the picture book, such as Marcia Brown, Barbara Cooney, Gail E. Haley, Crockett Johnson, Leo Lionni, James Marshall, Mercer Mayer, Gerald McDermott, Tomi Ungerer, Lynd Ward, and Kurt Wiese (to name just a few), as well as contemporary picture-book creators like Kevin Henkes, Mary Hoffman, Jerry Pinkney, Chris Raschka, Peggy Rathman, Jon Scieszka, Simms Taback, Wells, Mo Willems, Ed Young, and Paul O. Zelinsky. In addition, the picture book inspired Weston Woods to produce biographies of authors, as seen in *Mr. Shepard and Mr. Milne* (1973), *Tomi Ungerer: Storyteller* (1982), and *Beatrix Potter: Artist, Storyteller and Countrywoman* (1993), educational documentaries like *The Lively Art of Picture Books* (1964), *Gene Deitch: The Picture Book Animated* (1977), and experimental films, such as the child-created *Alexander and the Car with the Missing Headlight* (1967) and the American/Russian animation project *Here Comes the Cat!* (1989, 1992 film). From its earliest projects, Weston Woods has been dedicated to the celebration of racial, ethnic, and cultural diversity and committed to the preservation of the ancient art of storytelling. And from the beginning, the studio has been a pioneer in bringing highly regarded books for children to the screen, in a way that returns children and their parents to the literature itself, rather than off to the toy store in search of a commercial tie-in to the movie version of a book.

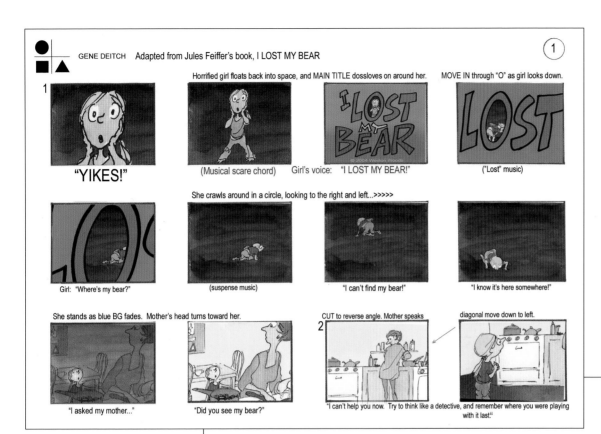

GENE DEITCH   Adapted from Jules Feiffer's book, I LOST MY BEAR

1

"YIKES!"

Horrified girl floats back into space, and MAIN TITLE dossloves on around her.

(Musical scare chord)   Girl's voice: "I LOST MY BEAR!"

MOVE IN through "O" as girl looks down.

("Lost" music)

She crawls around in a circle, looking to the right and left...>>>>>

Girl: "Where's my bear?"

(suspense music)

"I can't find my bear!"

"I know it's here somewhere!"

She stands as blue BG fades. Mother's head turns toward her.

"I asked my mother..."

"Did you see my bear?"

CUT to reverse angle. Mother speaks

2

diagonal move down to left.

"I can't help you now. Try to think like a detective, and remember where you were playing with it last."

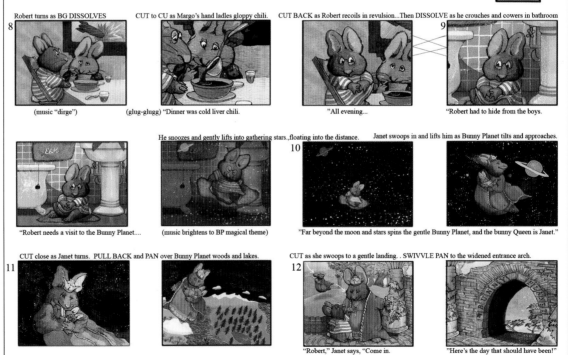

Robert turns as BG DISSOLVES

8

(music "dirge")

CUT to CU as Margo's hand ladles gloppy chili.

(glug-glugg) "Dinner was cold liver chili.

CUT BACK as Robert recoils in revulsion...Then DISSOLVE as he crouches and cowers in bathroom

9

"All evening...

"Robert had to hide from the boys.

He snoozes and gently lifts into gathering stars.,floating into the distance.

"Robert needs a visit to the Bunny Planet....

(music brightens to BP magical theme)

Janet swoops in and lifts him as Bunny Planet tilts and approaches.

10

"Far beyond the moon and stars spins the gentle Bunny Planet, and the bunny Queen is Janet."

CUT close as Janet turns. PULL BACK and PAN over Bunny Planet woods and lakes.

11

CUT as she swoops to a gentle landing. . SWIVVLE PAN to the widened entrance arch.

12

"Robert," Janet says, "Come in.

"Here's the day that should have been!"

Top: Animators create storyboards as a visual guide to the scenes of each film. This storyboard page for Jules Feiffer's *I Lost My Bear* includes Gene Deitch's directions for animating the title of the film.

Bottom: Deitch's storyboard for Rosemary Wells's *Voyage to the Bunny Planet.*

Top: The studio adapts books, such as William Steig's *Doctor De Soto*, into a range of media formats, including video and audiocassette tapes, 16-mm film reels, and filmstrips. Additionally, the studio provides educational materials to accompany the films.

Bottom: A sample of recent Weston Woods products, such as a CD music sampler, DVDs, and a recording of Caldecott and Newbury Awards acceptance speeches. To display these products, Schindel invented a hanging plastic bag, named the Monaco bag.

The legacy of Weston Woods is a vital one that began in the 1950s when the company's films were aired on television programs like *Captain Kangaroo.* Indeed, most adults of a certain age remember growing up with the film versions of such familiar books as Robert McCloskey's *Make Way for Ducklings* (1941, 1955 film), James Daugherty's *Andy and the Lion* (1938, 1955 film), and Virginia Lee Burton's *Mike Mulligan and His Steam Shovel* (1939, 1956 film), which were among the first group of Weston Woods films shown on television and which were in continual circulation on *Captain Kangaroo* well into the 1970s. The actual payment for airing these films was extremely modest (three hundred dollars for a first-time showing, one hundred fifty dollars for each rerun). With the exception of some highly visible names like Disney, the children's media market was not particularly lucrative nor its contributors especially well paid. But the exposure that Weston Woods received from its association with a national program like *Captain Kangaroo* was enormous and lasting, even though the films were aired without a credit line for the studio. Still, the buzz had begun, and because of the positive reception of these early efforts, Weston Woods chose to continue to focus on making quality films based on quality books.

From these first films, which were not animated, Weston Woods went on to build an expanding catalog of products—from animated and live-action motion pictures to audio recordings. The studio has experimented with or ventured into productions using nearly every kind of medium, from 16-mm and 35-mm movies to laser discs, from vinyl recordings to videotape, and from audiocassettes to CD-ROMs and DVDs. In fact, a good number of titles exist simultaneously in print and in a number of these formats, whether old-school (film and audiotape) or modern (web-based). Its recent series of titles in the Playaway format, for example, consists of a small compact-listening device with a pre-loaded soundtrack.

The Weston Woods catalog has grown to more than four hundred titles, with each year bringing the release of fourteen new titles, as well as the re-release of older titles in new formats (a process known in the media and advertising world as "repurposing"). It's a

③

. . . on a rope he tied between two trees.

(truck out)

cut

He looked not at the towers but a the space between them and thought,
what a wonderful place to stretch a rope;
a wire on which to walk.

cut

cut

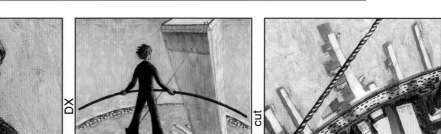

cut

cut

DX

V.O: Once the idea came to him he knew he had to do it !
If he saw three balls, he had to juggle.
If he saw two towers, he had to walk !   That's how he was.

In these storyboard pages, animator Michael Sporn illustrates his approach to the animation of Mordicai Gerstein's *The Man Who Walked Between the Towers*. Vertiginous close-ups, dissolves, and cuts heighten the tension in Gerstein's interpretation of Philippe Petit's fabled walk between the towers of the World Trade Center in 1974.

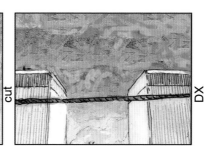

⑫

(Wind blows)   Dissolve

DX

cut

V.O: Philippe put on his black shirt and tights. He picked up his
twenty-eight-foot balancing pole.
All his life he had worked to be here; to do this.

As the rising sun lit up the towers . . .

cut

. . . out he stepped onto the wire.

V.O: Out to the very middle he walked . . .

(Camera trucks out quickly at first . . . then slowly)

One of the latest incarnations in the evolution of the media formats the studio uses is the Playaway® series, a preloaded MP3 audio recording of a book's content.

clever strategy for updating and re-presenting existing titles, whether individually or as part of compilations that are more popular for the family DVD and rental markets. Often this process is accompanied by new soundtracks and narrative voices, and it sometimes involves the photographing of original artwork. Today the company is updating its titles to be compatible with iTunes and other digital formats. In some respects, these innovations have been in response to technologically savvy children and parents, and also to the growing "wired" audience that is always in search of the latest electronic materials.

Regardless of the new packaging and recycling, the astonishing range and quality of Weston Woods films have remained unchanged. In this exceptional body of work, you'll find Wanda Gág's *Millions of Cats* (1928, 1955 film), which some historians feel opened the creative pathway for the emergence of the distinctly American picture book of the twentieth century. Here, too, you'll find Maurice Sendak's masterpiece *Where the Wild Things Are*, which won the Caldecott Award in 1964. The book was adapted by Weston Woods in 1975, after more than five years of work and the development of an innovative animation technique. The wry, sly books of William Steig—such as *Brave Irene* (1986, 1989 film) and *Sylvester and the Magic Pebble* (1969, 1993 film)—became Weston Woods films well before Steig became a household name as the literary creator behind the Shrek franchise. The subtle collages of *The Snowy Day* (1962, 1964 film) and other books by Ezra Jack Keats have become quietly dazzling Weston Woods movies and are among the studio's first fully animated films and its most sublime. The memorable drawings of Robert McCloskey have their solid, sturdy home in the studio's versions of *Make Way for Ducklings, Lentil* (1940, 1956 film), and *Blueberries for Sal* (1948, 1967 film). The moving story *Zlateh the Goat* (1966, 1973 film) by Nobel Prize–winning author Isaac Bashevis Singer was the subject of a hauntingly beautiful live-action film shot in the Czech countryside.

In the six decades that Weston Woods has been creating films, individual producers on the staff, and the studio as a whole, have received nearly every possible recognition for excellence in children's media production. Paul Gagne, the company's director of production, is the recipient of multiple Andrew Carnegie Medals for Excellence in Children's Video from the American Library Association for his part in the Weston Woods adaptations of Henkes's *Owen* (1993, 1995 film), Judy Sierra's *Antarctic Antics* (1998, 2000 film), Cronin's *Giggle, Giggle, Quack* (2002, 2003 film), and Willems's *Knuffle Bunny* (2004, 2006 film). Gagne has shared a number of these awards with one of Weston Woods' other producers, Melissa Reilly, including Carnegie Medals for their film versions of Peter Reynolds's *The Dot* (2003, 2004 film) and Christine King Farris's

March On! (2008, 2008 film). In 1984 Weston Woods was nominated for an Academy Award for Best Animated Short Film for William Steig's *Doctor De Soto* (1982, 1984 film), and in 2005 it was on a short list for potential Oscar nominations for its production of *The Man Who Walked Between the Towers.*

Weston Woods has been the recipient of major recognition from the children's media community—including the studio's induction, in 1986, into the Children's Television Hall of Fame, along with *Mr. Rogers* and The Children's Television Workshop (*Sesame Street*). Mort Schindel has also been honored for his contributions to children's media with such accolades as the Award of St. Mark from the Venice Film Festival (1968), the Regina Medal (1979), one of the first Eric Carle Honor Awards in 2006, and in 2007, a lifetime achievement award from the Connecticut Center for the Book for the role that Weston Woods has played in returning children to reading. When one mentions to Mort Schindel the growing list of awards that he and the studio have received, he casually demurs, pointing out that the field was initially and, to some extent, still remains so small that Weston Woods couldn't help but win so many prizes. "Hardly anyone was doing what we were doing," he notes, "and so we had the field to ourselves. I guess they had to pin the ribbons on us."[1] That joking answer is in keeping with Schindel's inherent modesty about what the studio has been able to accomplish, and it underscores the vision he has brought to the enterprise from its inception. Though it is hardly true today that Weston Woods is alone in the highly competitive market of children's media (whole commercial networks are now dedicated to children's television programming, and PBS has aggressively devoted a good deal of its time and resources to developing new animated and live-action programs for children), these commercial challenges have forced the studio to keep finding innovative ways to reach its ever-expanding audiences.

Looking back on the history of Weston Woods, one is led to wonder how this remarkable journey could have taken place. With its limited resources, it seems altogether improbable that Weston Woods would become one of the most respected leaders in the production of quality films for children and, in fact, a pioneer in the field of "edutainment" (a word first coined by Schindel to describe the work of the studio). A studio doesn't simply appear one morning like the village Brigadoon, or the magic pebble that Sylvester, the main character in Steig's picture book, accidentally finds. But the story is no less compelling for being real. It's full of its own serendipities and travails; its own dramas and struggles; its own string of surprising occurrences and discoveries; its own exciting passage from a run-down log cabin in the midst of a boggy Connecticut forest to a world-class presence in the global media market.

Chapter 2

The Luck in "Tough Luck"

I had to do my own thing…even if I had to start something new to be the head of.

—Mort Schindel

In his acceptance speech for the Distinguished Alumni Award from Columbia University Teachers College in the summer of 1994, Mort Schindel, as has been noted earlier, attributed whatever good fortune he had achieved to "tough luck." By this Schindel clearly did not mean to refer, even ironically, to the "luck" of having had a privileged childhood in an upper middle-class family in New Jersey in the 1920s. His father, Abraham Schindel, had been the successful and beloved manager of the most prominent department store in the state of New Jersey, Bamberger's. The Schindels had a lovely home in Orange as well as a summer house on the Jersey shore. His father and mother, Ruth Schindel, were responsible pillars of the community—active leaders in their temple, generous with their time and donations outside the home, civic-minded in their social activities. The Schindel children—Robert, the eldest; Mort, nicknamed "Mutt"; Louis, "the Thinker"; and Elaine, the youngest—were cared for by a uniformed nanny and attended private schools, to which they were driven by a chauffeur. They rode horses, took sleigh rides, and were the proud owners of the latest inventions for childhood amusement, like scooter bikes. They even went to a birthday luncheon in 1923 for the silent film child star Jackie Coogan. Ruth Schindel had wanted her children to become a string quartet, but she soon discovered that Mort had little aptitude for the violin. The closest the children came to a musical ensemble was a photograph taken with their mother around the family's piano. On weekends the children would go to Bamberger's with their father, and while he worked, they had their run of the store, including the toy department. Schindel's impression of Louis Bamberger, the department store magnate and frequent visitor to the Schindel home, was that of a kindly uncle, "a simple, good-hearted, modest little man who

Morton Schindel (seated, fourth from left) at a birthday luncheon for the child film star Jackie Coogan (seated, far right), ca. 1923.

The Schindel family chamber ensemble (from left): Robert, Elaine, Ruth, Louis, and Morton playing the violin, ca. 1930s.

happened to become very fortunate." But Bamberger also offered advice to Schindel that he never forgot. "Do good work," Bamberger told Schindel, "and people will beat a path to your door."[1]

Yet there was something "tough" about the luck of this idyllic childhood. Schindel and his siblings seldom saw their father, who was constantly engaged with work. Their mother, too, was occupied with her many social commitments, like running the volunteer service for one of the area's largest hospitals. Indeed, Schindel says he always remembers his mother with her ear to the telephone receiver, making one of her endless daily calls. Though they were loving parents, the Schindels were also distant, emotionally reserved, and not particularly involved in their children's lives. As an adult, Schindel once remembered, poignantly, the sense of abandonment he felt as a toddler seeing his parents back out of the driveway in their car to go on a vacation—perhaps the one that was recorded in an article in the local newspaper in which they traveled to Egypt and the Middle East and were photographed riding a camel—while he and his siblings were left behind with their grandmother and a nanny. In fact, tellingly, Schindel says his parents did not introduce him to books as a child, except on those rare occasions when his father might read an installment of one of Howard R. Garis's Uncle Wiggily stories, which were syndicated in the daily newspaper. This absence of any meaningful contact with literature during childhood would make Schindel's discovery of it as an adult a particularly powerful experience.

"Tough luck," for Schindel, meant being dismissed in high school as someone without any distinctive language skills and thus destined for a career doing something with numbers. After high school, Schindel went to the University of Pennsylvania's Wharton School to study for an undergraduate degree in economics. His parents assumed, Schindel recalls, that he would follow in his father's footsteps and go into some aspect of the retail business—the same line of work that ultimately claimed the life of his father, who collapsed of a heart attack in December 1939 in an aisle of the department store he was managing at the time. (When Bamberger's was bought by Macy's years earlier, Schindel's father became one of the key managers for the Kresge department store, founded by Sebastian Kresge.) Still, despite the uncertainties of the retail business, after graduating from college and taking a grand, if brief, tour of Europe, Schindel was prepared to settle down and do just as his father had done: work tirelessly to get ahead. As was expected of him, he had even found an entry-level job and was beginning the long process of working his way up the ladder in the retail industry, when, in 1939, he found himself coughing blood

Saranac Lake in the Adirondacks became famous during the late 1800s for its "cure cottages" and sanitarium for the treatment of tuberculosis. Schindel lived in the healing environment of the lake during the early 1940s on the recommendation of his physician.

into a handkerchief on a hot, dusty July day in Manhattan, and discovered that his life had suddenly changed.

Schindel was diagnosed with tuberculosis, and in the days just before the discovery of streptomycin, an early antibiotic, there was no cure for the disease other than bed rest. He was unable to work, often depressed, and grieving the sudden loss of his father and the resulting instability of the Schindel family. But by 1941, he somehow felt well enough to embark on two major passages in his life. In that year, he married his childhood sweetheart, Ellen Bamberger, the niece of Louis Bamberger, because, like so many things in his young life, their union was expected of him—expected of them both. Mort and Ellen had known each other since childhood, and their mothers were close friends; the families assumed that the children would naturally, inevitably, get married. Schindel also felt well enough in 1941 to start his first business, ELMOR (a combination of Ellen's and Mort's names), with Charles Marti, a neighbor and a Swiss engineer, making machinery parts for the United States government as part of the war effort. Schindel used the four-thousand-dollar legacy his father had left him to launch the venture, which turned out to be a success.

But the strain of the company pushed his health to its limits again, and Schindel found himself selling his interests in the business and using the profits to move with Ellen, at the urging of his doctors, to Saranac Lake in upstate New York. Since the late-nineteenth century, the lake had been a famous cure spot for tuberculosis: Robert Louis Stevenson had stayed there to convalesce from his bouts with the disease, as had the composer Béla Bartók. Schindel's physician told him that his best chance of staying well would be if he would not work. "What am I supposed to do?" he asked. "Be an artist," the doctor replied.[2]

The "tough luck" that brought him to Saranac Lake as a young tuberculosis patient became a turning point in Schindel's life. In accepting the Regina Medal years later, he reflected on this moment, "I had never used a pen or a paintbrush in my life, and what's more, I'd never used what I now recognize as my intuition or feelings. Both my home life and the business school that I went to taught me to beware of feelings. I can still hear the professor saying, 'Use your head, man.'" Later in his Regina address, Schindel noted about this period: "Now I had a professional sanction for not going back to the department store business and being my father all over again. At the same time, of course, it behooved me to figure out some way to spend my life. The society that I came from was one that put very little value on people in creative fields."[3]

While mulling over this transformation, Schindel stayed at one of the "cure cottages" on the lake. There he made the acquaintance of Lee Eisler, an older patient, who introduced him to literature and the world of ideas—in particular, books like S. I. Hayakawa's *Language in Action* (1939), which Schindel credits with opening his eyes to the complex nature of language. Through his conversations with Eisler, they found themselves becoming interested in film. Eventually this led them to give a course using films that they borrowed through the lending library of the Museum of Modern Art. More important, Schindel began taking photographs and even made his first short film, a documentary about the locks of the rivers connecting the chain of lakes of which Saranac Lake was a part. He explored these waterways with his small motorboat. Years later, Schindel mused about his own activities when compared to that renowned member of the lake community mentioned earlier: "While Einstein was off sailing, thinking great thoughts about quantum theory, I was mostly drifting in my boat." But he was following the doctor's orders and trying to figure out how to be an artist.

Schindel had grown up using his father's home movie camera and had learned how to edit the family's home films. With World War II ending, he recalls, "people were coming out of the armed services who had some exposure to filmmaking, and they were starting businesses of their own. Many people were imbued with the idea that within five years all of education would turn to the audiovisual media. Somehow or other, the notion got to me that here was an art that was a new one...there literally were no textbooks. There was not a way to learn this whole thing except through teaching oneself."[4] And perhaps as important, this was a field in which there was little, if any, competition. It provided an artistic path that would allow him to make small movies for the educational market and to do so independently, with the least amount of deadline pressure from the studios that were beginning to open, like Coronet Instructional Films, Young American Films, Encyclopaedia Britannica, and McGraw-Hill Text Film.

Before embarking on his career of making his own films, Schindel went back to New York to try to get a job with one of these companies. He was told he had no experience, no credentials, and didn't belong in that field. He also realized that the educational film producers to whom he applied had no credentials as educators, so he decided to go back to school for a master's degree in curriculum design at Columbia University's Teachers College. He was the first person in their master's program to specialize in film production. After Teachers College, Schindel had brief jobs in this nascent educational film industry, and with one of these companies, Teaching Films, Schindel began making films in the late 1940s about curriculum-related topics— reading, science, and social studies. One of his more successful projects at the time was a filmstrip, now long vanished, about Singer sewing machines. Young American Films, which Schindel was briefly associated with, was at work on projects including a film about manners called *How Do You Do?* (1946) and the ever-popular *Why Punctuate?* (1948). On the West Coast, the prolific Sid Davis, a stand-in for and friend of the actor John Wayne, had begun making even more didactic, cautionary tales—like *Live and Learn* (1956)—whose storylines (minus their modern details) could have been lifted from the pages of a nineteenth-century illustrated magazine in which young readers were meant to be scared into correct behavior. His horrific tales about the often bloody travails of childhood, which were financed in part by Wayne, earned Davis the nickname "The King of Calamity."[5]

The main house was in disrepair and the property was an overgrown, marshy thicket when Schindel purchased Weston Woods, ca. 1950.

Schindel found, almost from the start, that this new life agreed with him: "Through sheer luck, within a couple of years after I went into the field, I became an independent film producer working alone in my living room. Once I adjusted vocationally, all of my physical problems and symptoms went away. I got to the point where I could happily work around the clock."[6] The only thing he couldn't change was the general dullness of the films that he (and everyone else) were making at the time, with their plodding plots and preachy pedagogy. And so, when luck again would have it, late in 1950, Schindel heard a public-service radio announcement that the U.S. Department of State was seeking people to work on an educational film project in Turkey as part of the Marshall Plan of Ideas, he jumped at the chance and the challenge. But things were complicated by a house.

After graduate work and living in New York City, trying to eke out a living, Schindel was determined to move with Ellen to a less stressful, more relaxing place, where he could make movies. Their search led them, in 1949, to the West Coast, where they were dazzled by Carmel Valley in California, with its nearby artists' communities. Back on the East Coast and still undecided about whether to move west, they got wind of a property in the woods of Connecticut that was cheap and close to the New York City train line. It was in a place called Weston, at the time (and since the days of King George III) a rough, unconventional part of the countryside that attracted "outlivers" of every stripe—artists, renegades, dreamers. These seekers "converged on the little town and became themselves," Christopher Plummer notes in his narration for *The Outlivers* (1987), a short documentary about Weston, which was partially filmed on the Weston Woods property.[7] Living in chicken coops and barns and tumbledown buildings of every vintage and variety, the community of Weston was certainly relaxed. Writer Ring Lardner Jr., the son of the famous journalist, would observe: "Weston is about as ideal a place for not working as I have found."[8]

But, of course, people did and do work—often quite hard—in Weston. Karl Godwin, who sold his swampy, run-down property along the unpaved Newtown Turnpike to Schindel in 1950, was a serious freelance artist, a commercial illustrator, and painter. Godwin created the portraits of famous people who were profiled in the popular *Reader's Digest* articles about "The Most Unforgettable Character I Ever Met." He had built the single-room, log-and-stone house that is now part of the main house at Weston Woods as a studio, with large windows to catch the northern light. But Godwin had another house and studio in nearby Westport, which his wife preferred to live in, so he had let the Weston house fall into ruins. When Schindel first saw it, saplings had grown through the windows; every kind of animal native to a New England swamp, including bees and snakes, had taken up residence and had to be evicted before he and Ellen could move in. Schindel's and Ellen's families both thought he was making a terrible mistake by buying the property, and family legend says that his mother-in-law wept when she saw it, saying that she couldn't imagine a daughter of hers living in a place like that.

Yet Schindel thought it would be perfect: it was certainly affordable (the astronomical prices for houses and land in Weston were still decades away); it was rural, yet close to New York City and its business opportunities; they could repair enough of the place to live in while they restored the rest; and Schindel thought he would not need much space for his film work, since he would just be editing on the premises film that had been shot elsewhere. And so, with family money, in the early spring of 1950, they began to settle into life in the Connecticut woods and into the slow process of rebuilding the main house, which Schindel sees as one of his most satisfying projects. It would take years, but like the movies he would begin creating there, "the house has been made and remade with no restrictive budgets and no demanding time schedules. Most of it is hand fashioned. There are no two rooms that even vaguely resemble one another. Still, it all fits together and is as livable as it is aesthetically pleasing."[9]

At the time, though, Schindel's work on the property and his burgeoning studio would continue in fits and starts because he was soon taken in a new direction. He

An engineer and landscape architect (both pictured) helped Schindel redesign the main house and grounds. The upper floor of the house had to be supported by beams while the land was being excavated.

Top: Two of Schindel's assistants in front of a media truck that was used to distribute films throughout Turkey when he worked for the U.S. Department of State, ca. 1953.

Bottom: The back of the media truck opened to reveal its cargo of films, film projectors, and generators to an audience of children.

was appointed to one of the positions he had applied for abroad. The Marshall Plan's educational mission in Turkey had ambitious goals of aiding in the development of the physical, social, and intellectual infrastructures of Europe in the wake of World War II. The information departments in European embassies were looking for people trained in communications to work in Turkey, setting in motion a pilot program of public-service instruction using the latest media. Schindel's assignment was to design, produce, distribute, and even screen movies in rural Turkish villages about subjects relevant to the lives of the inhabitants, like preserving freshwater supplies and raising poultry. At times, the film crew had to ford rivers by muleback in order to provide generators for villages without electricity. Schindel thought an appointment with the State Department would be a good opportunity to try something related to film that also offered him a way to compensate for the fact that he had not been able to serve during World War II. Both of Schindel's brothers had served in the Pacific, and he felt as though he had not done his part.

In many respects, Schindel's years in Turkey, from 1951 to 1953, provided him with an intensive, hands-on course in managing a large office (he had more than thirty employees); producing and distributing films; and experiencing firsthand the logistical difficulties and positive effects of bringing the unfamiliar medium of film to audiences in the Turkish countryside. Schindel's experience in Turkey served as preparation for his work in the United States, when he would bring literature to American children in previously untried ways. The obsolete railroad cars and media trucks that he made into information centers were used to transport films for screenings in remote Turkish villages and would, decades later, become "repurposed" into media-mobiles that would carry children's films and other media to remote village libraries and underprivileged neighborhoods in the United States.

By 1953, when Schindel's appointment abroad was completed, he and Ellen had had two children—Cathy, born in 1950, and Jeanie, born in 1951. (Their son, John, was born in 1955). The family was back in Weston. Although Schindel had been offered the opportunity to duplicate his successful program in Greece, he wanted to remain connected to the program in Turkey, where he hoped to significantly expand his film project into a national media program. He had applied to the Ford Foundation for funding to continue this work, and while he was waiting for word about the grant back in Connecticut, in yet another example of "tough luck," his proposal was turned down, even though the foundation had "nothing but praise for the program." Instead, another door of opportunity opened, which would send a wave of consequences rippling through the rest of his life.

Chapter 3

Launching the Ducklings

The imagination must have an address. —Isaac Bashevis Singer

It seems fitting that Weston Woods should trace its origins as a studio to Schindel living among the irrepressible sounds of real children echoing through the woods, as opposed to some idyllic solitude. The "voice" that Schindel ultimately found for his films was directly inspired by the exclamations and comments from his own children. Schindel recognized the value of his children's responses to the books he was reading to them—works that he thought, at first glance, held little promise for film adaptation. (Schindel reports that cartoons like *Tom and Jerry* and *Popeye* had initially colored his thinking regarding suitable animation material.)[1] But the books thrilled his two young children, Cathy and Jeanie, who were three and five years of age. They asked to have them read over and over again, repeating favorite lines with their father and interacting with the details of the pictures they examined while sitting in his lap. The energy and excitement that Schindel's children brought to the books became the wellspring of recognition upon which the studio was eventually launched. Schindel would later summarize the importance of this experience in *From Page to Screen* (1981), the documentary film he made in which he explained his rationale for founding Weston Woods:

> *My kids were an important part of my work in those early days.…*
> *I first became involved with picture books reading them to my*
> *daughters. The excitement and the way they noticed little details*
> *was an inspiration—the way Cathy counted Mrs. Mallard's eggs*
> *[in* Make Way for Ducklings*] every time we read the book to be*
> *sure they were all there and Jeanie dressed up like the shy little kit-*
> *ten in* Millions of Cats. *I was challenged by the idea that films*

Promotional image of Schindel and his daughters, Jeanie (left) and Cathy. While reading to his daughters, Schindel realized the importance of picture books to children, ca. mid-1950s.

might open up these wonderful books for children all over the world—for kids who might not have the chance to see them on the printed page. And I hoped the age-old tradition of storytelling could be preserved and transferred to the audiovisual media.[2]

Schindel was aware of the fact that virtually no one in the realm of media production was paying attention to the rich vein of potential source material that could be found in picture books. The developing medium of television struck Schindel as surprisingly devoid of any substantial, imaginatively challenging works for children, and he saw an opening. As early as 1949, Schindel had come across James Daugherty's *Andy and the Lion* (1938, 1955 film); he noted that Daugherty called the book, on its opening page, "a tale of kindness remembered and the power of gratitude." As an emerging educational filmmaker, Schindel thought ("naively," he later added) that values like these should play an important part in any school curriculum, and the picture book was a natural, secular way to introduce them. Daugherty and Schindel had met in Weston while Schindel was still living in New York, and soon after this meeting he approached the author with the idea of making the book *Andy and the Lion* as a live-action film, something Daugherty was eager to try. Children were found to play the roles of Andy and the other human characters for the production. Costumes were designed and sewn, and Schindel had found an old, tattered lion suit for the other title role. Despite such preparations, the project unraveled. "It just didn't work," Schindel said.[3] His idea was delayed several years until he returned from Turkey in 1953 and was finally able to begin producing films in the place that would officially be known, a few years later, as Weston Woods Studios.

While in Turkey, Schindel had observed a simple film technique that used a moving camera to pan over a still picture. This bare-bones approach to cinematography left an impression, and through it he saw a way that he could use the actual illustrations from children's books without having to go through the expensive process of fully animating a story or working through the myriad complications of live-action movies. Early educational films had nearly always been live-action motion pictures; only large commercial studios like Disney or Warner Bros. could afford to spend over seventy thousand dollars for a seven-minute animated film. Schindel knew that to make his films he would need to be resourceful.

In 1954, Schindel wrote his first contract to produce a film adaptation of *Andy and the Lion*. The process of making that film began again, but now, because of his children's enlightening responses, Schindel realized that "the charm of the story lay mainly in Daugherty's illustrations."[4] He was determined to preserve these images

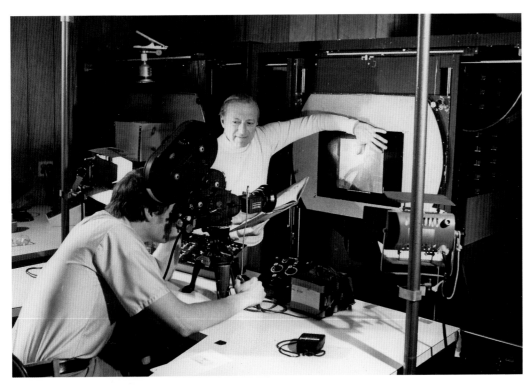

Top: Schindel works with a cameraman on an iconographic film, ca. 1976. The camera remains locked down while the image to be shot is mounted on a hand-cranked rig whose vertical and horizontal movements can be closely controlled.

Bottom: A close-up of a shot from James Daugherty's *Andy and the Lion*. The cameraman was able to control the movements of the easel by remote control.

onscreen. Securing the rights to make a movie version of *Andy and the Lion* had caught the publisher, Viking Press, pleasantly by surprise. At the time, virtually no one was vying for production rights for children's books; if filmmakers were interested, they expected to be paid by the publishers for their efforts, since they considered their films to be part of the promotional campaigns for the books. Schindel had no track record in the field and was thus an unknown quantity to publishers. Yet, two important factors convinced them of his seriousness: Schindel offered an advance and a royalty for permission to adapt the book and he had retained the well-respected law firm of Paul, Weiss, Rifkind, Wharton and Garrison to help him with the contract. Mortimer Caplin, Schindel's attorney at the firm, said Schindel was known as the firm's "smallest client but also our fastest paying," and added, "We always got a check from him within the same week that we sent out his statement." Caplin was instrumental in developing the basic rights agreement and future contracts, with their refinements, that eventually became the model for the industry standard.

Daugherty was enthusiastic about this newfound opportunity to make a film of his book. His frequent meetings with Schindel led to a professional relationship that in turn became a personal friendship. For Schindel, work on the film signified, he would later say, "a turning point in [his] career."[5] He returned to the "propaganda picture" he had seen in Turkey, wherein the camera panned over an image, and began to see, in his mind's eye, his camera "moving on those pictures of James Daugherty's."[6] Schindel had no idea what to call this technique, but in the agreement that he signed with Daugherty's publisher, Schindel indicated that he intended to "impart to said [Daugherty's] illustrations an illusion of motion through camera movement upon said illustrations." In the contract, Schindel referred to this as "still animation."[7] Later he came up with the term "iconographic" to describe the elaborate

The Iconographic Technique in Schindel's Words

"…to make a film out of *Andy and the Lion*, I [put] the pictures from the book on the wall, put the camera on a tripod, and panned the camera around the pictures. Well, it just didn't work. It turned out that when you move the camera, you can't maintain control over the picture. And also as you turn from left to right, you no longer have a flat picture in front of you. The picture is at an oblique angle. So I decided I had to come up with some kind of equipment that would keep the picture at a flat angle at all times, which meant the camera would be stationary and the picture would move. That was our next innovation, to make the first equipment ever devised for the iconographic medium. I simply took a normal drawing board and mounted it on vertical and horizontal garage-door tracks with gears. As you cranked the thing, it would move the picture across or up and down in front of the camera. I still have that device. It's been revised and improved many times, and today the whole board moves electronically. But the rig was not an end in itself; it was a necessary device to release the motion that illustrators had drawn into [those] beautiful books for children."

ballet of camera shots that danced across each page of Daugherty's and other books as they became films (see sidebar).[8]

In 1954, Daugherty introduced Schindel to the legendary group of children's librarians at the New York Public Library—Frances Lander Spain, the coordinator for all of the city's children's libraries; Maria Cimino, the director of the Central Children's Room; and Augusta Baker, the library system's famed resident storyteller. These and other professionals in the field of children's literature were enthusiastically impressed with the adaptation of *Andy and the Lion,* and the New York Public Library became Schindel's test-screening site of choice for the early Weston Woods films. Baker impressed on Schindel the importance of having the right narrator for each of the films. The voice of the narrator should tell a story, she explained, not sound like he is announcing the news. And so Schindel undertook the task of finding the right dramatic voice for his projects. To help with this task, Baker screened audition tapes of possible narrators for future films. Through her sensitive ear, Schindel found Owen Jordan, an actor and radio show host who shared Schindel's excitement for books that Jordan also read repeatedly to his own children. Jordan went on to narrate many of

Opposite: Schindel uses Robert McCloskey's *Lentil* to demonstrate the preproduction process of making an iconographic film: details from the original illustrations are selected and outlined; black frames are used to isolate the chosen detail.

Top: Camera-ready artwork from Daugherty's *Andy and the Lion*, with the framings for each shot drawn on a tissue overlay as a guide for the camera operator. The rectangles, marking the framing for each shot, are connected with vector lines that guide the sequencing movement from image to image.

Bottom: Storyboard for Marjorie Flack and Kurt Wiese's *The Story about Ping*, with the camera framings drawn in a copy of the book. On the right is an exposure sheet with timing instructions for the camera operator.

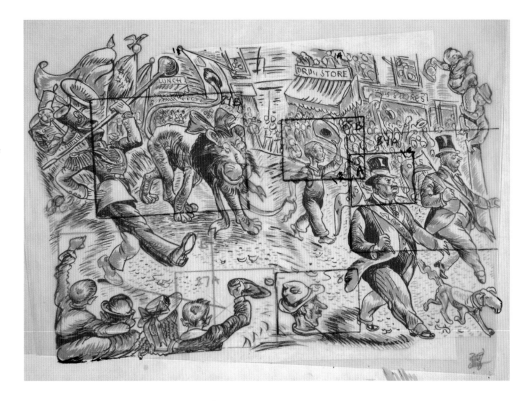

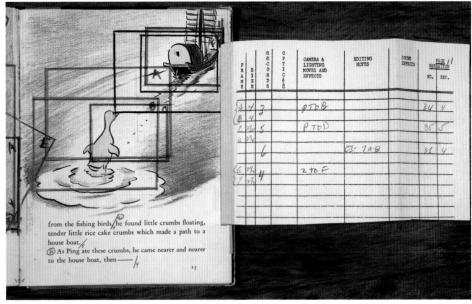

the early films produced by the studio and became, to borrow Schindel's phrase, "the golden voice of Weston Woods."[9]

Following the screening of *Andy and the Lion,* Frances Lander Spain contributed a particularly important, crystallizing comment about the film. Years later Schindel still recalled her words: "Mrs. Spain asked how I had gotten Mr. Daugherty to make so many new drawings for my film. That was the moment when I realized that the months of work I had put into that first film were worthwhile and that Jimmy Daugherty might be right when he said to me, 'What you are doing will find its way further than you can imagine in your wildest dreams.' There were no new pictures in that film, only details that I had revealed with my camera that even someone who had read the book many times had overlooked."[10]

Schindel's First Films

Schindel began reading hundreds of picture books and keeping an elaborate chart of award-winning titles. Through this process, he began to develop his list, which, in addition to *Andy and the Lion* (a 1939 Caldecott Honor book), included the following titles, in their order of production: *Millions of Cats* (1928) by Wanda Gág, *The Story about Ping* (1933) by Marjorie Flack and Kurt Wiese, *Make Way for Ducklings* (1941) by Robert McCloskey, *Hercules* (1940) by Hardie Gramatky, *Stone Soup* (1947) by Marsha Brown, and *The Red Carpet* (1948) by Rex Parkin.

To dramatize Ping's abandonment, Schindel redrew Wiese's original picture for the establishing and closing shots from *The Story about Ping*. Later Schindel recalled, "This was the only drawing of my own that I ever included in any of my films."

Buoyed by the film's warm reception, Schindel moved forward into a two-year development period, with forty-two thousand dollars in start-up funds that he had borrowed from family and another fifteen hundred dollars from the Westport bank. He decided to make seven films in this first production cycle (see sidebar). To select the books for adaptation, Schindel consulted again with major librarians, including those at the New York Public Library, as well as with educators at the Bank Street College of Education and the Child Study Association of America.

While at work on these early films, Schindel wore nearly every hat in the studio—art director, director, cameraman, and editor—alongside his new assistant, Bill Stoneback, whom Schindel hired to help with production. About all that was left to others were the voices for the narrations and the music, which Schindel commissioned from his cousin, Arthur Kleiner, who had been a composer in his native

Left: This artwork from the filmstrip of Hildegarde Swift's *The Little Red Lighthouse and the Great Gray Bridge* has tissue overlays with diagrammed shots indicating the specific sequence of images for the camera operator to shoot, i.e., long shots, close-ups, etc.

Bottom: Artwork from the filmstrip version of Wanda Gág's *Millions of Cats.*

Vienna. Kleiner emigrated to New York in the late 1930s with the help of Schindel's father and eventually became the music director for the Museum of Modern Art. One of Kleiner's duties there was to provide original music for the museum's screenings of silent films, and so the leap to Weston Woods films was a smooth one for him. Nevertheless, Schindel was surprised by Kleiner's minimalist score for *Andy and the Lion;* he had expected something far more complete, something that filled all the "spaces" around the pictures and the words. However, Kleiner convinced his cousin that less could indeed be just right, especially where music was concerned. Kleiner's essential idea was that the music should not overpower the art

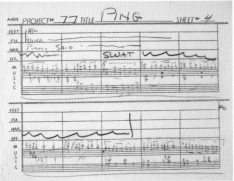

Top: Bill Stoneback checks the timing for voice recording of *Andy and the Lion.*

Bottom: A page from Arthur Kleiner's score for *The Story about Ping.* Music was added after the voice track in order to sync the pace of the narration with the tempo of the music.

of the book or the quality of the narration. These three elements should be in harmony, he believed, which required a score that was minimal, suggestive, understated. From Kleiner's approach, Schindel learned what he called "the eloquence of silence," and incorporated it into the aesthetic he was developing for his films.[11] And from this, too, Schindel discovered that the music and orchestration for each of his projects needed to be organically related to the books themselves and to grow out of the culture of the books.

Schindel would gain valuable knowledge from the challenges that each Weston Woods film presented. Securing the rights to film Wanda Gág's *Millions of Cats* (1928, 1955 film) was one of Schindel's big, early hurdles. The book was so famous that its publisher, Coward-McCann, was reluctant to give permission for a film adaptation, claiming that the publisher had no rights to the book because the rights to the book belonged to "the children of the world."[12] But Schindel was able to convince the executives at Coward-McCann that the Weston Woods film version would remain true to the story. He insisted that no liberties would be taken with the illustrations, the words, or the spirit of the original. Schindel's work, in fact, stood in opposition to the direction taken by the Disney studios with their feature-length animated versions of *Snow White* (1937) and *Pinocchio* (1940) and their film adaptations of such modern classics as Munro Leaf's *Ferdinand the Bull* (1936, 1938 film), *Bambi* (1928, 1942 film), Burton's *The Little House* (1942, 1952 film), and Hardie Gramatky's *Little Toot* (1939, 1958 filmstrip), all of which were completely remade in Disney's signature animation style and not in a manner that preserved the original illustrations. For example, *Ferdinand the Bull*, known to his devoted fans by Robert Lawson's black-and-white illustrations, morphed into a color cartoon version of himself. Burton's folk-art style in her 1942 book, *The Little House,* was transformed by the film's art director, Mary Blair, into something graphically jazzy and edgy. *Little Toot* would be given a full-throttled theme song, of course, performed in swing time by the Andrews Sisters. In sharp contrast, the enduring ethos of Weston Woods Studios was to create films that were an extension of their source material: the films were intended, as has been said, to complement and revitalize the experience of the books themselves. In his first film adaptation, *Millions of Cats*, Schindel even offered to give the publisher final approval of the project. He invited Coward-McCann to send its children's book editor, Alice Torrey, "to look at what I've done…and critique it," promising to scrap the whole project if it was deemed unsatisfactory, and going so far as to declare to the publisher that "I'll throw the whole thing away—you have no obligations." And in the end, Coward-McCann granted permission to make the film.

With *Make Way for Ducklings* (1941, 1955 film), *Stone Soup* (1947, 1955 film), and *Hercules* (1940, 1956 film), Schindel worked closely with each of the respective author/illustrators, Robert McCloskey, Marcia Brown, and Hardie Gramatky; in the process, each became an adviser and close personal friend. All of these artists were drawn to Schindel's sense of inclusiveness and to the exciting prospect of having their work transformed so faithfully into film. This collaborative approach represented yet another innovative step for the company: rather than treating the books as mere property to be used by the studio as it chose (à la Disney), Schindel and Weston Woods regarded their relationship to the authors as one based on creative consensus.

Schindel modified this aesthetic compact in only a few instances, such as in the adaptation of Marjorie Flack's *The Story about Ping* (1933, 1955 film), a story about a group of ducks living on a boat that sails along the Yangtze River in rural China. The book itself doesn't begin with a picture of Ping's boat; rather, it ends with that image. Schindel realized that in order to have the book make cinematic sense, it required an establishing shot of the boat. This prompted Schindel to use the last

The first public screening of Weston Woods films took place at the Museum of Modern Art on January 6, 1956. This was also the first use of the name of Schindel's new studio.

illustration at both the beginning and the end of the film to set the scene.[13] And in the production of *Make Way for Ducklings*, Schindel wanted to have the narrator in the film count Mrs. Mallard's eggs (as Schindel's children had eagerly done). But before he would take such a liberty, he consulted McCloskey. To Schindel's surprise, McCloskey said he liked the idea, and that he had often wished he had added a count of the eggs to the book's original text.

Before Schindel released any of these early films, he went back and remade the lot, incorporating all of the refinements. Reflecting on this, he added, "As a result, I don't have the usual embarrassment of having to apologize for my early attempts."[14] When he was far enough along with his productions he was able to show them, through Ellen's Bamberger family connections, to the renowned media mogul Lew Wasserman, who was then the head of MCA, the corporation that owned Universal Studios. Schindel hoped Wasserman would be interested enough in his films to provide him with an entrée into possible outlets for these works. Wasserman reportedly loved the films and called them an "artistic triumph." But in the next breath he said they represented a "financial disaster" and were a waste of Schindel's increasingly scarce resources, even though each film cost approximately thirty-five hundred dollars to make plus his time—a fraction of the going rate for full animation at that time. Wasserman simply did not see a market for Schindel's productions on television, and he was even less hopeful about their future as films, since there was no commercial venue for them. The most successful work of children's cinema during the 1950s, Albert Lamorisse's *The Red Balloon* (1956), had sold only eight hundred copies, even though it was recognized as the best-selling children's film at that time.

In 1956, at the urging of Kleiner, Schindel was able to hold a screening of his first eight films at the Museum of Modern Art. The program was shown in the middle of the day in order to be accessible to authors, illustrators, and people in the media and publishing worlds. The museum promptly purchased a number of films for its permanent collection, and within a few short hours, the names Schindel and Weston Woods were no longer unknown to the New York cultural community. The *New York Times* and the *New York Herald Tribune* covered the screening. The *New York Times* reported, "Neither 'puppetized,' dramatized, nor put in cartoon form, the books are virtually unchanged from their original state. They are to be 'brought to life' by…storytelling technique, original music, sound effects, and skilled camera work…"[15]

Schindel had hoped the Museum of Modern Art debut would spark interest in the films for television. However, thoughts were mixed about who would comprise the audience for such films. Some critics felt that Schindel's films were too entertaining for the school, library, or other educational markets, but that they might be right for television. Others thought the opposite was true: the films were too slow-moving for television, too bookish, and couldn't possibly compete with the action-driven cartoons that were popular on television, but they might be right for educators and librarians.

Schindel was distressed. Early in 1956, as his two-year development period was running out—and with it, his funds—he tried to sell his films to one of the new television shows, *Captain Kangaroo*. He was told that the show already had its own films in production, including the *Tom Terrific* cartoons that were being produced by Terrytoons under the direction of a new animation supervisor, Gene Deitch (who was known as one of the rising young stars of the animation world). Deitch had moved back east, following his apprenticeship in California with the famed former Disney animator John Hubley, to take on the challenging job, as he put it, "of turning a loser cartoon studio into a winner."[16] Schindel first met Deitch in 1957 when Schindel went in search of a job at the CBS studios as a hedge against his uncertain prospects as an independent film producer. Though their meeting was cordial, Deitch refused to hire Schindel because he lacked the technical training in animation. Schindel would later tell Deitch, "It was the greatest favor you could ever have done for me."

Deitch's "favor" and the uncertainty about how to market the Weston Woods films forced Schindel to move ahead with his plans and to develop his own approach for spreading the word about his work. "I'm in the woods (in more ways than one)," Schindel recalls having said to himself at the time, "and I need a way to work my way out...[and so] Weston Woods was formed."[17] Schindel went to the Town Hall in Weston and formally registered the company. In the wake of the Museum of Modern Art showing, he used a fifteen-hundred-dollar loan from the bank to do publicity mailings about his films to key libraries across the country that had established film-lending programs. Upon request, Schindel also sent out a 16-mm preview copy of his films. Libraries could keep the copies and order others, or they could return them without charge. Schindel kept checking his mailbox for returns, and eventually he went to the post office, thinking there must be a pile of films waiting for him. But it turned out that most of the libraries had kept the films, and were asking for more.

Schindel's luck continued to change when a few years later in 1956, the *Captain Kangaroo* television program was in desperate need of films to provide both a narrative interlude for the show and a break for the actors. Production on the *Tom Terrific* cartoons had been delayed, and CBS (the show's network), as Schindel recalls, came to Weston Woods with an offer to use its films for a limited period of time.

Top: After first previewing his films for the librarians at the New York Public Library, Schindel assembled a focus group of his true target audience, ca. 1950s.

Right: Captain Kangaroo (Bob Keeshan) reading from *Millions of Cats*, one of several Weston Woods films that gained national exposure on the television program, 1956.

The contract between *Captain Kangaroo* and Weston Woods called for thirteen films to be shown over a twenty-six-week period, with each film repeated once. Schindel had finished another two films by this time *The Little Red Lighthouse and the Great Gray Bridge* (1942, 1955 film) by Hildegarde Swift and Lynd Ward and *Jenny's Birthday Book* (1954, 1956 film) by Esther Averill. He was also working on four others including *Lentil* (1940, 1956 film) by McCloskey, *Mike Mulligan and His Steam Shovel* (1939, 1956 film) by Burton, and *Hercules* by Gramatky. When David Connell, the producer of *Captain Kangaroo*, asked Schindel when the remaining films would be done, he replied that the studio didn't have a fixed production schedule, and that the films were done when they were done, however long that might take. Despite the bluntness of this answer (surely the response of an artist), Schindel was energized by the opportunity, and the films were finished in time for their scheduled television premiere. Though CBS paid only a token amount to air the films, the network provided Weston Woods with an incomparable chance to showcase its productions; the films would reach an audience of millions each day and because of the public response to the films, they would be shown on the program over and over for the next fifteen years. "And besides," Schindel quipped about the new sense of urgency that had swept over the studio, "CBS was our only customer."

Chapter 4

A Golden Age Arrives

We may see how all things are
Seas and cities, near and far
And the flying fairies' looks
In the picture story-books.

—Robert Louis Stevenson, "Picture-books in Winter"

This composite was created to celebrate the national press coverage of the first Weston Woods films in *Newsweek* magazine, September 10, 1956. The article discusses the Picture Book Parade and reproduces the Weston Woods logo.

After the debut of Schindel's films on *Captain Kangaroo,* CBS decided to extend the initial contract for another three months while the *Tom Terrific* cartoons were being completed. Each morning during the six months that the Weston Woods films were on the air, they reached approximately four million children "from Maine to Hawaii."[1] Parents, librarians, educators, and other media professionals also saw the films; they were an equally important audience that Schindel hoped would pave the way for his films in a new and growing market.

One reason for the initial success of Weston Woods during the 1950s is that it presented an alternative to the norm of children's entertainment. The ever-increasing supply and influence of adrenalized cartoons, comic books, and other forms of media led to a public concern among parents and professionals about the kinds of materials that were being directed at children. This unease is addressed by Dr. Benjamin Spock in his popular early child-care books as well as in Dr. Fredric Wertham's outspoken criticism of the violent content of comic books. In this environment, Weston Woods stood in positive contrast to some of the prevailing trends, as was noted by such public voices as the New York Public Library's Frances Lander Spain in the *Saturday Review of Literature,* "Those of us who are disturbed by the quality and subject matter of films for children are delighted and grateful that there are now these films which we can enthusiastically recommend."[2] The *Captain Kangaroo* show was certainly pleased by the upscale, book-oriented appeal of the films, as recognized by the press. *Newsweek* from September 10, 1956, proclaimed, "During the past eight weeks, CBS's highly popular children's program, *Captain Kangaroo,* has organized what may be the largest reading circle in history, and injected genuine artistry into children's TV entertainment."[3] One of the photos accompanying the article featured Bob Keeshan (a.k.a. Captain Kangaroo) reading from *Millions of Cats* and surrounded by a display of books that had been adapted by Weston Woods (see p. 45). And from the perspective of children's book publishing, *Publishers Weekly* saw the arrival of Weston Woods and its films as "just about the best thing to have happened to juveniles in years."[4]

Along with the television exposure he was receiving, Schindel began his first advertising campaign, sending out more than one thousand single-page flyers to a mailing list of educators, librarians, and media professionals, urging them to try Weston Woods films without any obligation. Schindel cast his net wide in describing the possible venues and purposes for his films, which included teaching "elementary language arts" and "intermediate remedial reading."[5] And he broadened the educational mission of his films to encompass library story hours, church-based showings for youth groups, and screenings for chapters of the PTA and other child study groups. He also suggested that the films might be included in the educational curricula of teachers colleges and in disciplines like language arts, children's literature, and library science.[6] In order to facilitate the introduction of his films to the educational establishment, Schindel offered a free preview service for the films, in keeping with a branding philosophy similar to the Bamberger stores. The retail giant based his

Below: Hardie Gramatky was one of the many artists whom Schindel befriended during the early years of the studio. Gramatky, who lived in nearby Westport, drew this picture of his classic book, *Hercules*, for Schindel.

Right: Artwork from the filmstrip version of Gramatky's *Hercules*, named after the fire truck that plays a starring role.

Top: For the documentary movie *American Songfest*, host Robert McCloskey was filmed in an outdoor bathtub at Weston Woods playing the harmonica, reenacting a scene from his classic tale, *Lentil.*

Right: The original illustrations of McCloskey's *Lentil* were in black and white, and were hand-colored for the iconographic film production by McCloskey himself. The author also played the harmonica for *Lentil*'s musical score.

success on the store's innovative, hands-on customer service policy, always with a no-obligation, money-back guarantee. Following Bamberger's example, Schindel wanted his customers to be fully satisfied.

In the midst of these business developments, Schindel continued to work, with undiminished drive, adding more films to the studio's catalog. Among this next wave of productions were iconographic film versions of *Georgie* (1944, 1956 film) by Robert Bright, *Lentil* (1940, 1956 film) by Robert McCloskey, *Mike Mulligan and His Steam Shovel* (1939, 1956 film) by Virginia Lee Burton, *Hercules* (1940, 1956 film) by Hardie Gramatky, *The Camel Who Took a Walk* (1951, 1957 film) by Jack Tworkov and illustrated by Roger Duvoisin. These were soon followed by *The Five Chinese Brothers* (1938, 1958 film) by Claire Huchet Bishop and illustrated by Kurt Wiese, and *Curious George Rides a Bike* (1952, 1958 film) by H. A. Rey. And there would be many other films to come: as reported in *Publishers Weekly*, Schindel was busy buying up the rights to adapt more than a hundred other picture books into films.[7]

Schindel referred to this second group of films, in conjunction with his first group, as the Picture Book Parade. The idea of naming a group of selected products the Picture Book Parade was spawned by his interest in establishing a distinct

Top: Artwork from the iconographic version of *Curious George Rides a Bike*, Schindel's favorite story by H. A. Rey. Weston Woods made an update of this film in 2007, featuring new narration by actor David de Vries, the current "golden voice of Weston Woods."

Right: Artwork from the filmstrip version of Virginia Lee Burton's *Mike Mulligan and His Steam Shovel*. The studio produced an updated version in 1996, restoring the full text of the original book, which had been abridged for the original iconographic film production.

Opposite: Publicity mailers for the Picture Book Parade, c. 1956.

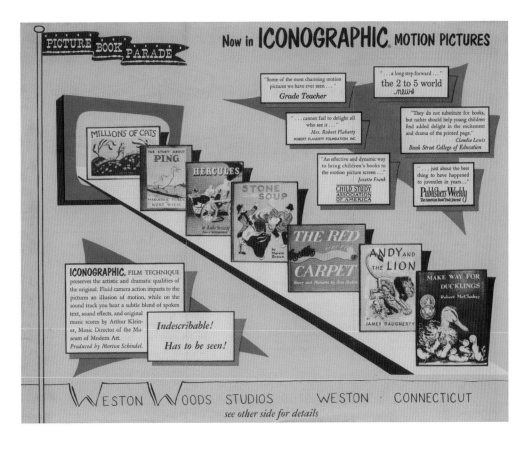

identity for Weston Woods Studios. Schindel noted in an early brochure that the films were available for airing on television and, ultimately, Schindel hoped the Picture Book Parade would result in a television show featuring his films, an idea he would continue to explore for the next several decades.

The combination of an unconventional but successful advertising campaign and the overwhelmingly positive press reactions fueled financial earnings and professional recognition. By the end of 1957, the income for the studio had grown from nothing to approximately seventy thousand dollars from broadcasting fees, purchases, and rentals of this first group of films. Meanwhile, a number of the early films produced by Weston Woods were being screened at both American and European film festivals, and several of these films won the studio's earliest awards such as first prize at the American Film Festival for both *Georgie* and *The Camel Who Took a Walk*. Schindel had also been invited to present programs of his films for library groups in the United States and Canada, as well as to deliver talks for educators and filmmakers at professional conferences.

At one of these conferences for librarians in 1957, Schindel was approached with the idea of doing films without soundtracks, allowing librarians to tell the stories of the books while a film was running. Schindel had to explain that this would not make for a happy arrangement, since the speed of the film would be too fast with the pace of the librarian's narration. However, Schindel knew that the studio could use the books' illustrations to make 35-mm filmstrips, thus allowing the librarian to advance the frames to the desired speed of narration. The expansion of the studio's product line to include 35-mm filmstrips required that the pictures in the book be shot and that, in some cases, the artwork of the picture book be redesigned. When picture books are shot on standard film, their horizontal orientation causes white bands to appear above and below the original picture. (In today's technology, black

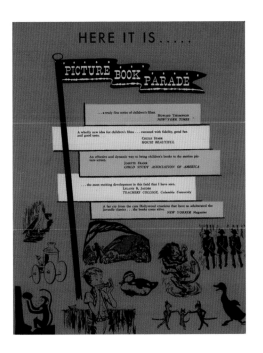

bands appear when a film that is shot in a widescreen format is viewed on a television screen.) To eliminate these bands, Schindel had to ask the illustrator of a book to paint extensions so that the picture being photographed would completely fill the frame, exemplified in the extensions that Gramatky painted (and signed) for the filmstrip version of *Little Toot* (1939, 1958 filmstrip). If the original artist was not available to do these extensions, Schindel would hire highly skilled artists to mimic the original style of the illustrations and to provide the necessary expansion to the various backgrounds for the films.

While Schindel's vision of a television show waited in the wings, by 1959, Weston Woods had produced filmstrip versions of all sixteen of its motion pictures, and the studio was packaging eight of the filmstrips in their labeled canisters, together with eight booklets of the story texts. But Schindel's marketing innovations did not stop here. One could also purchase filmstrips with LP recordings in yet another new product line. This line consisted of texts and audio elements from the first sixteen films, using Owen Jordan's original narrations, which, as Schindel described them, "blended with illustrative music and subtle sound effects that accentuate the mood and action of each story."[8] There were four stories per record, two on each side, and the cover art for each

READ ME A STORY

LONG 33⅓ PLAYING

Ages 3-8

Faithful reproductions of beloved stories from the Picture Book Parade, in words and music.

MAKE WAY FOR DUCKLINGS
Robert McCloskey

ANDY AND THE LION

STONE SOUP

HERCULES
BY JAMES

THE STORY ABOUT PING

MILLIONS OF CATS
BY MARJO KUR

WESTON WOODS STUDIOS, INC. • WESTON, CONNECTICUT

Read Me A Story, an LP containing six audio recordings of books included in the Picture Book Parade, features Schindel's children (from left) Cathy, Jeanie, and John on the cover, ca. 1958.

Opposite: Two signed illustrations from the filmstrip version of Hardie Gramatky's *Little Toot* show the artist's extensions to the original pictures.

album showed the three Schindel children reading together. Schindel also packaged the LP records alone, for a series the studio called Read Me A Story. Arthur Kleiner's original music for the films was also made available separately on two LPs. Schindel realized that to justify the considerable investment in each property, he would have to try to maximize the use of all of the film's assets through filmstrips and other products. There was a growing interest in audio-visual materials throughout the 1950s, but it was only a small fraction of the major interest that would occur in the late 1960s, with the arrival of federal subsidies for media purchases. Despite Weston Woods' early television exposure and marketing efforts, sales nevertheless flattened out. At the same time, the field of children's media programming was growing. As Schindel later said to one interviewer, the educational scholar Jill May, "we discovered back then that there really was no significant, viable market for what we were doing. We had to help develop the market and wait. Things change very slowly, and luckily, we realized early on that we probably would have to wait for awhile for a new generation of teachers and librarians who were taught in college to use children's literature and audiovisual techniques."[9]

These ever-widening activities and busy production schedules required that Schindel play an increasingly vital role at the studio, a role that would continue to evolve and refine itself over the next few years. He began to focus more on the conceptual ideas and aesthetic judgments concerning the studio's work, as well as the business and public relations aspects of running the studio, while slowly stepping back from a daily, hands-on involvement in film production. Such a redirection of Schindel's attentions was essential, given the scope of the studio's work. As early as 1963, the

New York Times marveled over what the studio had become: "Weston Woods is the only American movie plant for young (3–13) audiences that incorporates production, promotion, and distribution" in a single, "self-sustaining operation." The *Times* went on to note that such a centralizing of efforts was "unusual in the nontheatrical movie world."[10] By now the Weston Woods staff had grown to include people who could edit both film and sound and those who could take care of mailings, bookkeeping, and correspondence. But when he was nearby, Schindel never failed to pick up the phone in the main office and handle inquiries or orders personally (again, in deference to the business role models of his forebearers). This first-person approach was the modus operandi of the studio. The office space was tight at Weston Woods; everything from production to mailing was packed into the original garage next to the main house on the property. In this small log-cabin structure, recently renovated to include a concrete-and-flagstone floor with radiant heat, Schindel and his staff were working elbow to elbow with one another in what was becoming a flourishing cottage industry. The running joke, Schindel recalled, "was that if we weren't careful, we might accidentally send out someone's sandwich instead of a film."

During this period, Weston Woods expanded from its original purpose—to make literary films for children—into an umbrella structure for the creation and purveyance of culturally educative media for children. Thus, while the Picture Book Parade was trying to find and build its market, Weston Woods Studios was seeking not only to produce and distribute these films, but to become engaged in other media work. Indeed, in the wake of the Soviet Union's launch of its Sputnik 1 satellite in 1957, and the ensuing preparation of American students for careers in science, Schindel was approached by Robert Davis, a university researcher who was running a pioneering math education program in the Weston school district called the Madison Project. With funding from the National Science Foundation, Davis commissioned the studio to film the class sessions for future study. In conjunction with the project and as a service to the community, Schindel created a mobile video studio, similar to the ones used for taping television news events. The project went on for several years, using a cast of real children and an actual classroom setting. But when this arrangement with the Weston schools fell through in the third year of the project, Davis asked Schindel if he would be willing to construct a studio on the Weston Woods property, a facility large enough to hold a classroom set, where production could continue. Schindel agreed and built the barnlike structure that would eventually be used as the primary studio facility for Weston Woods. But two years later, Davis joined the faculty of Webster College in St. Louis, Missouri, and took with him the Madison

A production still from the live-action adaptation of McCloskey's *The Doughnuts* showing an actor carefully stacking the output of the commercial doughnut machine that was used in the film's production. Schindel estimated that over 16,000 doughnuts were made on the machine.

Project, which has since become a model for innovative math education.

The studio space, with its soundstage, would not remain vacant for long. In 1963 it became the site for Weston Woods' first live-action film, *The Doughnuts* (1943, 1963 film), based on a chapter from McCloskey's *Homer Price*. Another landmark for Weston Woods, it was the first live-action dramatic motion picture for children produced in the U.S.A. by the studio. Schindel was concerned by how few noneducational films were being made for older children, and he was looking for an opportunity to try a movie that would reach this audience, especially children with reading problems. *The Doughnuts,* with its wry humor and quirky characters and storyline, appeared to be an ideal way to enter this field; furthermore, McCloskey's text was essentially "laid out like a movie script," and ready for filming.[11] Shooting for the film was done on the weekends, because the actors were either at school or at their regular jobs. During the course of its production, more than sixteen thousand doughnuts were made. (Ever resourceful, Schindel had managed to locate a fully functional 1940s doughnut machine through an advertisement in *Baker's Weekly*.)

One of these doughnuts still survives to this day, in a virtually petrified form, and is among Schindel's most cherished objects, carefully framed as though it were a crown jewel in a diadem of accomplishments. And the doughnut machine occupies a corner of the gallery on the Weston Woods grounds, a favorite stop for visitors. Over the years, *The Doughnuts* would become one of the studio's most successful early properties and would set the stage for other live-action films that the studio would make in the coming years such as Isaac Bashevis Singer's *Zlateh the Goat* (1966, 1973 film), McCloskey's *The Case of the Cosmic Comic* from *Homer Price* (1943, 1976 film), and Don Freeman's *Corduroy* (1968, 1984 film).

Morton Schindel (left) and Robert McCloskey in the back garden of Weston Woods, ca. 1960. Schindel and McCloskey worked on a variety of projects together, from film adaptations to documentaries, and became close friends as a result.

During the course of creating several film adaptations of the author's works (including *Time of Wonder* [1957, 1961 film], and *Blueberries for Sal* [1948, 1967 film]), McCloskey and Schindel had become good friends. McCloskey was living near Weston during the winters and was a frequent visitor at the studio, generously offering suggestions and sharing ideas with Schindel. He had been enormously impressed with McCloskey's ideas, particularly with his 1958 Caldecott acceptance speech for *Time of Wonder,* in which McCloskey stated, "With everyone clamoring for more scientists, I should like to clamor for more artists and designers. I should like to clamor for the teaching of drawing and design to every child, right along with reading and writing."[12] From Schindel's perspective, McCloskey—as an artist and as a person—was a significant influence on his life. In fact, it was McCloskey who underscored for Schindel the principle of the organic nature of creative work—whether picture books or films—that would guide Weston Woods in the coming decades and that still serves as part of the studio's ethic. As Schindel would later note in his acceptance of the Regina Medal in 1979, "From Bob [McCloskey] I learned another lesson that was critical to the development of my work—the difference between art and commerce. Commerce, I came to realize, is usually an activity that's motivated, shaped, and timed to the needs of the marketplace. Art is a self-generated activity, one that depends on the intuition and taste of the artist, where the product is finished when it is satisfying to its creator—not because a deadline has been imposed and time has expired."[13]

Schindel would produce the studio's first documentary in 1964 about McCloskey and his work, as part of the studio's Signature Collection, a separate line of films meant to amplify the range of the studio, especially its interest in the individuals who created the books that Weston Woods filmed. Whereas today children's book publishers readily make available interviews and biographies of authors and artists as an integral part of promoting their books, at the time, the documentary profiles that Weston Woods was producing were another, particularly valuable, step in a chain of innovative practices, since these documentaries provide the earliest—and sometimes the only—filmed record of a number of our most gifted artists from this period, Robert McCloskey among them.

A retiring, modest, and naturally reticent man, McCloskey had initially resisted the idea of a film about himself. Eventually, McCloskey agreed to become the subject for a documentary, in part to spare himself having to make so many public appearances, repeating the same observations and explanations about his work. He was somewhat baffled by the attentions of many of his fans and confessed jokingly to Schindel, "To tell the truth,

Mort, I think they like to touch me and smell me!"[14] Though barely twenty minutes long, work on the film turned out to be an ambitious and demanding project: Schindel rented an airplane to shoot on the island in Maine where McCloskey spent his summers and a helicopter to shoot in the Charles River Basin and Beacon Hill areas of Boston, where *Make Way for Ducklings* takes place. Schindel also found himself setting up his tripod in the Boston Public Garden to photograph the city's famous swan boats and pond for one of the film's establishing shots.

Throughout the 1960s, Schindel continued to make iconographic movies and filmstrips. There were explorations into the sheer magic of words, like Ann and Paul Rand's *Sparkle and Spin* (1957, 1963 filmstrip); new versions of La Fontaine fables from Brian Wildsmith like *The Rich Man and the Shoemaker* (1965, 1972 filmstrip); plenty of nursery standards like Randolph Caldecott's *Hey Diddle Diddle* (1882, 1962 filmstrip), Edward Lear's *The Owl and the Pussycat* (1871, 1971 film), and Beatrix Potter's *The Tale of Peter Rabbit* (1902, 1962 filmstrip); and multilingual books like Antonio Frasconi's *See and Say* (1955, 1963 filmstrip). Through the influence of McCloskey, Schindel's dedication to arts education continued to grow, and he made short films like *Paint All Kinds of Pictures* (1963, 1968 filmstrip) based on a book by Arnold Spilka, and *A Picture Has a Special Look* (1961, 1963 filmstrip) by Helen Borten. Schindel also adapted Miroslav Sasek's singular books about geography and culture (which have been experiencing a revival in recent years): *This Is New York* (1960, 1962 film), *This Is Venice* (1961, 1964 film), *This Is Israel* (1962, 1964 film), and *This Is Ireland* (1962, 1965 film). Weston Woods was also the distributor for a film version of *Madeline's Rescue* (1953, 1959 filmstrip) by Ludwig Bemelmans.

The outpouring of creative activity at Weston Woods would lead Schindel to later confess that he felt he might soon be running out of material that lent itself to being filmed iconographically, since not everything that he acquired, he noted, was possible to adapt in that form. And then he was referred to Ezra Jack Keats's *The Snowy Day* (1962, 1964 film) by its enthusiastic editor, Annis Duff. This quietly affecting story about a boy's experience of a first snow was "one of the few books that I ever read that gave me goosebumps. . . . It evoked all sorts of images," Schindel remembered later.[15] He had also remembered Duff's appearance at the Caldecott ceremony where Keats had received the award because she "looked like something out of a fairy tale in her gown," Schindel recalled. "It was ice blue with snowflakes appliquéd onto the skirt."[16] But despite the magic that surrounded the book for him, Schindel knew his studio could not make it into a film. "I looked at the artwork through the viewfinder of our camera," he said, and saw that "the hard line of Keats's collages

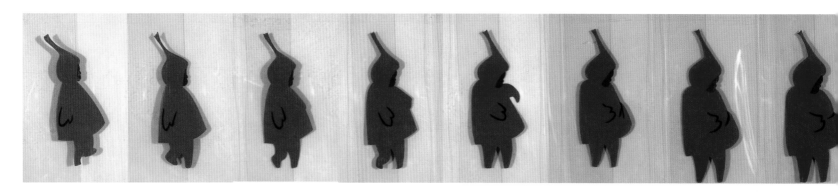

could not be projected in the iconographic medium. *The Snowy Day* wanted to be an animated film." But that leap, given the expense of animation and the precarious finances of the studio, was "a whole new ball game. I didn't have the faintest idea how to go about getting into it."[17]

As luck would have it, not long after *The Snowy Day* appeared, an animator named Mal Wittman visited Weston Woods, looking for a project to do with the studio. He screened several of his films for Schindel, who thought Wittman's work looked promising but was reluctant to offer him the Keats project. "I had learned," Schindel said, "that you don't hand people assignments if you're looking for good work. They have to do what they want to do. I told him that…he would have to tell me which book he wanted to adapt."[18] But Wittman didn't know what to do next, so Schindel sent him to the Central Children's Room in the New York Public Library. "A week later, Mal was back with a heavy briefcase. After talking for a while, he got up the courage to ask whether I wanted to see what he had brought along. The first book he took out of his briefcase was *The Snowy Day*! Our first animated film project was on its way."[19]

The film was done in consultation with a somewhat difficult Keats, as Schindel tactfully recalls. But the project went smoothly and no upsetting creative differences occurred—even Wittman's atypical selection of spare guitar music by Barry Galbraith

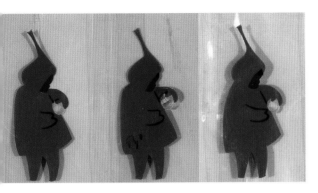

This sequence of animation cels from the film adaptation of Ezra Jack Keats's *The Snowy Day* are about an eighth of those actually required to animate the simple movement of Peter packing a snowball. Individual cels like these, painted on clear celluloid (from which the drawing gets its name), are the final, top layer of the finished picture that is ultimately photographed. The background is typically one piece of art, as opposed to a separate sequence of drawings.

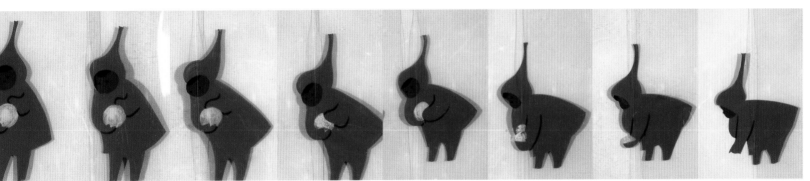

(not the usual score by Kleiner) was approved. Schindel had thought that Augusta Baker's voice would be perfect for the part, especially since she was a close friend of Keats and may well have been the inspiration for Peter's mother in the picture book. Baker had done an audition tape of the story for Schindel and Keats, but they had their doubts about whether or not hers was the right voice. So they let her make the decision after listening to the reel of auditions that included her own reading among those of other possible narrators. "As she was listening to her own performance," Schindel recalled in his tribute to Baker in 2005, "even before it was finished she broke out in uproarious laughter and said, 'Certainly, that is not the right voice for that delicate little film!' Together we selected the recording that is heard to this day: a light, bright, fragile little voice that even cracks partway through, delicate as a snowflake."[20] The narrator was Jane Harvey, who had sung with the Benny Goodman Orchestra and who would become a torch singer later in her career.

Weston Woods went on to make a number of other film adaptations of Keats's books during the 1960s, including *Whistle for Willie* (1964, 1965 film) and *Peter's Chair* (1967, 1971 film). But the breathtaking simplicity of *The Snowy Day* would remain a triumph and serve as a prelude to the future; it would lead the studio into a major new direction: animation.

Chapter 5

A World of Wild Things

Each new decision to build [the studio] was a step into the unknown. The phenomenal thing is that it was possible to build a successful business with my heart, rather than my head. I was a driven, compulsive person. I knew no other way. —Mort Schindel

One of the unexpected and obscure influences of the Cold War is that Sputnik made possible the Weston Woods that we know today. Although this evolution would take nearly a decade, the launch of the Soviet satellite in 1957, as earlier mentioned, eventually led to major support from the United States government for the purchase of audiovisual materials in American schools. The passage of the Elementary and Secondary Education Act (ESEA) in 1966 brought good fortune once again to Weston Woods' door. Schindel reports that in March of the same year one could watch this dramatic sea change in the growing thickness of the daily stack of orders that the studio received for its films. In 1967, the year following the implementation of the ESEA, orders from school libraries had easily quadrupled. The labs that supplied the films and other media to Weston Woods were overextended, so much so that Schindel agreed to pay for weekend and evening shifts to fill the studio's orders. And, of course, Schindel added, "everyone at Weston Woods gave up whatever they were doing to type, wrap, and ship orders."[1]

Along with this sudden surge of new business came an expanded public profile for the studio. In 1973 the American Library Association was holding its annual meeting in New York, and Schindel was asked to invite all interested attendees for a day trip to Weston Woods; and, he remembers, "seven hundred librarians were our guests for lunch or dinner and a tour of our facilities that week."[2] In his extensive notes about Weston Woods, Schindel repeatedly reports that he was virtually an outsider when he began his work, and librarians had been his staunchest allies. Not only had they helped to critique and launch his films, but they had also provided him with a constant stream of product suggestions. Along with this generous service, librarians hosted Schindel at conferences and made him a part of their community. The hospitality was one way, Schindel said, that he could thank them.

Schindel's business was growing and tours of the property for old or new colleagues, teachers, librarians, or aspiring young filmmakers became more frequent. With endless patience and enthusiasm for each visitor, Schindel's guided tour included the family's living quarters, his inventions and furniture designs, and an architectural history of the studio buildings. Schindel always regarded his guests not as a peevish obligation or imposition, but rather as a way to engage and inform part of what he has referred to as the studio's "unpaid sales force."[3] Generating goodwill among the audiences that Schindel hoped to cultivate through personal contacts was a principle, borrowed from Louis Bamberger's ethos, that Weston Woods put into practice from the start. Schindel also acknowledged that the boundary between private and public spaces at Weston Woods was beginning to blur: "In time I realized that I was so identified with Weston Woods and its buildings that I couldn't distinguish timber and concrete standing on dirt in the backyard from myself personally."[4] Schindel maintained a virtual open-door policy to anyone interested in the work of the studio; his hospitality was and remains legendary to this day.

As the studio expanded, Schindel saw that Weston Woods was reaching its limits in the production of iconographic films: "We began to exhaust the supply of those books that could effectively be adapted in this medium."[5] Having had a taste of working in full animation with Ezra Jack Keats's *The Snowy Day* (1962, 1964 film) and another work by Keats, *Whistle for Willie* (1964, 1965 film), Schindel was interested in pursuing other animation projects. Meanwhile, the staff Schindel had assembled at Weston Woods was ably handling production of the iconographic films to which the studio had already committed, thus allowing Schindel the chance to follow opportunities to grow as a filmmaker. "The whole Weston Woods program was taking off independently of my input," he observed. "My hope that the work could be perpetuated by others was being realized, and it gave me the freedom to think about new directions," including fully animated films.[6] Schindel had an inkling that he was experiencing "growing pains against [his] own standard dimensions," but he knew he had to engage those challenges: "I have always been concerned that our reputation at Weston Woods was greater than what our production merited. It is possible that part of what motivated me to try new things was to see whether there was some way that I could make our achievements catch up with what people thought of us."[7]

One of the limitations to pursuing these fresh animation projects was money, despite the growing success of the studio's catalog of iconographic films. Given the expense of making fully animated films, Schindel was worried about his new project commitments, and he spoke to his accountant, Manny Zimmer, about his concerns. Schindel recalls that Zimmer told him not to worry, that when Schindel did run out of money, he would know it, and he added that all Schindel would have to do in that case was to stop spending until some money came back in again. "I began to see my bank account like a sink," Schindel recalls. "All I would have to do is plug up the drain and the sink would fill up again." He still speaks appreciatively of Zimmer: "His observation proved to be essentially correct and very unorthodox for someone in his profession—a quality for which I retain an affection for him."

As Schindel was looking for new ventures, coincidentally, they came looking for him in the form of an entrepreneurial American producer, William Snyder. Snyder's production company, Rembrandt Films, had distributed such motion pictures as *White Mane* (1953) and the puppet films of the Czech animator Jiří Trnka. He had also bought the movie rights to the Madeleine books, and was proposing to Kreslený Films in Czechoslovakia (the hub for short film production) that their animation studio in Prague produce eight films a year for his company and the American market. This was in the late 1950s, and the Czech film industry was (and indeed would remain) eager to have the hard currency of the West, and so an agreement was made between the Czechs and Snyder. But there were difficulties with the early productions, and to "spruce them up," back in America, Snyder urged Gene Deitch, who had developed a reputation as an "all-around creative handyman," to come to Prague for a brief stay to complete several of the pending films.[8] Deitch had been unhappy with the corporate life he had led at Terrytoons, so he struck out to form his own production company; however, to stay afloat he had to make television commercials, rather than projects on which he really wanted to work, such as *Munro* (1959, 1960 film), an animated film based on a story by Deitch's friend Jules Feiffer. Snyder offered to finance the *Munro* project if Deitch would make the film in Prague at Krátký Films. Deitch agreed and left for Prague, thinking he would be there for a few weeks, perhaps a month. The experience changed Deitch's life as he recalls in his book *For the Love of Prague* (1997):

> …*perhaps it was an infant memory, something I could not imme-*
> *diately identify, that caused my sense of euphoria on that first visit.*
> *Having at first expected some horrible police-state experience, I had*
> *instead met a bunch of friendly animators, and found much in com-*
> *mon with them. And I met Zdenka [Deitch's future wife]. So I felt very*
> *relaxed and relieved, but still I also felt strange; I couldn't figure out*
> *what it was. It was much later, as Zdenka said, that I realized that it*

Zdenka Deitchová and Gene Deitch annotating animation cels for Maurice Sendak's *Where the Wild Things Are*, Prague, ca. 1974. Deitch met Zdenka while working at his first animation studio in Prague, where she was the director.

was the old-fashioned clothing, and mainly the smell of coal. That was the infant memory. In Chicago at that time when I was born, most people heated their homes with coal. I hadn't smelled that coal in the air since babyhood, but the same smell in Prague evoked that powerful nostalgia, and feeling that I was somehow at home! [9]

And indeed he was. Deitch would remain in Prague, having fallen in love with the city and, more important, with Zdenka Najmanová, the enormously talented and energizing director of animation at the Barrandov Studio, where Snyder had arranged for his films to be made.

In 1961 Deitch's *Munro* won an Oscar for Best Animated Short Subject, and Deitch would become instantly famous in animation circles for this satiric fable about the absurdities of an authoritarian bureaucracy that drafts a four-year-old boy into the army. Among the other projects brought to him by Snyder, Deitch worked on the films *Madeline's Rescue* (1953, 1959 film) by Ludwig Bemelmans, *Anatole* (1957, 1960 film) by Eve Titus, and *The Happy Lion* (1954, 1960 film) by Louise Fatio. But there was also a steady stream of contracted orders from America, including *Tom and Jerry, Popeye,* and *Krazy Kat* cartoons—animated shorts that fed an increasingly hungry television market.

Deitchová and Deitch in their apartment, Prague, ca. early 1970s.

Schindel made his first of many trips to Prague in 1967, bringing with him two book projects that he initially planned to coproduce as animated films with Snyder: Barbara Emberley's *Drummer Hoff* (1967, 1969 film), illustrated by her husband, Ed Emberley, and Celestino Piatti's *The Happy Owls* (1964, 1969 film). Schindel's interest in these books may well have had to do with the times. Written in nursery-rhyme form, *Drummer Hoff* was an unsparing portrayal of the vainglorious futility of war. When it emerged during the height of the Vietnam War, some considered it to be a controversial, political work for children. *The Happy Owls* took a slightly different, though no less provocative, approach concerning the need to find peace and harmony in the world and to be in touch with nature, rather than the chaotic clatter of the barnyard. Together these texts represented for Schindel one of his core beliefs about children's books and their rich, deep power. "To me," Schindel told Leonard Marcus in an interview from 2005, "a good children's book . . . is almost like a psalm from the Bible. . . . There are messages, there are morals, there are things by which you can guide your life. There is a ladder on which you can grow."[10] Schindel had been working with the idea of the children's book as a "psalm" since it was first introduced to him by Marcia Brown when the two became friends in the late 1950s, while the studio was adapting her book *Stone Soup* (1947, 1955 film). Elsewhere Schindel would remark, in a similar vein, "A highly selective library of good books represents something like a testament."[11] For him, an expression of these individual feelings and values is found in children's books and the communities they create: "Like people with the same religious or cultural background who gravitate towards one another, people with the same experience in children's literature find themselves comfortably on common ground."[12]

In Prague, Schindel found himself on just such common ground with Deitch, nearly ten years after their first encounter at Terrytoons. At their second meeting, Deitch was now eager to join forces with Schindel, especially on books that had both substance and beauty. Although he was no stranger to life in the commercial fast lane, Deitch was nevertheless sensitive to the possibilities of working on books like the ones Schindel offered and was well versed in making challenging films. Indeed, *Munro* had taken years to produce. Due to the book's critique of authoritarian and absurd adult behavior, and given the McCarthy-haunted 1950s, potential backers of the project were easily frightened, making funding difficult to secure. Working with Schindel offered Deitch an opportunity, at last, to do the kind of children's films he had always dreamed of doing. "Up until then," Deitch commented, "my first eight years in Prague were devoted to doing the same old American kinds of films, and while they were interesting to make and afforded us great opportunities to develop our craftsmanship, they weren't what I wanted to make ideologically. . . . I think that Mort had great . . . *unsureness* as to whether I could readapt myself to his kind of thinking, after having spent so many years doing zany, wild comedies with so much violence, etc., which he abhorred."[13] But Deitch and Schindel took the leap and established a lifelong collaboration. Deitch continues to produce and direct films for Weston Woods, including *The Emperor's New Clothes* (1984, 1990 film) by Nadine Bernard Westcott, *I Lost My Bear* (1998, 2004 film) based on the book by Feiffer, *Diary of a Worm* (2003, 2004 film) from the book by Doreen Cronin, *Emily's First 100 Days of School* (2000, 2006 film), and *Voyage to the Bunny Planet* (1992, 2008 film) by Rosemary Wells.

To capture the marionettelike quality of the robotic soldier in Barbara and Ed Emberley's *Drummer Hoff*, Gene Deitch and his animation team constructed a puppet with hinged limbs.

Opposite: Deitch's storyboard page for *Drummer Hoff* also focuses on the herky-jerky movements of the robotic soldiers.

In *The Picture Book Animated*, a documentary film produced by Weston Woods, Deitch cites the first project he would direct at Weston Woods, Barbara and Ed Emberley's *Drummer Hoff*, as an example of his ideological approach to filmmaking:

> *Tucked into each book when it arrives is always a note from Mort, to guide me in my first step; to find the core of meaning a motion-picture version might project. In each book it's different, and my film adaptation must grow from the unique character and content of the books. Something always clues me in as to what the book is really about; Ed and Barbara Emberley's* Drummer Hoff *is a fine example of what I mean. Hidden among the bright colors of this outwardly lighthearted book are hints of its real depth. As the grandly uniformed soldiers strut along, intent on constructing their mighty cannon, they ignore the flowers underfoot, the birds and insects that watch them. In our film, I was able to show the soldiers actually stepping on the flowers and shooing away the birds, actions that support what I felt to be the meaning of the last page of the book: the ultimate triumph of nature over the posturings of humans and their sometimes destructive machines. I believe that within* Drummer

Hoff *is truth, powerful and basic, and expressed in highly distilled simplicity. Yet, the simple rhyme and design of the book remain—the fun is still there. We've tried only to project the ideas in the book, so that when the child returns to it, after seeing the film, he or she will love it more, and see it more. As our aim is always to project the book, we tried to always find the most valid way to adapt its graphic style to motion. The woodcut illustrations of* Drummer Hoff *suggested these paper puppets which could be animated in the still, formal way you would expect these figures to move.*[14]

After finishing a detailed storyboard—a scene-by-scene visual scripting of the major action of the film, Deitch would then tape-record a careful explanation of his ideas for Schindel to listen to as he "read" the storyboard; this audio narrative provided a sense of the voice that would be fitting for the film. In addition, Deitch would send potential musical clips and audio effects for the soundtrack. Once Schindel approved Deitch's outline, the film would move into more complicated levels of production that could combine the talents of an entire studio team. Depending on the complexity of the project, it might take a year to produce a fully animated film and, in some cases, much longer. Although the cost of production was always a consideration for the studio, it was not the major factor in deciding whether to make a particular film. Schindel had maintained from the outset that he had "one guiding principle: the book is always our director." He continued,

We could spend up to three or more years on a single project, to ensure that the animation, narration, and music are true to the authors, illustrators, and readers. I added a clause to our contracts that required us to work with the editor, author, and/or illustrator throughout the production of each title. . . . When an artist puts paint on a canvas, he may paint over it multiple times until he is satisfied that the piece is just right. That is the way our films are made. Once we made a commitment to a project, we threw away the budget and the time schedule.[15]

Schindel has frequently called Deitch the "unsung genius of Weston Woods."[16] This is not hyperbole when one considers the creative range and seemingly endless inventiveness that Deitch displayed in his films for the studio. From the beginning of his association with Weston Woods, Deitch was producing truly unique films, each with its own array of aesthetic challenges, to be sure, but each bearing the distinct stamp of his unique style.

Animation cel from Deitch's adaptation of *The Three Robbers* by Tomi Ungerer. The dark, menacing appearance of the robbers at the opening of the story is quickly undercut by Ungerer and Deitch's lively humor.

Among the perennial favorites of these early films is *The Three Robbers* (1962, 1972 film) by the Alsatian author/illustrator Tomi Ungerer. The book follows three tall-hatted highwaymen who terrorize the countryside, robbing coaches and scaring innocent citizens. The robbers brandish such comical weapons as a sneeze-inducing pepper blower; a double-edged, wheel-disabling ax; and an unloaded blunderbuss for show. In the end, we discover that the robbers are genuinely kindhearted people after they find a little girl as part of one of their hauls and decide to act as the foster parents to her and all the other orphaned children in the countryside. In many ways, these imaginative details and the whimsical story line were the perfect vehicle for Deitch's special touches and sense of humor. Even the rough sound effects for the conceptual draft of the film, recorded in the closet of Deitch's Prague apartment, played into the buoyant mood of the story. In his ad hoc studio, Deitch hummed a musical score into a cassette recorder and sent the results to Schindel. Everyone at the studio found Deitch's inspired, spontaneous riffs to be the perfect fit for Ungerer's improvisational tale. In fact, the "boo-boo-boo-boo" with which Deitch opened and closed the film has become a kind of signature sound for this initial run of remarkable films.

The set of blocks that Deitch used as models for the animation of *Changes, Changes* by Pat Hutchins is prominently on display at the Weston Woods Museum.

Top: The cover of Hutchins's *Changes, Changes*, which was adapted by Gene Deitch using drawings of blocks as the main characters.

Right: An animation cel from *Changes, Changes* with the two busy "block" people building one of the structures that is created during the course of the film.

Bottom: Invented by conductor František Belfín, the "Plank-o-Plonker," a wooden musical instrument fashioned from ordinary two-by-four planks, provided the key rhythmical elements for the soundtrack of *Changes, Changes*.

Original "Plank-O-Plonker" (Czech:"Prknofon") used in CHANGES, CHANGES. Actually, <u>wooden mallets</u> are used for playing. Note <u>saw</u> for tuning!

Sounds and music would again play an inspired role in a film Deitch directed the next year, *Changes, Changes* (1971, 1973 film), based on the book by Pat Hutchins. On one level, the book uses the predicaments of two old-fashioned wooden dolls who live in a world of toy blocks to illustrate basic geometric shapes. Yet, on another level, the book is about the nature of narrative itself, and how even the tiny steps of the toys—much like the hesitant steps of young children—can lead to clever, funny, and at times exciting consequences. To propel this action, Deitch came up with a thoroughly wooden musical score—as he explained in *The Picture Book Animated*: "Everything in the book is made of wood, so why not use pieces of wood, tuned wood, for the music? A xylophone and a marimba were the only actual instruments to qualify. For our bass drum, we used a wooden crate! There were lots of wood-blocks and rattles, and one glorious instrument invented for the occasion…a rank of ordinary two-by-four planks sawn to calculated lengths, hung and struck with wooden mallets…surely the only musical instrument on earth that is tuned with a hammer and saw."[17]

In Deitch's view, each project presented a group of new artistic obstacles. He stressed that "…in every film there is a special problem that has to be overcome and that requires a new way of animation, a camera effect, a new way of getting color onto the cels. I try to face the problem and to come up with something that seems fresh."[18]

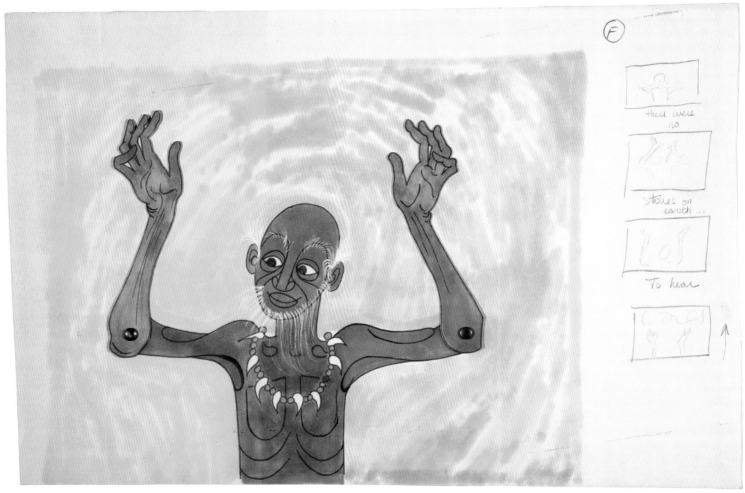

In order to mimic the specific gestures of the storyteller from *A Story, A Story*, author Gail E. Haley and Deitch created a model with movable arms held together with rivets at the elbows.

In *A Story, A Story* (1970, 1973 film), the Caldecott Award–winning picture book by Gail E. Haley that Deitch directed, the challenges lay in providing the right background sound as well as in creating a culturally correct, gestural vocabulary for the African storyteller who narrates the tale of Anansi, the most ancient "spider man" who became the archetypal storyteller. To be sure of the film's African musical tapestry, Deitch consulted with anthropologists in Czechoslovakia who specialized in African cultures; and to be sure of the storyteller's gestures, Deitch invited Haley to Prague to demonstrate for him and the rest of the animation team the proper movements for her main character, which he filmed for later reference.

Deitch would use a similar modeling device for Diane Paterson's book *Smile for Auntie* (1976, 1979 film). Perhaps the first children's book about irony, it is centered around an old-world "Auntie" figure, bedecked in old-fashioned shoes and a

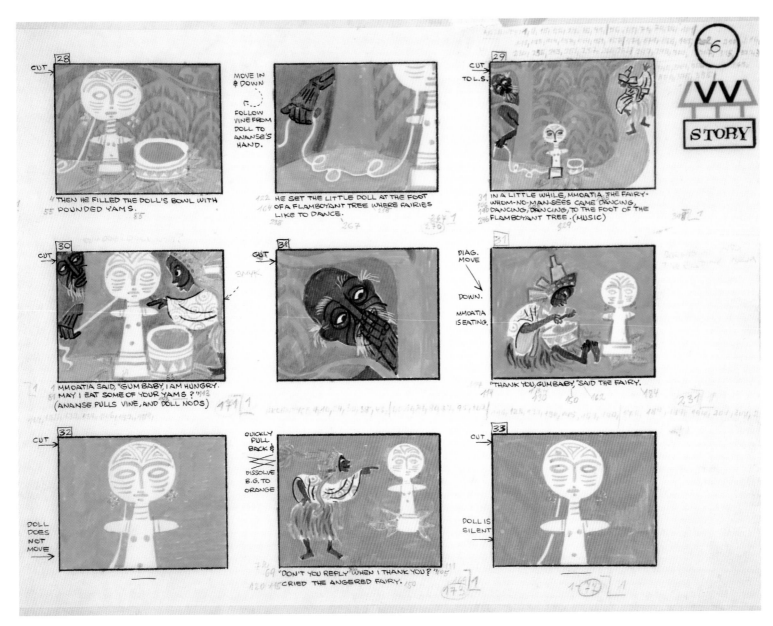

28 CUT →
THEN HE FILLED THE DOLL'S BOWL WITH POUNDED YAMS.

MOVE IN & DOWN
FOLLOW VINE FROM DOLL TO ANANSE'S HAND.

HE SET THE LITTLE DOLL AT THE FOOT OF A FLAMBOYANT TREE WHERE FAIRIES LIKE TO DANCE.

29 CUT TO L.S.
IN A LITTLE WHILE, MMOATIA THE FAIRY-WHOM-NO-MAN-SEES CAME DANCING, DANCING, DANCING, TO THE FOOT OF THE FLAMBOYANT TREE. (MUSIC)

STORY

30 CUT →
MMOATIA SAID, "GUM BABY, I AM HUNGRY. MAY I EAT SOME OF YOUR YAMS?" (ANANSE PULLS VINE, AND DOLL NODS)

31 CUT →

DIAG. MOVE
DOWN.
MMOATIA IS EATING.

"THANK YOU, GUM BABY," SAID THE FAIRY.

32 CUT →

DOLL DOES NOT MOVE

QUICKLY PULL BACK & DISSOLVE B.G. TO ORANGE
"DON'T YOU REPLY WHEN I THANK YOU?" CRIED THE ANGERED FAIRY.

33 CUT →

DOLL IS SILENT

When creating a film's storyboards, Deitch attempts to reflect the visual style of the source book, as can be seen in this storyboard from Haley's *A Story, A Story.*

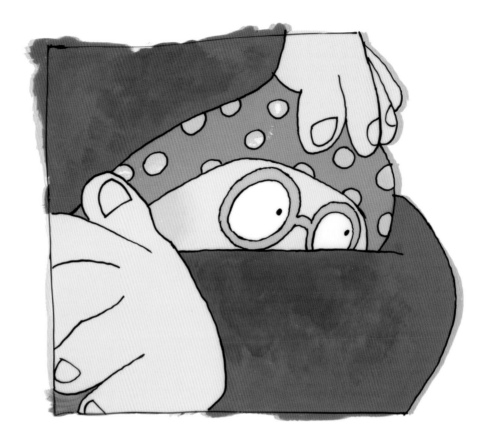

babushka, who tries to coax a baby to smile with a series of tricks, absurd poses, facial expressions, and sound effects. Nothing works; the baby is too serious a creature to be tickled by ordinary vaudeville shtick and refuses to satisfy the grown-up with any sign of amusement. But as soon as Auntie delivers on her threat to "go away," the baby exhales a rolling wave of laughter. Here Deitch opts for no music at all—just the sounds of Auntie marching around the frame, out of breath from her antics, sending the film into vibrations from her somersaults and heavy steps. To capture the action correctly, Deitch again turned to the author for a visual key to Auntie's gestures. Deitch also hired Helena Růžíčková, a famous Czech film actress, and had her dress like Auntie and reenact the story, again to be filmed for later reference for the studio's animators. The film ended up winning a string of awards, including a CINE Golden Eagle; it was named Outstanding Film of the Year at the London Film Festival and Best Children's Film at the Zagreb International Animation Film Festival.

Deitch's first body of work for Weston Woods also included *A Picture for Harold's Room* (1960, 1971 film), a sequel to Crockett Johnson's popular picture book, *Harold and the Purple Crayon* (1955, 1974 film), featuring the same nightshirted artist. The

technical problem with *A Picture for Harold's Room,* Deitch discovered, was that it could not be told sequentially, from the beginning to the end. Had he tried to animate the act of Harold drawing, not only would it have been impossible to perfectly match the lines, but this would have also produced a jerky motion between the frames. The solution, Deitch found, was to work backward from the completed pictures, erasing the lines until there was nothing left, while filming in reverse order after which the film could be run forward with smooth, seamless continuity.

In his adaptation of Quentin Blake's *Patrick* (1969, 1973 film), the sticking point for Deitch was getting a feeling for the main character. Deitch and the animators developed an idiosyncratic walk for the young fiddler, Patrick, with his shoulders tipped back and his long legs carrying him forward into his music-touched ramble. (Deitch would later demonstrate this gait with great élan in *The Picture Book Animated*). The other key element for Deitch was identifying just the right music to embody Patrick's generous spirit and his ability to bring joy and healing through his playing. As Deitch explained, he just happened to be playing a recording of an Antonín Dvořák violin concerto at home one evening when he came to a passage that brought Zdenka, who was in the other room of their apartment, to exclaim, "Patrick!" Once Deitch had the rhythms of the concerto, he also had the rhythms he needed for the film.

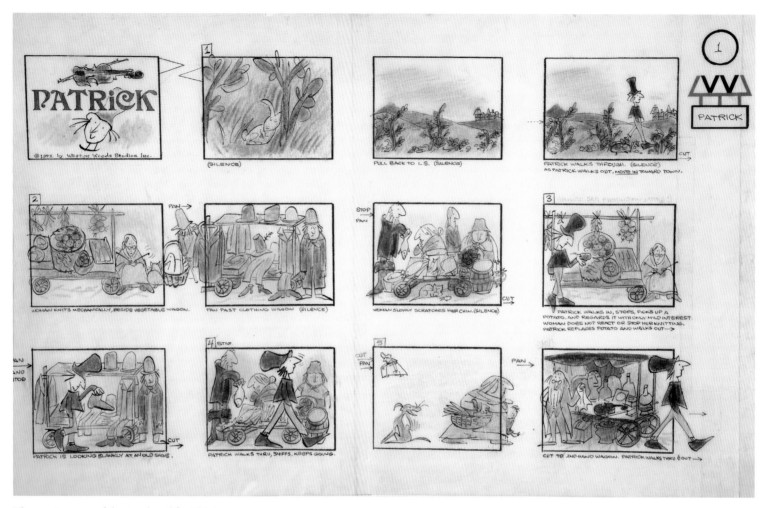

The opening page of the storyboard for Blake's
Patrick with annotations below each frame
describing the scene. The irrepressible Patrick
appears throughout the frames, literally walking out
of the last frame into the next page.

But nothing Deitch had done before quite prepared him for what he called "the Mount Everest of children's books," Maurice Sendak's *Where the Wild Things Are* (1963, 1975 and 1988 film). When Sendak and Deitch first met in Prague in 1969, Deitch reports, they "had some long walks through old and dark corners of the town" and agreed that they wanted to make "a magical film."[19] Sendak had two concerns for the project. First, according to Deitch, he explained that the film should "go beyond the book,"[20] but exactly what that might mean would take years—as well as a number of starts and stops—to realize; Sendak's second consideration was to underscore the centrality of Max in the story, urging Deitch to remember that in the book "everything is Max."[21] But how that might translate into a soundtrack, the beginning point for all of Deitch's productions, took some doing. Deitch recalled:

> *I wanted all of the sound effects to be within Max's home experience. So to create the Wild Things' dance rhythm, I restricted myself to domestic sounds, specifically those which might express Max's feeling of isolation: a gas oven lighting (a mother who was too busy for Max); a door slam (Max was shut in or out); a car starting (the father going off to work); a baby crying (competition). All of these sounds, repeated over and over on the tape loop, were used to heat up the music, which I distorted simply by spinning the record with my finger and letting the sound reverberate in my tape recordings. It took weeks to get all of these elements positioned just right onto the four tracks of my Quadro recorder.*[22]

Next came the animation art and how to translate Sendak's meticulously crosshatched drawings onto the animation cels while remaining faithful to Sendak's visionary illustrations. This, too, was a challenge and eventually called for "a new technique, developed especially for this film by one of the studio artists, Rudolf Holan, [who] made it possible to transfer the book's original rendering style directly onto our animation cels."[23] The character and background drawings for the film took well over a year. Next, Deitch had to figure out how to make the Wild Things move. Sendak had told Deitch that he wanted the creatures to have "slow, heavy, dreamlike movements"; in order to achieve this, Deitch had to devise "a way of photographing the phased drawings in an interweaving series of dissolves. This device, in combination with the slowed-down, wavering music and special effects, was part of our attempt to fulfill Maurice's wish for us to 'go beyond the book.'" But despite the innovations, consultations, and years of work on the project, things did not go smoothly. After making quite a bit of the animation for Max, for example, Deitch screened it for Sendak,

Morton Schindel (left) and Rudolf Holan, the background and character painter, reviewing animation cels for Maurice Sendak's *Where the Wild Things Are*, Prague, ca. 1974. Holan spent over a year adapting Sendak's distinctive cross-hatching style into images that could be animated.

Left: Deitch at work on the storyboards for *Where the Wild Things Are* in his Prague studio, ca. 1974.

Right: A sequence of cels shows how the movements of one character are rendered. (See lower right-hand corner of storyboard in photo at left.) To make the characters' gestures deliberately jerky and dreamlike, Deitch chose to leave out cels from the animation sequence.

Opposite: Sendak gave Deitch and his animators detailed instructions for Max's movements and the emotions that fueled them.

who was not pleased with many of Max's movements. To guide Deitch and his team of animators, Sendak drew sketches of how he wanted Max to act. In 1975 the film was finally released to both critical acclaim and debate: there were some who felt that the film went well beyond the book, and others who thought Deitch's animation of the Wild Things was a quavery distortion of the original art. After initially liking the auditory elements of the film, Sendak found that, in the end, he had reservations about the score, which led to the music eventually being redone in 1988 with a new, Mozart-inspired soundtrack by Peter Schickele. When asked by a reporter about the added expense and time spent on the new music, Schindel repeated his unwavering principle: "We take as long as it takes to make the film what it wants to be."[24]

Sometimes creative differences cannot be resolved, as Deitch explained in his account of William Steig's *Sylvester and the Magic Pebble* (1993), one of the last films that he made during this prolific period. According to Deitch, Steig had wanted his son, Jeremy, to compose the score for the film, but Deitch felt the son's music was not right for this project. Deitch was certain he could persuade Steig to change his mind once he heard the piece that Deitch had commissioned from a contemporary Czech composer. In the end, Steig refused to listen to this new work, insisting that the film be released with his son's score. "[Steig] loved the animation," Deitch recalled, "but the film was released in a crippled form, the music bland, the atmosphere lost. It was one of my most crushing defeats, yet my esteem for Steig's work goes on."[25]

In some respects, Deitch gave the studio's films their distinctive look—a look that was in harmony with the printed books themselves—and every one that passed through Deitch's authorial hands bore the marks of his shaping. Over the years, Deitch

① Caught in mid action by Mother's angry voice - frozen, for a moment, in 'chasing Jennie' gesture · Threatening, with fork in hand.

② fills with rage - puffs up - spontaneously Threatens Mother with fork - very stiff - very angular - jerky - gestapo-ish - no curves or jumping about - goose stepping gestures!

③ aggressive Thrust towards Mother - Stiff bending forward snarling - running movement.

④ begins stalking Mother - more aggressive - very wolf-like (like Gene's pic. no. Ⓔ but not so curved) - should be angular + a bit scary.

⑤ begins to get nervous (he's gone too far) - Settles for a 'fuck you' gesture - an 'I'd-like-to-kick-you-gesture. Quick Thrust of leg + foot + kind of ineffectual snarl gesture

⑥ resorts, finally, to little boy tongue sticking out. Casually drops fork. He's cooling off.

⑦ really nervous - has he gone too far? false bravado gesture - but he's scared. (Then he's sent to room)

note : all of this should be more agitated - more stacato! · all sharp pointing stabbing gestures - Hitler means: harsh, sharp goose-stepping gestures.

M. Sendak

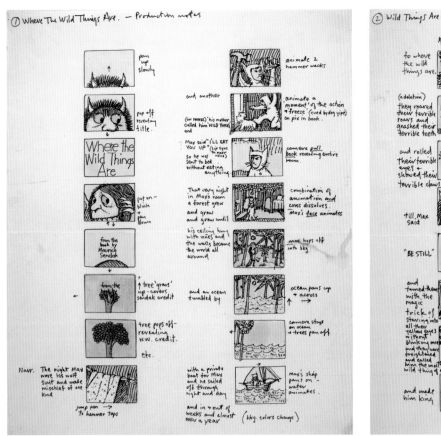

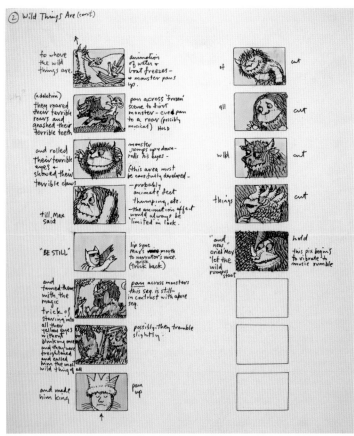

Production notes created by Weston Woods animators for the film adaptation of *Where the Wild Things Are.*

has won dozens of prizes and widespread acclaim for his films with Weston Woods. And given the breadth of his talents, Deitch's work with the studio is deserving of a book-length study in its own right. "Gene's contribution to the success of Weston Woods films is second to none," Schindel has claimed, adding, "I learn something with every new animated film I do with Gene….Each film is a new challenge for him, and he finds innovative solutions to the problems that the films presented. As he stretches his range, he pulls me along with him." What has kept Deitch from being more widely known, in Schindel's estimation, is the fact that he has been working in Czechoslovakia. Despite these distances, though, Schindel insists on an even larger assessment of Deitch's importance: he was "one of the unsung heroes of the children's literature field during its critical transition from picture books to the audiovisual age."[26] After many years of artistically collaborative work, Deitch wanted to work on other projects independent of Weston Woods, including an animated version of *Charlotte's Web* (1952), an ill-fated undertaking that Deitch describes in his online book, *How to Succeed in Animation.*

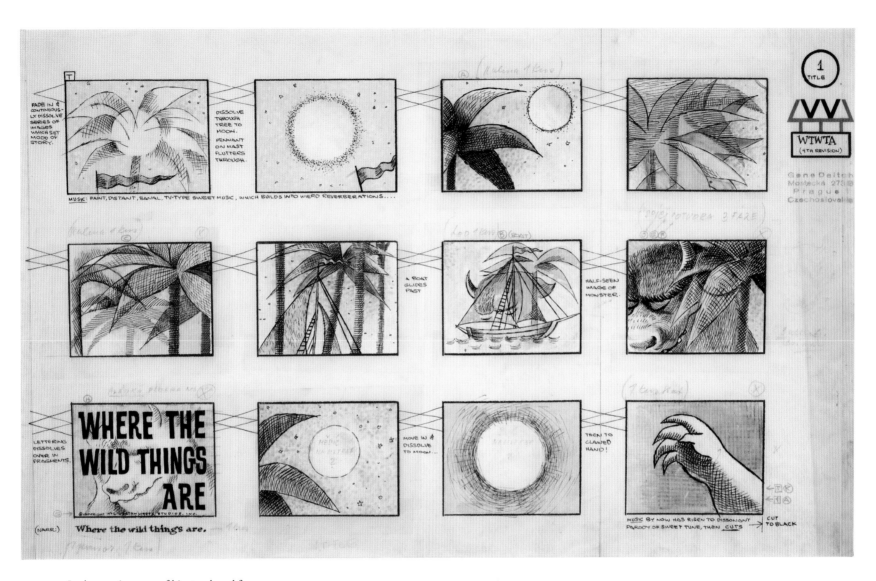

In the opening page of his storyboard for
Where the Wild Things Are, Deitch incorporated
some of Sendak's suggested adaptations. In a
manner similar to the book, the title sequence
previews elements from the story.

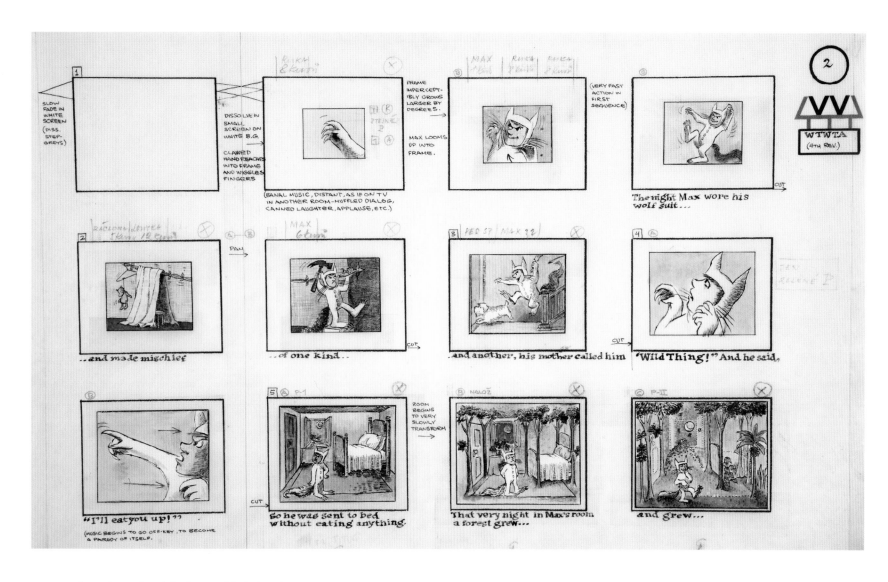

Some viewers found the focus on Max's clawed hand to be more menacing than the original illustrations. These concerns were soon overcome by the sheer kinetic energy of the film and also by the novelty of scenes that do not appear in the book, including Max's reaction to being called "Wild Thing!" by his mother.

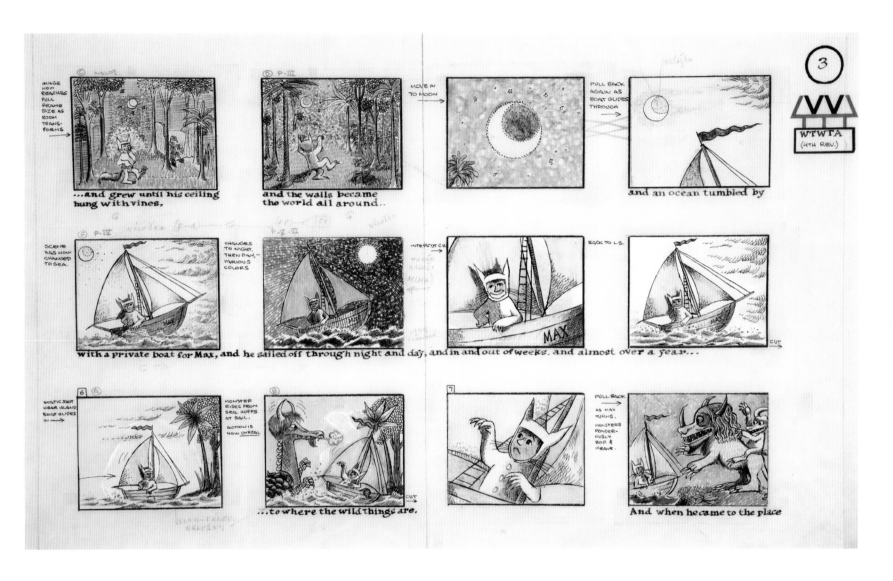

Deitch illustrates Max's haunting journey from
his room to the land of the Wild Things, depicting
the passage of time through images that are only
hinted at in the text.

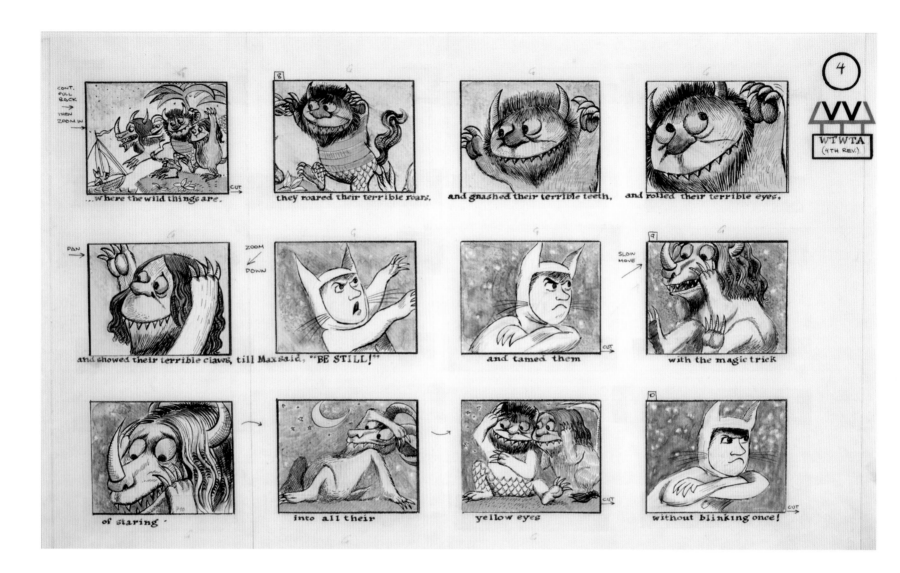

... where the wild things are.

they roared their terrible roars,

and gnashed their terrible teeth,

and rolled their terrible eyes,

and showed their terrible claws, till Max said, "BE STILL!"

and tamed them

with the magic trick

of staring ·

into all their

yellow eyes

without blinking once!

Max's first encounter with the Wild Things made full, effective use of the disjointed style of animation that Deitch, Holan, and others on the creative team had invented precisely to convey the meeting of two forces: a little boy and his very own monsters.

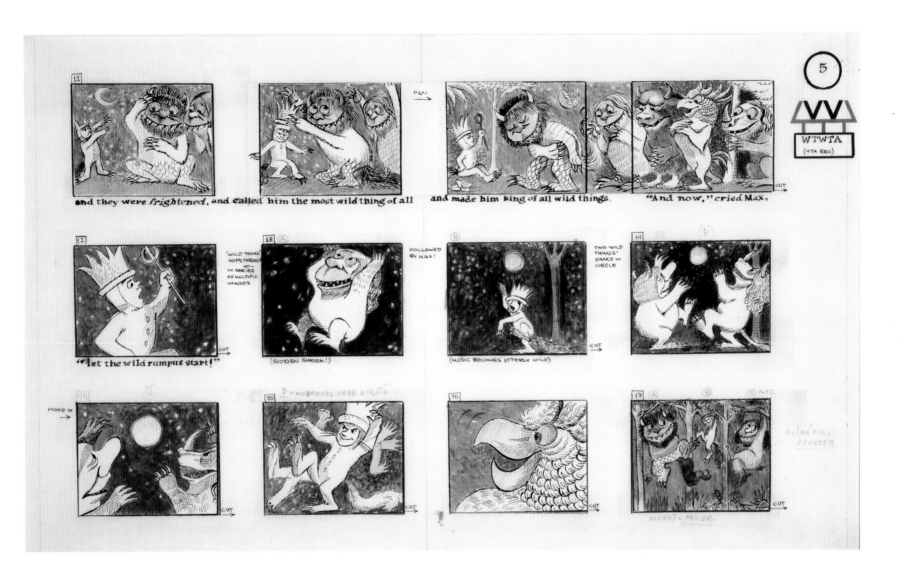

On this page, Deitch represents Max's coronation, which is followed by the famous "Wild Rumpus" scene. While the images of the rumpus are not accompanied by text, the soundtrack in both versions of the film was full of booming, crashing, bellowing sounds.

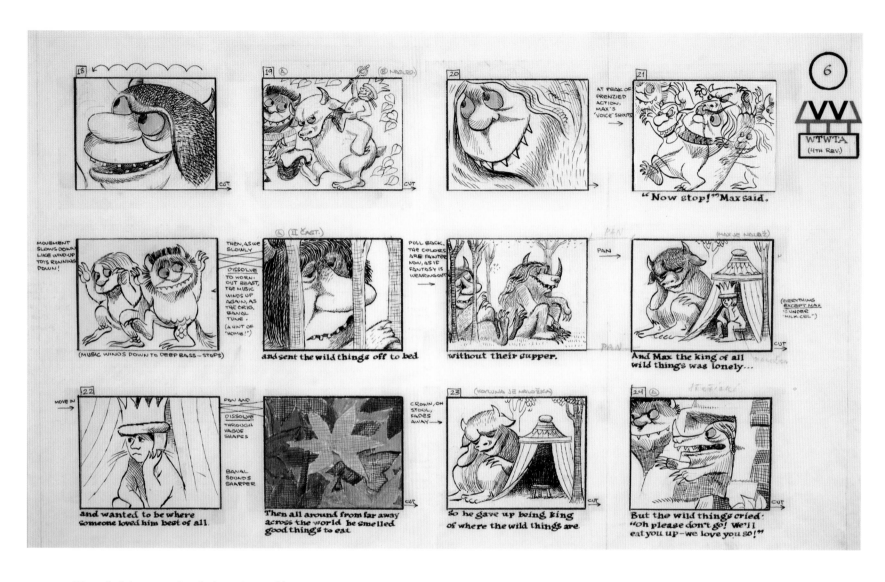

The end of the rumpus is only drawn in pencil here,
since Deitch indicated the colors and other visual
textures on previous pages. The only page that is in
full color is the one reminding Max of home.

The final storyboard page begins in black and white, with Max taking leave of the Wild Things, and then moves back to the colors of the original book as Max returns to his room. The final pan to the moon was in the storyboard, but not in the actual film or the book. The film ends with a shot of Max's supper sitting on the table under the window in his bedroom, and the moon can be seen outside the window.

An animation cel from Michael Sporn's adaptation of William Steig's *The Amazing Bone*. Actor John Lithgow narrated this film, the first of several projects he has done for Weston Woods.

Meanwhile, as the production schedule of Weston Woods films continued to grow, it was necessary to find talented directors who could maintain the high standards set by Deitch. One of these new filmmakers, Michael Sporn, had worked with the renowned animation team of John and Faith Hubley and was already recognized in his own right. Sporn was asked to create the animation for a group of films from books appearing in the 1970s and 1980s, including Wells's *Morris's Disappearing Bag* (1975, 1982 film), Steig's *The Amazing Bone* (1976, 1985 film), Stephen Kellogg's *The Mysterious Tadpole* (1977, 1986 film), and James Stevenson's *What's Under My Bed* (1983, 1990 film). Perhaps the most successful of Sporn's films was the adaptation of Steig's *Doctor De Soto* (1982, 1984 film), which is regarded as a pivotal Weston Woods film from this period. Sporn, like Deitch, has continued his association with the studio, most recently with his acclaimed adaptation of Mordicai Gerstein's *The Man Who Walked Between the Towers* (2003, 2005 film).

Above: *Doctor De Soto* was the first Weston Woods film to be nominated for an Academy Award. Although it didn't win this highly competitive and coveted prize, the nomination nevertheless helped to place the studio among the leading producers of short animated films for a general audience.

Right: Two animation cels (top) and a production still (bottom) from Michael Sporn's adaptation of William Steig's *Doctor De Soto.*

Chapter 6

Beyond the Picture Book

The storyteller joins the ranks of the teachers and sages…he is the man who could let the wick of his life be consumed completely by the gentle flame of his story.

—Walter Benjamin, "The Storyteller"

Within the first decade of the studio's opening, it was clear to Mort Schindel that the primary concern of Weston Woods was storytelling, regardless of the medium in which this ancient practice might take place. For Schindel, it wasn't a theoretical question of "hot" or "cool" media, terms that had been introduced by Marshall McLuhan's *Understanding Media* (1964) to describe the growing dominance of visual culture over print culture. Speaking to Rex Lardner, reporting for the *New York Times Book Review* in 1969, Schindel dismissed McLuhan's idea that "the medium is the message," along with the argument that because they engaged more of the sensory experience of their audience, visual media were superior to books. Rather, Schindel argued, "An advantage a book has over a film or a filmstrip is that these media are designed to go from beginning to end at a specified pace. But with a book you can go at your own pace. You can savor certain sentences or paragraphs.... You can skip pages if you like. A child can touch the picture the artist painted. He can look at the picture upside down if he wants. With a book, the reader is in complete control." Schindel went on to turn McLuhan's famous phrase on its axis by asserting, "the medium is the messenger." Surprising the interviewer, who had begun by expecting Schindel to be an unapologetic, outspoken defender of the value of the audiovisual media that he produced, Schindel instead insisted that "the book is the most personal and direct of all media of communication."[1]

The mantle of the bibliophile was not a new one for Schindel, who had built his reputation on his preservation of the integrity of the books on which his films were based. In fact, as we have seen, this position allowed Schindel to build trust with skeptical editors and publishers early on in the life of the studio, and it remains one of its core values. In the same *New York Times* interview, Lardner observed, in glowing terms, that "Morton Schindel of Weston, Conn., has done more in the past decade and a half to encourage children to read—a useful accomplishment, many think, for both learning and enjoyment—than anybody since Charles Dickens." And to add to his encomiums, Lardner went on to quote "a noted librarian," who had called Weston Woods "one of the world capitals of children's literature."[2]

As these kinds of accolades directed toward the studio's film work began to appear in print, Schindel was expanding the scope of Weston Woods to include other, more traditional approaches to storytelling. One of these forms was oral storytelling, which Schindel had become intensely interested in during the 1960s.

Schindel's fascination with this ancient tradition had been piqued by his contacts with Augusta Baker and other storytellers from the New York Public Library and by professional storytellers (and authors) like Marcia Brown. In 1958 Brown told him that in his dedication to storytelling, whatever medium it might take, he was engaged in a crucial act of cultural preservation. He was, she said, "a voice in the wilderness."[3] At the time, there was not a great deal of cultural value placed on traditional storytelling, except in those small pockets of awareness, like the children's rooms of public libraries, where the practice continued to flourish. But Schindel felt that the studio could help move storytelling beyond its appeal as a quaint relic of the past—an activity that now took place on a back porch, around a kitchen table, or perhaps at a folk festival—and into a more prominent, mediated position.

On a visit to the Chicago headquarters of the American Library Association during this period, Schindel met with Mildred Batchelder, the longtime, revered executive secretary of Children's Services and Young Adult Services at the ALA. Batchelder showed Schindel a series of in-house recordings that the ALA had begun to make of a number of storytellers, including Ruth Sawyer, the Newbery Award–winning author of *Roller Skates* (1936), who had achieved fame both as a writer and as an oral storyteller. Through Batchelder, Schindel became aware that "a generation of wonderful tellers of stories for children was passing on without their talents having been recorded for posterity." The act of preserving the work of some of these storytellers, Schindel thought, "would be a worthwhile contribution to the library profession."[4]

Ruth Sawyer became the first of a number of storytellers whom Schindel recorded over the years, making their work available on tape and LP recordings. The project was close to Schindel's heart since Sawyer was the mother-in-law of Robert McCloskey, though she and Schindel did not meet during the filming of *Make Way for Ducklings* (1941, 1955 film). Sawyer was in her eighties when Schindel approached

Schindel (right) gave Augusta Baker (center) and Elizabeth (Betty) Fast, the director of the Children's Library in Groton, CT, a tour of Weston Woods in a 1915 Ford Model T, a prop purchased for the live-action film *Homer Price*, ca. 1970. During the studio's early years, Baker, a talented storyteller, served as the final arbiter in any auditions of narrative voices for Weston Woods films.

her about recording a group of her stories, along with her comments about the art of storytelling. Schindel remembers that she was quite "frail," but "her voice was strong, and her delivery, even in conversation, had a dramatic quality that I had never before encountered." It was a difficult recording session, with many stops and starts and an even more difficult editing job afterward. "The job took weeks, which could not be justified or explained except by my need to pay my respects to a person who had left her mark on a profession into which I was now finding my way. She had borne a torch well and long that something in me now needed to take in hand and keep burning."[5] Despite some early reservations, Schindel ended up with enough material to do two LP recordings of Sawyer's stories, and just before her death in 1970, a third album of her tellings of Christmas legends, *Joy to the World* (1966, 1969 sound recording). To accompany a new edition of the book, the studio also produced a cassette recording of her reading *Journey Cake, Ho!* (1953, 1967 sound recording), which McCloskey had illustrated, and which Weston Woods began to distribute through its catalog.

With filmstrips and other variations on the studio's product line, Schindel continued to remain highly sensitive to the needs of his customers. Librarians, as previously mentioned, were responsible for adding a key product line to Weston Woods: filmstrips that could be shown with or without sound, at a pace that could be determined by the librarian. Since most children's librarians at public libraries are also trained as storytellers, they were excited about using the filmed versions of the picture books that Schindel was producing. But they wanted to have the option of providing the narratives themselves, thus accompanying the visual texts of the films, and so Schindel made available filmstrip versions of the stories that allowed the storyteller to control the pace of their particular tellings. The idea made perfect sense to Schindel when librarians suggested it to him, and he began to package the filmstrips with LP recordings (and later audiocassettes) of the stories, which could be used by the librarian if she or he wished.

For collections of filmstrips and LPs, Weston Woods designed ever more elaborate packaging, often with special pullout compartments for the small booklets that contained the texts of the stories and round die cuts to hold the filmstrip canisters. The filmstrips could be purchased individually with their text booklets, in sets (a box of four stories), series (eight filmstrips in boxes with sliding drawers), or a library (ten filmstrips, booklets, and recordings in a large storage case).

By introducing so many children to classic works of literature through their film and filmstrip versions, Weston Woods was building a new audience for the books themselves, a good number of which had gone out of print. Publishers soon realized

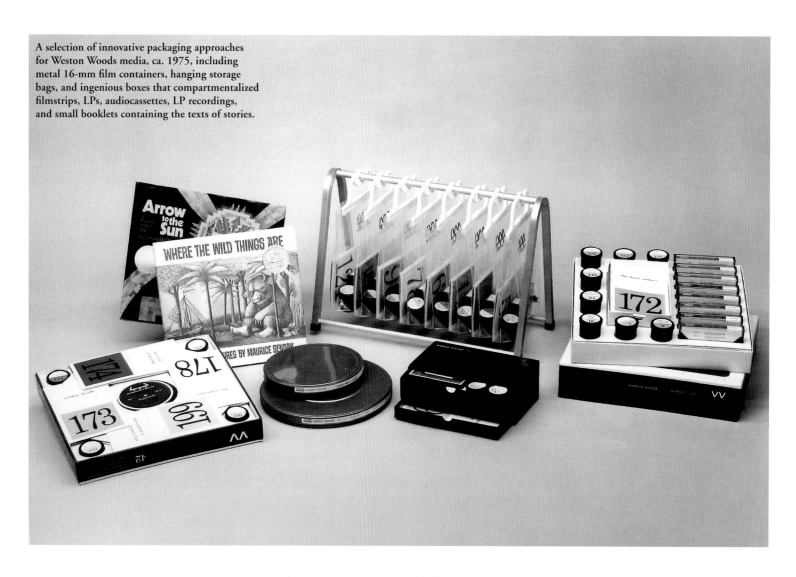

A selection of innovative packaging approaches for Weston Woods media, ca. 1975, including metal 16-mm film containers, hanging storage bags, and ingenious boxes that compartmentalized filmstrips, LPs, audiocassettes, LP recordings, and small booklets containing the texts of stories.

that inexpensive, paperback editions of these Weston Woods–revitalized works were an easy way to fill a niche.

The public school library market was expanding as was the size and shape of the paperbacks that accompanied the films; it became clear that there must be a better way for librarians and other consumers to store and retrieve the filmstrips, books, LPs, and later, cassettes. Again, the genie of innovation came to Schindel's rescue—this time from an unlikely source. Schindel had bought a shirt that came in a plastic bag that hung on a rod for display. While unsealing it, he had an idea for a kind of packaging that would literally sort out Weston Woods' growing product line. In 1976 he spun off a new company named Monaco (named after himself and his then wife, Nancy) to produce the bags, which he called "hang-ups," to hold these media materials.

Schindel (left) happily demonstrates the versatility of the Monaco bags to a group of visiting librarians, ca. 1975.

Jackie Torrence, a famed storyteller, was featured on storyteller recordings and on a video called *The Story Lady*.

These sturdy plastic sacks, complete with handles and sealing snaps, were an instant hit with librarians, who requested that the bags be produced in a wide range of sizes to accommodate the individual books, films, and recordings for each title. But librarians found that it was impossible to easily arrange and to keep the bags in order, since they slid over each other and ended up in unruly piles. This problem led Schindel to invent a simple aluminium rack with an adjustable rod from which the bags could be suspended by their handles (similar to a closet pole). These racks would sit on a library shelf and provide a way to organize and display the bags when they were not in use. Later he developed a freestanding, multitiered, turning metal rack system. Since patenting his original idea, Schindel's bags have gone global and are used in such places as pharmacies, craft stores, laboratories, and parts departments around the world. In fact, Schindel has confided that the sales on the bags produced by Monaco have provided a cushion of capital that has kept Weston Woods financially afloat, beyond its critical successes and its rising sales.

Over the years, this kind of steady support has allowed Schindel, as the mythologist Joseph Campbell discussed in *The Power of Myth* (1988), to "follow his bliss." The pursuit of this bliss led Schindel to produce the Storytelling Circle, a series of LP recordings of storytellers by such notable artists as Laura Simms, David Holt, Diane Wolkstein, Rafe Martin, Heather Forest, Jay O'Callahan, Barbara Freeman, and Connie Regan, to name just a few. This series included compilations of storytelling performances from the famous National Storytelling Festival, held each year since 1973 in Jonesborough, Tennessee. The festival was initially sponsored by the National Association for the Perpetuation and Preservation of Storytelling (NAPPS), now the International Storytelling Association. Especially important were the stories of the dynamic African-American storyteller Jackie Torrence, who was known both in her home state of North Carolina and nationally as "The Story Lady." Torrence was recognized for her tellings of Brer Rabbit and Appalachian mountain stories, as well as for her tales about such mythic figures as John Henry, Annie Christmas, and High John the Conqueror. Weston Woods produced a collection of Torrence's stories titled *Legends from the Black Tradition* (1982). Although the storytelling recordings never sold in great numbers, they were an act of unflagging devotion for Schindel that kept him close to the original, oral source of stories—a subject that has always fascinated him. In 2006 the International Storytelling Center conferred on Schindel its Lifetime Achievement Award for "blazing new trails for the power of storytelling."[6]

Pete Seeger and other folksingers provided still another variation on this theme for Weston Woods, which distributed an animated version of Seeger's book

The Foolish Frog (1973, 1973 film), which he had written with his brother, Charles Seeger. This shaggy-dog story about a banjo-playing farmer who meets an ostentatious frog—to great, nonsensical consequences—was set to music by Seeger, with Gene Deitch's folk-art-style animation. In a similar vein, traditonal songs like *Frog Went A-Courtin'* (1955, 1961 film) and *Over in the Meadow* (1957, 1968 film) became books adapted from their original lyrical sources by John Langstaff with illustrations by Feodor Rojankovsky. The songs were recorded in Langstaff's strong baritone voice, and these vocals provided the music for the two films that were based on these lyrics. A classically trained singer and music educator, Langstaff had founded the Christmas Revels in 1971 in Cambridge, Massachusetts, as a way, he explained, to "draw people together through the power of ritual, music, dance, and drama. There's a need for art that connects us to each other."[7] Given these shared purposes and affinities, it's no wonder that he and Schindel became good friends, and in 1969 Langstaff was one of the featured artists in Weston Woods' first portfolio, an elegantly designed catalog that celebrated those staunch defenders of children's literature whom Leonard Marcus would coin in the title of his 2008 book, the "Minders of Make-Believe."

Reflecting then current music curricula of most American schools, the Weston Woods catalogs of the 1960s, 1970s, and 1980s were filled with books based on musical "stories" that had been drawn from familiar children's songs, poems, and nursery rhymes, many of them folk favorites. By the late 1980s, a number of these musical works had become Weston Woods films, and Schindel began to produce LPs that featured filmstrips based on picture book classics like Randolph Caldecott's *Hey Diddle Diddle* (1882, 1962 filmstrip), Edward Lear's *The Owl and the Pussycat* (1871, 1971 film), and Eugene Field's *Wynken, Blynken, and Nod* (1889, 1971 film), as well as American standards like *The Star-Spangled Banner* (from the book by Peter Spier published in 1973, 2002 film) and *Yankee Doodle* (with Stephen Kellogg's rollicking illustrations from 1976, 1976 film).

Continually seeking novel ways to introduce stories to his audience, Schindel frequently sent promotional mailings of small, flexible vinyl records (also known as floppies) of the soundtracks of new Weston Woods releases, along with the catalogs. Additionally, Schindel used these recordings as a way of keeping in touch with the studio's ever-widening circle of friends, particularly during the holiday season. Among these audio communiqués were Ezra Jack Keats's *The Snowy Day* (1962, 1964 film), Gail E. Haley's *A Story, A Story* (1970, 1973 film), and Maurice Sendak's *Where the Wild Things Are* (1963, 1975 and 1988 film). When asked about these records, Schindel waved them aside as a kind of promotional greeting card. Yet the mailings

This production still from *The Foolish Frog,*
Pete and Charles Seeger's retelling of the traditonal
folk song of the same name, exemplifies the
broad scope of source material used by the studio,
ca. early 1970s.

also made an important point, subliminal as it may have been: it was essential for the stories that the studio was telling visually to also be *heard.*

These audio "experiments" expanded to include cassette tapes in the 1970s, when this medium began to replace LP recordings. Another tradition that Schindel initiated at this time was to record the Caldecott and Newbery Awards acceptance speeches that were given at the annual summer conference of the American Library Association. As a sign of gratitude towards the ALA for its unwavering support (exemplified by the permission given by the ALA to reproduce the seals of the Caldecott and Newbery Medals on the covers of its products), the studio provided all attendees with complimentary cassettes.

The studio stood at the beginning of what would become a seemingly omnivorous and omnipresent interest in the backstory—the curiosity and fascination with prior experiences—of artists and other prominent public figures whom we admire. Today we take for granted the Internet's ability to provide firsthand exposure to events like awards speeches. At an earlier time, however, Weston Woods provided this same information through its recordings. Similarly, today we expect to find, with the stroke of an ENTER key, readily available background material about authors and illustrators and the works they create—on publishers' web sites, blogs, or through other, easily accessible information sources. Once again, Weston Woods was ahead of the curve.

For Schindel, though, there was a larger purpose in the telling of backstories: educating the viewers, both children and adults, about the nature of books and about the talented individuals who created them. This broader sense of purpose, coupled with Schindel's profound admiration for the artists he was working with, led the studio to produce a series of documentaries about the writers and illustrators of notable children's books including McCloskey, James Daugherty, Keats, and Sendak. Generally, these documentaries were just under twenty minutes, and shortened versions of them were folded into the VHS and DVD compilations made by Weston Woods in the 1980s and 1990s. These "meet the author" segments continue to be an integral part of the studio's documentation of the artists whose works it has adapted, a focus that one can see most recently, for example, in its Author's Library, which features *Getting to Know Simms Taback* (2005), *David McPhail: The Film* (2007), and *Virginia Lee Burton: A Sense of Place* (2008).

Schindel decided to tell the story of the studio's productions using the very medium in which they were made, since the 1960s brought more and more visitors to Weston Woods (at its peak, more than a thousand guests annually) and tours were not always possible for the number of people who expressed interest. This led Schindel to produce the documentary *The Lively Art of Picture Books* (1964), which was meant for a single screening at the annual conference of the American Library Association. The film, narrated by John Langstaff, provided an overview of the history of the picture book, with a group of interviews featuring three well-known practitioners of the art form: McCloskey, Barbara Cooney, and Sendak. The documentary proved to be so popular that there were repeated requests for it from librarians around the country, and eventually Schindel released a commercial version available through the Weston Woods catalog. Initially, the film had cost twenty-five thousand dollars to produce—not an insignificant sum in the 1960s. However, it was a cost that Schindel was willing to absorb to spread the word about the studio's primary purpose of celebrating the picture book. Over the years, the film would become a popular part of the studio's Signature Collection, and eventually would bring in more than six hundred thousand dollars in sales. Although the film was intended primarily for an audience of librarians, Schindel hoped it would reach academics—library science, college, and university professors who taught children's literature courses—a group that he was interested in cultivating. In some respects, *The Lively Art of Picture Books* had been made with this group in mind, given its historical rooting in Caldecott and the traditions of the picture book, as well as the attention it paid to contemporary artists. Schindel's documentary, in fact, contained the earliest filmed interview with Sendak and the only profile of James Daugherty on film. When *The Lively Art of Picture Books* appeared, Ruth Hill Viguers, the editor of the prestigious *Horn Book Magazine,* called the film one of the "milestones" that "have marked the progress of the picture book in the United States." She went on to describe it as "a stunning testimonial to picture books at their best."[8]

Schindel's interest in nonfictional storytelling would inevitably lead the studio to make or distribute other documentaries, some of which focused on figures from the history of children's literature. The highly regarded *Mr. Shepard and Mr. Milne* (1973) tells the story of the friendship behind the creation of the children's book *Winnie the Pooh* (1926). The film was produced in England at some of the actual settings for Milne's stories and Shepard's illustrations, and included an interview with Shepard. Other documentaries in the series, like *Children of the North Lights: A Portrait of Ingri and Edgar D'Aulaire* (1977) and *Edward Ardizzone* (1978), were likewise produced outside the studio but were distributed by Weston Woods, thus becoming part of the Signature Collection as well. One of the studio's later documentaries, *Beatrix Potter: Artist, Storyteller, and Countrywoman* (1993), based on the biography by Judy Taylor and narrated by Lynn Redgrave, won *Booklist*'s Editor's Choice Award and the Gold Apple Award at the National Educational Film and Video Festival.

But perhaps the most complex of the documentaries that Weston Woods produced was *Gene Deitch: The Picture Book Animated* (1977), which told the story of Deitch's creative process. This, too, was a celebration of Deitch's remarkable talents and Schindel's deep admiration for all that he had done to define the studio's work during its golden age. Schindel wisely let Deitch write his own narrative for the documentary, which begins with a reenactment of Deitch standing on the Charles Bridge in Prague opening a package that contains a picture book from Weston Woods, his next animation assignment.

Deitch had carefully scripted the entire documentary. In fact, it was meant to be structured like one of his films, with an unfolding sense of drama as it explores how he takes a picture book story and literally builds a film out of its elements, "fleshing out" aspects of the book that need to be given a physical life on the screen, right down to the walk a character might have. In the film, Deitch describes part of the process: "I remember how Quentin Blake and Mort Schindel and Zdenka and I all met in a London hotel room, trying to imagine how Patrick (the title character of the book *Patrick*, by Quentin Blake) might walk. How a character walks is often a visual key to his whole personality. Well, there we were, all galumphing around that hotel room, trying to find a walk that would express Patrick's dreamy inner life."[9] Deitch then demonstrated the walk, with shoulders back and hands in pockets, the walk that Patrick would finally adopt in the film (see p. 75). In fascinating detail, Deitch also described the music made on wooden instruments for Pat Hutchins's *Changes, Changes* (1971, 1973 film), and the haunting first soundtrack for Sendak's *Where the Wild Things Are*.

Gene Deitch: The Picture Book Animated was full of such creative revelations. We learn, for example, that two of Deitch's more difficult projects were his adaptations of Crockett Johnson's *A Picture for Harold's Room* (1960, 1971 film) and *Harold's Fairy Tale* (1955, 1974 film) because, as was mentioned earlier, to keep the lines of Harold's famous purple crayon steady, Deitch was "forced to shoot the entire film backwards," erasing the lines that Harold draws as the movie backed up to the beginning. In the final version, of course, the film is projected forward, and Harold's lines flow smoothly on the screen. This exploration of Deitch's approach to animation provided an energizing, human look at a remarkably vital talent, and the documentary was a solid success for the studio. In fact, the film continues to be listed in the studio's catalog and to be referenced widely, especially online, and particularly on sites devoted to the history and art of animation.

An animation cel from *Harold's Fairy Tale* by Crockett Johnson. Gene Deitch reveals the difficulties he encountered while animating Harold in the Weston Woods documentary *Gene Deitch: The Picture Book Animated*.

To animate this book, Harold's pictures had to be first drawn in their entirety. Animation cels of Harold drawing were then photographed in reverse order, with the purple line being erased from the background at regular intervals.

But Schindel, the founding father of the children's literary "edutainment" movement, tells his own story in the documentary film *Morton Schindel: From Page to Screen* (1981), in which he provides the viewer with a guided tour of the studio as both a tranquil physical space and a wellspring of creative activity. The film, which remains in print, is one of Schindel's ongoing projects that aim to document—through audio and video interviews, newspaper and magazine articles, autobiographical statements and position papers, product descriptions and other corporate records—a complete, unabridged history of the studio. In one respect, the film was intended as a means of explaining the studio to its audience. But in a deeper sense, it is Schindel's subtle testament to the studio's guiding principles.

Chapter 7

Experiments in Imagination

I feel that you and all these lovely people in your studio…are modern interpreters, modern instruments.…We're all simply interpreting the story and carrying it one stage further.…

—Gail E. Haley, *Gene Deitch: The Picture Book Animated*

A s the 1960s progressed, the staff of Weston Woods grew to the point where the studio could essentially run itself, without Schindel having to be present for every decision. This freedom allowed him to focus on highly experimental areas of production where he felt the studio might leave its mark. Schindel was restless, in search of the new, and "boredom is the dream bird that hatches the egg of experience" as the German critic Walter Benjamin suggests in his essay "The Storyteller."[1]

During this period, Schindel's connections with Gene Deitch and the Prague-based animation studio had become stronger. Schindel would visit Prague several times a year and attend art events such as mime and puppet shows, blacklight and magic-lantern theater performances, and avant-garde animation, all of which were popular in Czechoslovakia but which were unfamiliar to him, as they were to most Westerners (and Americans in particular). "When I was going regularly to Prague," Schindel remembers, "the directors there whose work reflected great talent almost never got their work shown out of the Eastern Bloc of countries for screenings."[2] This was especially true in the aftermath of the Prague Spring, those months of social, political, and artistic liberation in 1968, before the government cracked down again on anything and everything that could be seen as "dissent."

Out of solidarity with a number of Prague's filmmakers, Schindel was eager to explore the possibility of distributing their films, but he thought the films might be a difficult sell to his American audience of librarians, teachers, and educators. Schindel took up this challenge by working with Miroslav Stepanek, a Czech animator who created stop-action animation with puppets. He was so impressed with Stepanek's film *The Shooting Gallery* (1969) that Schindel sent a promotional version

The SIM collection
of stimulating, imaginative and motivating
non-verbal discussion films

THE GIANTS

The hostility of two animated antagonists
takes the form of faceless giants who ultimately abandon their cowardly masters in
a protest against violence and despotism.
Animated with documentary footage,
color, 10 minutes
Sale $150, Rental $10

JABBERWOCKY

Borrowing its title from Lewis Carroll's
famous nonsense poem, this film presents
a bizarre adventure in the subconscious. A
startling free association of ideas is created by the unexpected actions of a group
of childhood animated toys and games,
provoking viewer reaction and debate.
Animated, color, 14 minutes
Sale $150, Rental $15

MAITRE

Rejection makes an avant-garde artist
unable to function creatively until his fan-
tasies free him from the self-restraints imposed by others' criticisms.
Animated, color, 11 minutes
Sale $120, Rental $10

MIME OVER MATTER

The artistry of Czechoslo-
vakian pantomimist Ladis-
lav Fialka and his gifted
company conveys with
humor and pathos the
struggle between a man
and mechanical objects
he takes for granted.
Live-action, color, 12 minutes
Sale $150, Rental $12

Mr. Koumal

Each MR. KOUMAL series consists of three episodes
in which Mr. Koumal — the modern Don Quixote — is
pitted against life's trials and tribulations. A — CAR-
RIES THE TORCH, INVENTS A ROBOT, FLIES LIKE A
BIRD. B — FACES DEATH, CRUSADES FOR LOVE,
MOVES TO THE COUNTRY. C — DISCOVERS KOUMAL-
IA, GETS INVOLVED, BATTLES HIS CONSCIENCE.
Animated, color, 1½ — 2½ minutes each
Sale $35 each or 3/$100, Rental 3/$7

THE SHOOTING GALLERY

A pair of three-di-
mensional figures
breaks out of the
mechanical imprisonment of a carnival shooting gallery to find the joy of freedom. But shots from the gun
of a military figure send them plummeting to the
ground, flattening them out and restoring the gallery
to its oppressive, predictable order.
Animated, color, 6 minutes
Sale $125, Rental $7

This SIM catalog reflects the expanding interests
of the studio, including distribution of works
by Czech artists like the avant-garde animator
Jan Švankmajer, 1977.

of the film to the studio's mailing list. According to Schindel, the typical response was, "'It's a beautiful, very interesting picture, but we don't know the book.'"[3] Still, this initial lack of enthusiasm did not deter Schindel from wanting to bring what he thought were exciting discoveries to American audiences. And so he formed a new company, SIM, named after his young daughter of the same name (born in 1955) to travel down yet another creative avenue. In the promotional literature for these films, Schindel offered another meaning for the name of the company: SIM was an acronym for "Stimulation, Imagination, Motivation," which were qualities "that characterized all of the films that I acquired in Czechoslovakia for distribution under that label."[4]

The works that Schindel called attention to through SIM were meant to be, according to the company's 1973 brochure, "adventures in education through non-verbal films…[that] serve as insights into the human condition. They are an adventure in provocative education for any receptive mind." The SIM films were described elsewhere in the promotional material as "episodes in 'the life of the imagination.'"[5] Among the many SIM titles were Gene Deitch's *Mr. Koumal* (1969), "nine short ironic vignettes…featuring an animated Chaplinesque figure beset by life's poignant ironies" and *The Giants* (1969), a prophetic "black comedy" about "the futility of revenge," which Schindel described in the brochure as "a film aimed at older children, attacking violence and especially about how we rely on weapons (psychological as well as actual) to maintain the hostile stance, without which so many feel vulnerable." Of course the catalog included the film that inspired this venture, Stepanek's *The Shooting Gallery* (1970). This film about puppetlike figures that are eliminated when they depart from their role as targets was characterized in the SIM catalog as "a poetic drama which depicts the contrast between tender fantasy and wanton destruction." In addition, SIM distributed the live-action pantomime *Mime Over Matter* (1970), which asked its audience to consider the power of art to transcend the limitations of often absurdly mechanized modern realities. The brochure also explained the purpose of such an unusual array of productions: "Each SIM film, having an open-ended format, is ideal for subjective interpretation and group discussion…as in many great works of literature or music, no single conclusion can be drawn; there is no 'correct' or 'wrong' explanation. The films are full of fresh perspectives on ecology, values, politics, art, psychology, aesthetics, and a vast range of human emotions.…Abounding with creative animation, these films use the most advanced cinematographic techniques, incorporating 'wordless eloquence,' which leaves the audience speechless or draws them into effusive discussion."

While Schindel believed wholeheartedly in the talents of the artists, the principles that their films conveyed, and the educational purposes that these works might serve, he knew that SIM was a risky business venture. A hundred or so films were sold to high schools in New York City for use in language arts classes. Although it may have helped to spread the word about some talented Czech artists and to spark discussion among some American audiences, the series was not a financial success. In all likelihood, a collection of films on such pertinent topics would meet a very different, happier fate today.

But if Schindel's "Czech initiative" failed in the financial column, it paid dividends in the creative cachet that it created for the studio. For example, through SIM Schindel imported Jan Švankmajer's surreal, stop-action animation version of the famous nonsensical poem *Jabberwocky* (1872, 1971 film) by Lewis Carroll. In the wake of the political and artistic repression that followed the Prague Spring of 1968, the renowned Švankmajer could not get this film, or others, screened in Czechoslovakia. After meeting Schindel during one of his visits to Prague, Švankmajer implored him to take the film to America. Schindel was fascinated by Švankmajer's technique of using real objects to animate films; in *Jabberwocky*, for instance, the cast of objects includes antique games, toys, dolls, furniture, and clothing from the nineteenth century, along with one very lively black cat that disrupts both the action and the viewer's expectations at key moments. Included in the 1977 SIM catalog, the film was described as "a bizarre adventure in the subconscious." Though Schindel's experiment with SIM was short-lived, it nevertheless presaged other arts-related, educational possibilities for the studio to explore, adding to its already successful commitment to literature-based films.

Schindel's frequent travels to Prague also energized his interest in puppetry, a vibrant part of the Czech art scene. Puppet performances were familiar sights, whether in the open air, in cabarets, at the famous National Marionette Theater, or in Jiří Trnka's animated films. (The latter had been making their way to the United States since the 1950s and were distributed through William Snyder's studio, Rembrandt Films.) Once again, Schindel was drawn to a sophisticated form of storytelling that had been relatively neglected in the United States, except on children's television programs like *Howdy Doody, Captain Kangaroo,* and *Mr. Rogers' Neighborhood,* where the puppetry was fairly rudimentary. However, the arrival of *Sesame Street* on television in 1969 ushered in a magical time for this art form in America, which culminated in 1976 when Jim Henson's *The Muppet Show* began its fabled five-year run as one of the most popular shows on prime-time television.

Top: Robert McCloskey constructing one of his intricate puppets, which he made during an extended stay at Weston Woods, ca. 1970.

Bottom: Lisl Weil dances into existence one of her large drawings from *The Sorcerer's Apprentice.* Weil's popular performances inspired Schindel to film her interpretation of this classic piece.

Opposite: A study for the cover of a book adaptation of *The Sorcerer's Apprentice,* ca. early 1960s.

Meanwhile, closer to home and independent of Prague's puppeteers, Schindel's friend Robert McCloskey (an inveterate tinkerer like his semiautobiographical character, Homer Price), had been experimenting with puppets for years, often while on extended visits to Weston Woods. An essential part of his idea for a potential television show, his puppets were animal characters, subtly articulated by means of extremely intricate mechanisms made up of gears, tiny wires, pulleys, and levers—all of which were hidden from view. Always the consummate artist, McCloskey took his time with his puppets, as he did with his picture books. He was not interested in rushing his characters into production; instead, he sought a kind of mechanical perfection in his elaborate creations. Schindel was so impressed with what he saw that he showed McCloskey holding one of the puppets in a publicity photograph for his documentary about the writer, simply titled *Robert McCloskey* (1964).

After McCloskey's death in 2003, Schindel rescued the puppets from a tangle of wires and gear cogs in storage boxes and placed them proudly on display in Weston Woods' gallery building. Schindel even made a brief movie about them, with a vintage film clip of McCloskey demonstrating how they worked, as well as an interview with the costume designer who had made the first clothes for the creatures and who had helped to restore them to their original state.

Another experimental work that Schindel committed to film was an unusual version of Paul Dukas's musical composition *The Sorcerer's Apprentice* (1897, 1963 film) by the author/illustrator Lisl Weil. Growing up in Austria, Weil was formally trained as a dancer; as an adult, she became an innovative, multitalented performance artist who practiced what she called "visual listening." Weil states that in her work, "each note played, each measure, equals a line drawn by me. Every tone I draw, every color I use, depicts the mood of the music and its story. It shows the close relationship of all the arts."[6] As Lee Kingman, a scholar of Weil's work, explains: "This love of dance and music, combined with [Weil's] ability to draw so spontaneously, led to her remarkable performances for more than twenty years with the Little Orchestra Society of New York and other major orchestras. During the playing of such pieces as *Petrouchka* and *The Firebird,* Weil drew the characters and their stories—in perfect time and with dancelike gestures—on huge panels stretched across the stage."[7]

Schindel had seen Weil's performance of *The Sorcerer's Apprentice* and was so impressed that he decided to film her dynamic approach to this classic piece (even though Disney had popularized and, in some respects, laid claim to this story by incorporating it into the animated film *Fantasia* [1940], with Mickey Mouse as the conductor). For Schindel, it was a difficult project to film, and he was not altogether happy

In a study for her book, Weil illustrated the source of inspiration for her performance of *The Sorcerer's Apprentice*, the musical score from Dukas's famous orchestral work.

with the results; he thought the Weston Woods version lacked the electricity and in-the-moment energy of Weil's live stage performances. Schindel was working within the limits of film technology, before the advent of Steadicams, which would have allowed a better following of Weil's interpretation. Nevertheless, he again let Joseph Campbell's directive—to "follow [his] bliss"—steer his actions towards his desire to visually document an ephemeral event that had enriched the cultural lives of children.

Perhaps the most time-consuming and complex of Schindel's explorations of alternative modes of storytelling was *Alexander and the Car with a Missing Headlight* (1967, 1967 film), a film that he acquired for distribution after seeing it in Munich. The movie is centered on a boy who befriends a car that seems ready for the scrap heap. Together they escape from the junkyard and go on an adventure through city streets, where they are chased by a tenacious dog, and eventually across the ocean and through the jungles of Africa, making friends and meeting guides and helpers along the way. *Alexander* was the inspired work of a young German director, Peter Fleischmann, and the evolution of this film is a fascinating story in its own right. Schindel describes the process this way:

> *Peter was a young director studying cinema in Paris.* Alexander *was his idea of a children's fantasy. He wanted to involve children in the production. Through the grapevine, he heard about a school in some remote part of Paris—a poor area—where there was a teacher, Mademoiselle Tortel, with a creative bent. She emphasized the artistic expression of children. Peter tells of how, when he went there, he was immediately surrounded by walls full of children's art. It blew his mind and fired his imagination. He arranged with Mademoiselle Tortel for the children to do the art for his film. But he did much more. Fleischmann told his fantasy to the children. He listened to their comments, to how they improvised on his story. He allowed his original concept to find a new configuration, which was a blending of his ideas and those of the children. He took them on walks of Paris so that they could identify the buildings and squares that they would draw for the film. When the youngsters went to work on the art, it was rendered in anything from eight-foot murals to little four-by-six-inch pictures. Peter's one directive [to them] was that anything that moved had to be drawn on a separate piece of paper. When the backgrounds were all laid out, the moving figures and objects were cut out, and the children showed Peter how they would move. Only then were the graphics taken to a studio, where they were animated in accordance with the children's directives.* [8]

Upon completion, Fleischmann took the film back to Germany, where he had kindergarten students in Munich comment on the film, suggest changes, and make sound effects. The process took months of meetings, tapings, editing (including the addition of a few new pictures from the German children). When Schindel saw the film, he immediately wanted to bring out an English-language version of the production and distribute it through Weston Woods. To make an English translation of the film, Schindel found an obvious solution: enlist the help of children in the Weston area to provide a soundtrack that would have "the same sense of freedom and participation" exhibited by the German children. [9]

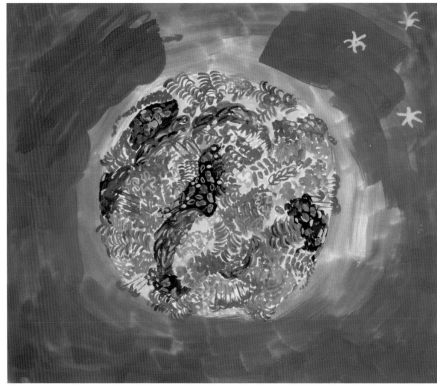

Top left and right: Original tempera paintings created by Parisian schoolchildren for the film *Alexander and the Car with a Missing Headlight,* directed by Peter Fleischmann, ca. 1965. Schindel arranged for the paintings to be shipped from France to Weston Woods so they could be preserved in the studio's archive.

Because there was no physical book upon which the *Alexander* film was based, Schindel decided to create one to preserve Weston Woods' connection with the written word. Viking Press agreed to publish the volume, which made use of the French and German children's original drawings that Schindel had shipped to the United States from Europe. Complications arose during production, however, due to the fact that the animation art had to be rephotographed and then laid out in book format. Although Schindel was "never quite satisfied" with the outcome, the book sold out its first print run of twenty thousand copies and the film was showered with critical plaudits while on the festival circuit. After several decades, the film continues to garner interest and remains in the Weston Woods catalog. In a broader sense, Schindel had reservations about "whether this film was an insight into the child's mind, meant primarily for an adult audience; or whether it would appeal to children as well. Clearly, it has successfully straddled the fence." What especially pleased Schindel, he continues, was that *Alexander and the Car with a Missing Headlight* "has motivated a number of youngsters to make animated films of their own and send them to me."[10]

Weston Woods would try to promote other experimental works, like *The Painting Ship* (1973), a short documentary by Rob Houwer, a colleague of

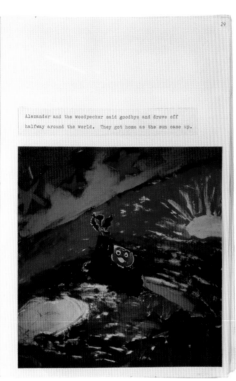

With the help of the woodpecker, Alexander flew up to the
sky and took a star to use as a headlight.
It worked perfectly.
The people in the castle were all very pleased.

Alexander and the woodpecker said goodbye and drove off
halfway around the world. They got home as the sun came up.

Reversing the usual order, Schindel first produced the film *Alexander and the Car with a Missing Headlight* and later adapted this title into a book, published in conjunction with Viking Press.

Fleischmann's, about an "open" art school for children housed on a barge in an Amsterdam canal. Although Schindel did not particularly like the film itself, he responded to the ideas it raised about aesthetic education—concerns that he, too, was exploring through SIM, as well as through his contact in the late 1970s with CEMREL (the Central Midwest Regional Educational Laboratory), based in St. Louis. With the help of Weston Woods and federal funding, CEMREL was interested in creating an entirely new approach to elementary education in America's schools, one that emphasized integrating the arts into the curriculum. In 1977, Schindel established yet another new company, one that would have a separate identity from Weston Woods and would be devoted to the publication of innovative educational materials—COMENIUS, named after the sixteenth-century Czech educator John Amos Comenius, who was an advocate for universal education and the creator of what is thought to be the first picture book for children, the *Orbis Pictus* (1658). Schindel wrote at length about how this revolutionary educational project might be approached, and even drafted position papers for, and statements of agreement between, CEMREL and COMENIUS.

Still, the concept couldn't quite make it off the drawing board and into pilot projects, despite growing support on the national level for programs that aimed to reinvigorate the educational experience. Perhaps the program was simply too bold for even those groundbreaking times. Not one to be deterred from offering unconventional ideas, Schindel was open to another proposal from educational consultant Dr. Bena Kallick to adapt some of the ideas into the curriculum plans that she called Literature to Think About. These were developed in the form of study guides to be distributed with Weston Woods' films. (To this day, brief study guides for each Weston Woods title can be downloaded free of charge from the Weston Woods/ Scholastic web site.) These materials provided teachers with cross-curricular activities for their students to amplify the experience of the books and their accompanying films. This approach kindled the idea for the television program *Reading Rainbow*, which aired in 1983. Two of that program's initial designers—Cecily Truett, who was a consultant to Weston Woods at the time, and Ronnie Krauss, who was on the Weston Woods staff—were present at one of the media think tanks hosted by Weston Woods years earlier. They were energized by the discussion and developed an early concept for *Reading Rainbow*. Although Weston Woods was not ultimately involved in the creation of the show, Schindel was delighted to see that the Weston Woods philosophy was spreading well beyond the studio and that he had been catalytic in helping to bring about this growth. Here again, Schindel was in the vanguard of an emerging spirit: finding innovative ways to connect the educational experiences of young people with new forms of media.

Weston Woods' horizons continued to expand beyond literature and film with its creation of Poetry Parade, a series of poetry recordings under the direction of Nancy Larrick. An educator, academic, and editor of volumes of poetry for children, Larrick brought together a number of well-known children's poets—Karla Kuskin, David McCord, Aileen Fisher, and Harry Behn—to read and record their poems. Declared in the brochure, the intent of the series was to take poetry out of the pedagogical restraints of the classroom and to provide selections of poems presented "in the informal way [that the poet] might read to children in his own living room." The poems were meant to act as an "open sesame" for children, not only to fine-tune their ears to sophisticated uses of language, but also to encourage their receptiveness to and hopefully their engagement with other forms of creative expression: "With several poems singing in their heads, children are quick to extend their participation to impromptu dramatization, picture painting, puppetry, and frequently to poetic creations of their own."[11]

In some respects, Larrick's series was an outgrowth of earlier work that the studio had done with poetry, including filmstrips and sound recordings based on Ogden Nash's *The Tale of Custard the Dragon* (1959, 1964 film) with illustrations by Nash's daughter, Linell; Richard Lewis's collection of Japanese haikus, *In a Spring Garden* (1965, 1968 film), illustrated by Ezra Jack Keats's Zen-like collages; and Doris Herold Lund's *Attic of the Wind* (1966, 1974 film), illustrated by Ati Forberg. As a culmination of this interest in poetry, the studio produced a filmstrip and an accompanying audiocassette titled *Karla Kuskin: Poetry Explained* (1980 filmstrip), a small but ambitious project that tried to make accessible both the creative process of a poet and the act of interpreting poetry.

Storyboard panels for the filmstrip production of *Karla Kuskin: Poetry Explained*, ca. 1979, an example of Weston Woods' experiment with the genre of poetry.

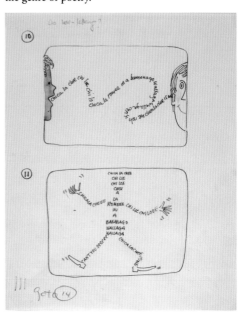

Artwork from the filmstrip *Karla Kuskin: Poetry Explained.* The graphic qualities of concrete poetry make it ideally suitable for adaptation to film.

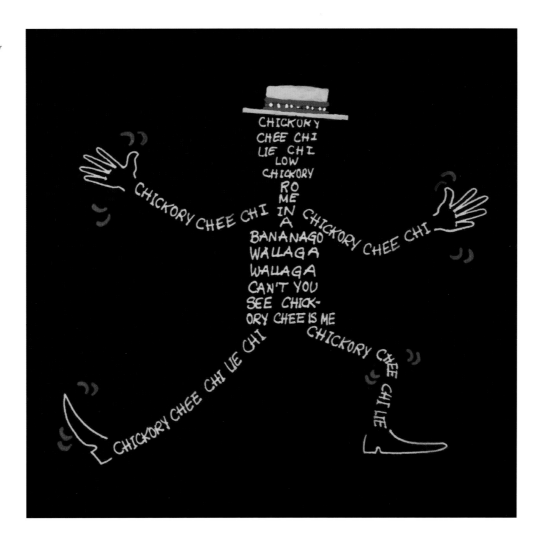

Poetry was not the only genre that Weston Woods would attempt to reimagine. In the 1970s, the studio began to produce a series of films as sound recordings and filmstrips (and, more recently, as animated movies) about famous figures from American history, based on the award-winning books of Jean Fritz. These humanizing stories drew on historical fact and were primarily set in Colonial America. The series began with books like *Can't You Make Them Behave, King George?* (1977, 1977 audiobook package), illustrated by Tomie dePaola; *Where Was Patrick Henry on the 29th of May?* (1975, 1985 audiobook package), illustrated by Margot Tomes; and then later continued with *Shh! We're Writing the Constitution* (1987, 1990 film), with illustrations by Tomie dePaola; *Who's That Stepping on Plymouth Rock?* (1975, 1998 film), illustrated by J. B. Handelsman; *Just a Few Words, Mr. Lincoln* (1993, 1999 film), illustrated by Charles Robinson; and *George*

Václav Carda played the lead role of Aaron in Isaac Bashevis Singer's *Zlateh the Goat*, a live-action film shot in the Czech countryside during the winter of 1972. Director Gene Deitch was struck by the boy's soulful face and the closeness of his appearance to Maurice Sendak's representation of Aaron.

Washington's Mother (1992, 2000 film), with illustrations by Dyanne DiSalvo-Ryan. Fritz's books about the founding fathers and other revered personages—together with their often humorous, all-too-human biographies and backstories—were a departure from the kinds of solemn hagiographic accounts of national leaders that schoolchildren were often told. One of the company's more successful series, these experimental films continue to be made available through revitalized iconographic animations.

Other innovative and memorable projects have not fared as well in the marketplace. One such work was the film based on the story *Zlateh the Goat* (1966, 1973 film) by Isaac Bashevis Singer, who won the Nobel Prize for literature in 1978. Maurice Sendak, who had done the illustrations, recommended it to Schindel over lunch one day at Weston Woods in 1969, during the early stages of making *Where the Wild Things Are.* The rights to produce a film of *Zlateh the Goat* were the most expensive rights the studio had acquired: a ten-thousand-dollar advance against a five percent royalty. This expense would be compounded by the cost of producing the work as a live-action motion picture shot on location in Czechoslovakia. Nevertheless, Schindel jumped in: "I had lived with the idea of doing *Zlateh* for so many years that I felt I had better do it, at any price, so I could get on with my life." [12]

Schindel approached Deitch about directing the film, but Deitch was hesitant. In the extensive production notes published by the studio in 1975, in conjunction with release of the film that same year, Deitch explained: "True, I did like *Zlateh* the best, but practical considerations, film experience, [my] cowardice, and other perfectly logical reasons led me to realize that it would be the most difficult to achieve on film. This story could not be convincingly produced as an animated film, my usual medium; and yet Mort and I both saw that it must spring visually from Sendak's inspired illustrations." [13] Deitch found himself in an aesthetically tricky situation in which life would have to at least try to resemble, if not exactly imitate, art.

Despite these reservations and his fear that he would not find an incarnation of Sendak's soulfully illustrated Aaron, Deitch was so overpowered by the story that he decided to continue with its production. *Zlateh* is the story of a boy from a poor family who takes their last remaining possession, their prized goat, to the market to sell. Along the way, the two are trapped in a blizzard, but Aaron survives the storm with Zlateh by burrowing into a haystack, keeping warm beside the goat, and being sustained by her milk. Sendak, who consulted closely with Schindel on the project, wrote to Deitch, describing his vision of the refuge in the film as kind of "heaven" inside the sheltering haystack.

Just as Deitch had anticipated, casting for the film was difficult, and at times astonishingly and ironically synchronistic, especially given the circumstances of the history of that region of Eastern Europe:

> We found a boy with a perfect face and, as I suspected, not among any characteristic Czech types. The boy, Václav Carda, who had a Gypsy mother, had the beautiful, long-faced darkness Maurice Sendak's drawings seem to suggest. Although the area where we shot much of the film is very near the Polish border and the true locale of Zlateh the Goat, *there is no longer a Jewish community there. The two young daughters were played by Gypsy girls. The only Jewish member of the cast was Jana Sedova-Popperova, who played the mother; she was once an inmate at the Terezín concentration camp.* [14]

Other problems followed the project: the search for the right location in the countryside; the wait for the right weather—snow (which was eventually solved by using an airplane propeller that blew white plastic flakes across the screen); and the coordination of cast members, most of whom were busy with other acting commitments. Postproduction work brought questions about the slow pacing of the film. Schindel asserted that the length was being used to convey the sense of "survival through three long days in a haystack.... Our heads told us that the people programming films for children would never sit still for the agonizingly long twenty minutes or so that the film would take." In the end, audiences and critics responded well to the production, which won a series of awards at both American and international film festivals. And when Singer won the Nobel Prize in 1978, the film was purchased by French and Swiss television, and was among the first videocassette releases offered by EMI in England. [15]

Deitch reported at the time, tongue in cheek, that "one critic said, 'Good as the film is, it is not perfect.' One creature, though, is perfectly happy. Today the real [on-screen] Zlateh or her offspring quietly munch the unruly grasses around an old cottage, perhaps telling goat stories about the meaning of those ghastly months when she was repeatedly subjected to bright lights and to hard white plastic pellets being blasted into her face by a roaring machine." [16] And Schindel was certainly happy, too, about the larger themes the film brought to the screen. As he wrote in the production notes, it was meant as "a visual expression of the drama of nature, the basic unity of all living creatures trying to survive…the trust and love of the goat for the humans who almost betray it…and how this might carry over to change and make more understandable the everyday life we must yet cope with." [17]

Chapter 8

Spreading the Word

Films are the key to worldwide dissemination of literature for children....It's because people everywhere are discovering that filmed adaptations of children's books, adaptations that faithfully mirror the book itself, play a vital role in getting good books into the hands of a lot of youngsters. —Mort Schindel

When Mort Schindel was transporting films and projection equipment in small vans and trucks to rural Turkish villages in the early 1950s, he could not have imagined that he would be doing something very similar a decade later in the small towns of Connecticut. After the initial successes of Weston Woods, Schindel had begun to think about ways to bring his films, and thus the children's books that inspired them, to children who could not get to a library or see his films on *Captain Kangaroo.* Like the Marshall Plan of Ideas that Schindel had admired and helped to implement in Turkey, he began to see an opportunity for spreading the word about books to children through the medium of film.

It was, perhaps, a natural next step for Schindel, as he wanted to broaden his audience by bringing his films to the children who were least likely to see them—young people in impoverished and rural areas. Outside of large public libraries, few places existed where children in America could see the kind of art films that he was making. Nor were there many, if any, opportunities for children to see films like his in a special, cinematic environment. (The studio had started to consider the importance of finding or inventing the right venue with the production of its live-action movies, like *The Doughnuts* [1943, 1963 film] and *The Sorcerer's Apprentice* [1897, 1963 film]). An account in the *School Library Journal* summarized the creative genesis of this project: "Months of frustrated design attempts came and went, during which time every conceivable type of environment was tried and rejected. Then, on one sunny afternoon, a school bus bulging with children on their way home interrupted Mr. Schindel's trip to town. After he had followed it awhile, frustrated at its repeated stops, an idea began to grow as each child stepped out and waved a cheerful

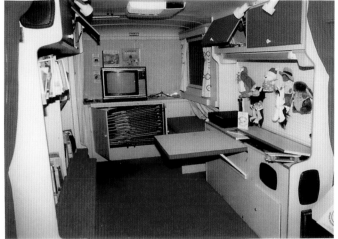

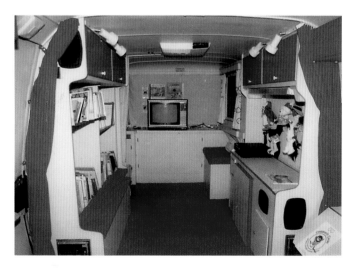

Equipped with collapsible tables, built-in bookshelves, televisions, and overhead storage compartments, the caravan was designed for a variety of purposes, all aimed at making children's literature accessible to underserved communities, ca. 1975.

Opposite top: The well-known children's newspaper *My Weekly Reader* featured the Children's Caravan on the front page of its April 24, 1968, edition.

Opposite bottom: As the Children's Caravan project began to develop in the 1960s, Hardie Gramatky (pictured here) and other artists and writers gave workshops on children's books and storytelling to drivers, ushers, and others who were part of the outreach program.

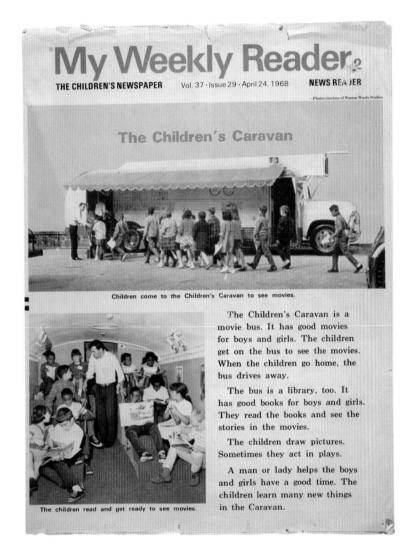

My Weekly Reader

THE CHILDREN'S NEWSPAPER   Vol. 37 · Issue 29 · April 24, 1968   NEWS READER

—Photos courtesy of Weston Woods Studios

The Children's Caravan

Children come to the Children's Caravan to see movies.

The children read and get ready to see movies.

The Children's Caravan is a movie bus. It has good movies for boys and girls. The children get on the bus to see the movies. When the children go home, the bus drives away.

The bus is a library, too. It has good books for boys and girls. They read the books and see the stories in the movies.

The children draw pictures. Sometimes they act in plays.

A man or lady helps the boys and girls have a good time. The children learn many new things in the Caravan.

good-bye. That afternoon, Mr. Schindel owned a school bus." [1]

Within a few months, the school bus had metamorphosed into a traveling movie theater, meant exclusively for children, called the Children's Caravan. The body of the bus was painted white, with one smiling face and one sad face (based on the classic masks from Greek drama), and the wheel rims were painted red. To prevent light from seeping into the bus during screenings, the windows had been removed and were replaced with a retractable awning that stretched along one side of the vehicle. The portable, covered entry area at the front provided shelter for the audience as it entered this "movie house on wheels." Inside, the seating area had been customized with red-carpeted risers and floor; framed illustrations from the films hung on the walls; and a gold curtain separated the projection area and the screen from the audience. Soon after this transformation, Schindel acquired a second bus, which was painted to match the first.

The interior of the second bus featured the set from *The Doughnuts,* complete with the fully functional doughnut-making machine used in the movie. Here, parents could have a cup of coffee and sample a cruller while their children enjoyed the show in the neighboring bus. Three volunteers from Weston, who dressed in red capes "with an Elizabethan look," drove the two buses, screened the movies, and managed the whole event. [2] On the Sunday before Christmas in 1963, the *Bridgeport Sunday Post* reported the debut of this "Mobile Art Cinema for Children" and conveyed Schindel's hope "to initiate mobile art cinemas for children in communities all over the country." For Schindel it was a dream, as he told the reporter, of "bringing art films to the supermarket." [3]

Top: Sketches showing the versatility of the Children's Circle logo.

Top right: Children's Caravan ushers in custom-designed uniforms receive safety instructions from a police officer.

In any case, by the end of 1964, Schindel had rethought and refined the project, and in the process had formed another company, Children's Caravan, Inc., to administer the programs of the "mobile art cinema." As the idea of the caravan became more focused, Schindel saw that he needed to find "a new way to get what was needed to the people who perhaps needed it most: the rural poor, who have seldom benefited from programs demanding heavy capital investment, as the urban areas have."[4] In 1966, Schindel began to approach federal agencies for possible funding, and the United States Office of Economic Opportunity agreed to provide the resources to rehabilitate eight buses as "cinemobiles" for use in communities of migrant workers in northern Michigan and New Jersey and in isolated areas of Appalachia. Just like the Turkish media trucks, the Children's Caravans had their own generating systems, since electricity was often not reliable or even available in the remote areas they served. The mostly young, idealistic crew members of each bus were trained at Weston Woods by Schindel and others, including Hardie Gramatky. They learned not only how to run the vehicles and the equipment, but how to talk to their audiences, which consisted of both children and parents. The cinemobiles showed a range of films, including the growing group of Weston Woods' films in the Picture Book Parade, as well as works by other producers, and each of the cinemobiles also provided paperback copies of the books on which the films were based. After the caravans left, these volumes were often donated to the community, in some cases to form the nucleus of a small library. As a whole, the experience was meant to be "a teaching moment," one that would give children the opportunity to watch films "right in their home environment, to enrich the vocabulary of *images* they need so desperately to form the concepts—otherwise meaningless—that they will encounter in their reading."[5]

The Children's Caravans have been on the road ever since—in newer models, of course, but with the same intent of providing a cost-effective means for introducing high-quality films (and the books they are referencing) to children (and, by extension, their parents) in locales where this kind of experience would otherwise be prohibitively expensive and thus unavailable. For a number of years, the buses have been among the major programs of the Weston Woods Institute, a nonprofit organization that Schindel established in 1982 in order to stimulate innovative approaches to cultural education for children, parents, and teachers. The media mobiles have since been renamed Literacy Caravans, and they now emphasize the development of reading skills. A number of Literacy Caravans are located in cities around the country, like the one that is part of the bilingual Lee y serás family literacy program in the San Francisco Bay Area, where Scholastic has a community-based, educational partnership with the Unity Council of Oakland, California. But these aspects of the media mobiles are just a narrow scope of Schindel's vision of a multifaceted, everexpanding project. Once the idea of the media mobile took hold, he had hoped to see the caravans serve a wide range of communities, from daycare centers and Head Start facilities, to migrant camps and Native American reservations, to museums and educational institutions. During an interview with Adrienne Schure for AARP in the aftermath of the events on September 11, 2001, Schindel asked: "How about making caravans to showcase different world religions? We might, for instance, have a caravan whose presenter is Islamic and another who is Jewish."[6] And Schindel's vision extended far beyond our country's borders, for he also thought that caravans could be a key resource for providing information within developing nations.

This kind of global aspiration was present nearly from the beginning in Schindel's thinking about Weston Woods and what it might accomplish. From the studio's earliest years, Schindel regarded picture books as a potential nonideological bridge to international understanding, and so he carefully selected works that were expanding boundaries beyond stereotypes in unthreatening ways, even during the Cold War.

A later model of the Children's Caravan is decorated with a mural of characters and scenes from Weston Woods films.

Schindel carefully maintained that the studio was "neutral and apolitical," a fact that, coupled with the quality of its films, made it possible for Weston Woods' productions to be easily incorporated into television programs in other countries.[7] During the 1970s, Schindel attended international conferences, hosted foreign visitors, and opened Weston Woods offices in Canada, England, and Australia; these activities helped to inform an international audience about the studio. By the 1980s, with the advent of home video, Weston Woods films had been translated into dozens of languages, among them Spanish and French, as well as Japanese and Mandarin Chinese. (The studio continues to make its films available in these and other languages.)

Schindel has stressed the international presence of Weston Woods—not merely from a business perspective, but from a sincere belief that the most exceptional and creative books, and the films based on them, might speak to a broader sense of cross-cultural understanding. Thus, Weston Woods has assiduously participated in international film festivals. As an indication of its growing international stature, the studio was invited in 1966 to the first International Children's Film Festival in Tehran. Along with Schindel, the guest list included the Canadian animator Norman McLaren (*A Chairy Tale*) and the French director Albert Lamorisse (*The Red Balloon*). The ten-day, red-carpet event was hosted by the Institute for the Intellectual Development of Children and Young Adults, a program founded by the Empress of Iran, Farah Pahlavi, in the decade before Iran's Islamic Revolution. Schindel was impressed by the festival's audiences, which consisted primarily of children. He marveled about the event in the *Horn Book Magazine* in 1967: "Over one hundred thousand school children actually saw films at the festival. On more than one night, Her Imperial Majesty and her son, accompanied by some of his schoolmates, appeared unannounced."[8]

Before returning to the United States, Schindel donated a complete set of Weston Woods films to the Central Children's Library of Iran. This gesture was standard business procedure for Schindel; he has always been well-known for his liberal distribution of complimentary copies of the studio's films, even before the advent of videocassettes and DVDs. Yet any business success was secondary to the larger "distribution" of the creative seeds represented by the films. And like so much of what Schindel did, the ideas and the practice came first, followed by the business model, or any blueprint for implementing the idea. In "Films: the Key to Worldwide Dissemination," a lengthy, unpublished position paper that Schindel wrote in the late 1970s, he argued that "for audiences of children around the world…films can [more easily] be made to cross boundaries—cultural, linguistic, and political—than

Opposite top: The Alsatian author Tomi Ungerer was one of many foreign authors with whom Weston Woods worked, ca. 1981. The studio completed several projects during the 1970s and 1980s with Ungerer, including film adaptations and a documentary.

Opposite: Three animation cels for the film *Moon Man*, the Weston Woods adaptation of Tomi Ungerer's *Alumette*. Animators manipulated these cels in layers over a background, creating one composite image.

books. A single print of a film can effectively communicate with millions of children, given the facilities of television for dissemination. And it is certainly far less expensive to produce a foreign language version of a film than to produce a book in another language."[9] The sound answer to Schindel's idealistic argument came, of course, in the increasing number of films that his studio produced or licensed for production in other countries. By 1965 the films on the Picture Book Parade had been translated into fourteen languages, and by 1975 the studio had provided licenses to thirty countries to show Weston Woods films.[10]

The diversity of the studio's titles reflected not only Schindel's spirit of internationalism, but also the changing face of children's book publishing, which was becoming increasingly drawn to books written and illustrated by authors and artists from other countries. This global expansion was part of the general movement in arts and letters toward an opening of the canon. Early on in its history, Weston Woods had adapted books by foreign writers and illustrators like Tomi Ungerer, Celestino Piatti, and Taro Yashima. During this time, the studio also produced films based on the popular This Is series, by the Czech author and illustrator Miroslav Sasek, including iconographic adaptations of the books *This Is New York* (1960, 1962), *This Is Venice* (1961, 1964), *This Is Israel* (1962, 1964), and *This Is Ireland* (1964, 1965). Done in the angular, midcentury modern style that was so prevalent among European artists, Sasek's travelogues for children were internationalism at its angular, charming best. A number of the books have been reissued, and they are reaching a new generation of fans who are drawn to their appealing retro style.

But of all the internationally oriented films that the studio produced, perhaps the most ambitious and thematically timeless was *Here Comes the Cat!* (1989, 1992 film) based on the picture book created by the American Frank Asch and the Russian Vladimir Vagin, who both wrote, illustrated, and participated in the process of animating the book in Cold War Russia. Perestroika was still a few years over the horizon, but already there were signs of a thaw between the two countries. In fact, Asch and Vagin had met at a Soviet/American children's book conference in 1986, struck up an immediate friendship, and agreed to collaborate on a book that might help to foster a more harmonious relationship between the two countries. The actual story was inspired by a dream that Asch had, in which a group of mice was being terrified by the looming shadow of a cat, only to discover that the creature wasn't dangerous at all, but rather, the cat came bearing cheese. After the publication of the book, Weston Woods decided to continue the exchange through a fully animated film that would be produced in Russia's Pilot Animation Studio in Moscow.

Top: Animation cel from *Here Comes the Cat!*, a pre-Perestroika collaboration between an American, Frank Asch, and a Russian, Vladimir Vagin.

Bottom: The Russian animators of *Here Comes the Cat!* improvised to include a sequence reminiscent of the famous Odessa steps scene from Sergei Eisenstein's 1925 classic, *Battleship Potemkin*.

From the start, it was a project meant for film. Indeed, the book contained a number of references to classics of the Russian cinema, including an homage to a well-known montage from Sergei Eisenstein's silent film *Battleship Potemkin* (1925): the baby carriage rolling down the broad Odessa Steps. The film was done in a vivid, Russian folk-art palette—bright reds and golds, greens and blues—with an overall feeling of a village festival, despite its dark, opening intimations. Enthusiastically received and the winner of a number of film festival awards, the project would prove to be prophetic of the relative ease with which the United States and Russia were ultimately reconciled in the early 1990s.

This growing spirit of rapprochement also led to Weston Woods' involvement in a Russian translation of their film based on McCloskey's *Make Way for Ducklings* (1941, 1955 film). When Raisa Gorbachev visited Boston's Public Garden in 1990, she had seen Massachusetts artist Nancy Schön's bronze sculpture of Mrs. Mallard followed by her eight ducklings. This sculpture had been installed in 1987 to commemorate the joy that McCloskey's book brought to the city's many visitors. Mrs. Gorbachev was captivated by the work, though at the time she didn't know of the book itself, since it had not been translated into Russian. In 1991, at the beginning of the Strategic Arms Reduction Treaty (START) talks, Barbara Bush presented Mrs. Gorbachev with a "sister" statue as a symbolic gesture of peace. Mrs. Gorbachev chose Novodevichy Park, one of Moscow's most beautiful spots, for the site of the duck-

Animation cel from Asch and Vagin's *Here Comes the Cat!*.

lings' parade. Because of his close friendship with McCloskey, Schindel felt comfortable offering to record a translated version of the *Make Way for Ducklings* film to be shown on Russian television; he also helped to persuade the book's publisher, Viking Press, to release a limited edition of the volume in Russian—once they could resolve, as Schindel recalls, how to translate the title idiomatically into the Russian language. One of Schindel's most cherished possessions, in a house filled with many, continues to be a bronze maquette of the statue.

While he was in the midst of one success, Schindel's attentions were already shifting toward new ideas and fresh possibilities, often reconstituting conceptual fragments that were present from a much earlier time. One of a host of plans that seemed to be constantly bubbling beneath the surface at Weston Woods in the 1970s and 1980s (and would continue into the new century) was his idea for a possible television show. His films had been shown in truncated forms on *Captain Kangaroo* because of the prevailing notion among educators and media specialists that children's short attention spans would not allow them to sit still for a full ten or twelve minutes. (The media research of this period would provide *Sesame Street* with one of its central tenets in the development of its quickly paced programming format.) Thus, the initial airing of Weston Woods films on television had had a disquieting effect on him.

Regardless of this early experience, Schindel remained intensely interested in television as a possible outlet, not only for Weston Woods films, but for the transmission of literature in general. He had long realized that TV was an unsurpassed medium for providing educational experiences to a wide audience, and in the late 1970s he observed that "face-to-face communication would be ideal but unrealistic; to reach a mass audience, it is necessary to resort to mass media."[11] More recently, Schindel explained his position about television in light of national concerns about literacy: "TV is the key to making any activity a nationwide effort. Certainly, literacy in all of its ramifications is a nationwide goal. The proper use of the medium should become an imperative, not an option. Broadcasting to homes and schools is obviously the key way to reach not only children but also their parents, teachers, and caregivers, all of whom need to meet the urgent needs of federally mandated programs such as Head Start, Even Start, and Ready to Learn."[12]

Robert McCloskey and the sculptor Nancy Schön inspect the bronze ducklings that were installed in both the Public Garden in Boston, ca. 1970, and later, Novodevichy Park in Moscow, ca. 1986. *Make Way for Ducklings* is an example of the universal appeal of children's books.

To advance the possibility of creating a television show, Schindel hosted think-tank gatherings at Weston Woods, as mentioned earlier. This first gathering, titled "TV Promotion of Children's Books," was held in the large living room at Weston Woods. Its objective was to draft possible television programs for national funding, with Schindel going so far as to prepare a few sample scripts. Among the participants

Schindel hosted a brainstorming session for a Weston Woods television program in the living room of the main house, ca. 1979. Participants included Marcia Brown (far left), Maurice Sendak (center, foreground), Schindel (far right, in profile), and McCloskey (center right, background).

were representatives from the media, library, and educational communities, as well as a number of writers and artists that included McCloskey and Maurice Sendak (who provided some hilarious sketches of hypothetical hosts for the program).

One of Schindel's first program ideas originated from an early Weston Woods product: The Picture Book Parade. While today the idea of a television program called *The Picture Book Parade* may seem dated, in the late 1950s, it was ahead of its time. Schindel began to brainstorm with his colleagues about what such a program might look like, right down to the opening of each show, with a conveyor belt "parading" the books toward the screen, their titles facing the viewer, while a friendly voice announced the arrival of the Picture Book Parade.

Continuing into the 1980s, these brainstorming sessions generated a variety of other potential programs. For example, the television show *Cric! Crac!* was meant to "motivate both children and their parents to be more interested in reading and storytelling by familiarizing the family audience with quality children's literature." Another project from the same year proposed a thirty-show series of half-hour programs for the Corporation for Public Broadcasting. This program used picture books to "combat

KREPLOCH! A NEW T.V. EXPERIENCE BY MORRI SCHINDEL AND A LOT OF SUPER STARS!

HOSTS I

"Hi Kids."

HOSTS II

Floss & Stan Dworkin

HOSTS III

Top: Maurice Sendak sketched a comedic series of proposed hosts for a Weston Woods television program, 1979.

Bottom: Schindel in costume as the host of the proposed television program, *A Story, A Story,* ca. 1988.

illiteracy through a 'remedial' program, an audiovisual curriculum for young adults who are reluctant readers."[13] Yet another proposal from 1989 involved an adaptation of David Macaulay's *The Way Things Work* (1988) as an experiment in video publishing that could be used for both English-speaking and international audiences. Other ideas did not make it into more finished forms. These included a Movie Van, which would use a traveling media mobile as its set; Story Caravan, a television program geared towards preschoolers; and *A Story, A Story* (1970, 1973 film), a proposal for the National Endowment for the Humanities featuring Schindel as the host.

While none of these programs received funding, they indicated the kind of innovative expansion that Schindel was hoping for, as he aimed to move the studio's productions into a more public sphere. Still, there were several small triumphs for Weston Woods on television. In 1989 a number of the studio's films were aired on the Boston-based program *A Likely Story,* and from 1989 to 1995, Weston Woods films regularly appeared on the Nickelodeon program *Eureeka's Castle.*

Over the years, Weston Woods has quietly, calmly, carefully, and consistently played a role in the "worldwide dissemination of children's literature" (to borrow Schindel's phrase). Through the stories it has told, the studio has visited cultures from Africa to the Arctic, from Western Europe to South America. Schindel's vision of Weston Woods as an internationally connected "vehicle" for storytelling has proven prescient, given the cross-cultural exchanges of the contemporary global village. Writing in 1968 in *Bookbird,* the journal of record for international children's literature, C. A. Waite noted Schindel's recognition of children's literature as an "international common market" of creative ideas, remarking on how something as simple as a refurbished school bus could be a harbinger for such dynamic and far-reaching aspirations.[14]

Chapter 9

Continuing the Tradition

When the time came to pick a successor, there were no lawyers or boardroom meetings— just the passing of a note between friends. —Mort Schindel

In 1996, as Mort Schindel was nearing seventy-eight years of age, a major event occurred in the history of Weston Woods: the studio became a subsidiary of Scholastic Inc., the largest publisher of children's books and related media in the world. This acquisition promised another feather for Scholastic's company cap, given the reputation of the studio. But the turning over of an independent, creative gem left some observers to wonder if this merger would simply be yet another example of the prevailing business practice of the time, especially ubiquitous in the publishing industry—the big fish eating the little fish. After all, Weston Woods was being absorbed into a large international corporation with an ever-growing portfolio of high-profile successes. A good part of this concern involved the question of how the studio would continue to operate and keep its creative integrity.

What wasn't commonly known about the acquisition when it occurred was that it had been in process for some time and that it had gone forward on amicable terms. Schindel and Scholastic's president and CEO, Richard Robinson, had been friends for many years. They had met at conferences, and Robinson was well aware of the reputation of Weston Woods within the children's publishing and media communities. Closer to home, Robinson's children, Ben and Reese, had visited Weston Woods and had grown up with the studio's films. Robinson had been drawn to Weston Woods because his father, Maurice R. "Robbie" Robinson, had founded Scholastic in 1920 and built it from the ground up, in much the same entrepreneurial way that Schindel had created his studio. At the outset, both Scholastic and Weston Woods were essentially family businesses and, in some respects, cottage industries; both had scrupulously developed their markets within the library and educational

Morton Schindel (left) and Richard Robinson, President and CEO of Scholastic Inc. at the Scholastic Headquarters in New York City, ca. 1996.

communities; both were idealistic about the roles they played in connecting children with books and literature; and both were visionary companies that prided themselves on their innovative work and corporate esprit.

In its earliest years, Scholastic had published classroom magazines, but soon added children's books to its product line. Its first volume, *Saplings* (1926), was a collection of writings by students who had won a literary contest that the new company sponsored in its magazine, the *Scholastic*. In the late 1940s, with the appearance of mass-market paperbacks, Scholastic launched the first of its book clubs for young people, and by the 1980s, along with being a leader in the mail-order sales of books, the company was a well-established organizer of school book fairs. The 1980s witnessed the beginning of Scholastic's astonishing run of highly successful book and entertainment franchises with the publication of the first of the Magic School Bus books (1986) and the launching of the Baby-sitters Club series (1986). The 1990s brought another commercial coup, beginning with R. L. Stein's Goosebumps books, first released in 1992, followed by the company's crown jewel, the Harry Potter series, which debuted in the United States in 1998.

By the early 1990s, Robinson had let Schindel know that he was interested in purchasing Weston Woods. Although there had been other inquiries about buying the studio, Schindel always regarded Scholastic as the place where Weston Woods would find its home—when it was time. "I did not shop around for the best deal," Schindel has remarked, adding, "we had mutual goals—worldwide dissemination. We had a product; Scholastic had the means."[1] In 1994, Schindel wrote a note to Robinson in which he announced, simply, "The time has come. If you are interested, let me know." According to Schindel, Robinson's reply was just as direct and succinct: "I'm interested." It would take several years to finalize the sale because of the myriad details, like those regarding Schindel's estate, that had to be resolved. The financial aspects were never in question, though, and Schindel reports having told Robinson, "I'm not going to negotiate a price with you because I don't consider it a business deal, but a legacy." For his part, Robinson wrote some figures on the back of an envelope when the two met to discuss the matter; the amount was agreeable to Schindel, and that, as they say, was that.

Scholastic acquired all of the existing Weston Woods company stock, along with the studio's backlist of titles. There were other understandings between Robinson and Schindel, one of which was that the studio would retain its unique identity and creative independence. They agreed that the individual character of Weston Woods would be maintained: the studio would have the editorial freedom to select its proj-

Top: Schindel (left) and Linda Lee, vice president and general manager of Weston Woods at Weston Woods, ca. 2005.

Bottom: Author Patrick McDonnell (left) with musician Bobby McFerrin (center) and Paul Gagne, director of production at Weston Woods, at the recording session for the adaptation of McDonnell's *ART*, ca. 2007.

ects and the time it needed to produce them, as it always had. During the transition, it was also determined that Weston Woods would remain in Connecticut, separate from the main New York offices of Scholastic. For additional storage space and to upgrade the studio's offices and production facilities, Weston Woods moved from the original studio grounds in Weston to offices in Westport, and eventually into a modest industrial space in nearby Norwalk. But the former studio grounds did not lie fallow; they became the site of the Weston Woods Institute.

Schindel had been preparing for this transfer of the studio's business and creative energies for quite some time by bringing key people into the company during the 1970s and 1980s. These principal figures included Linda Lee, the current vice president and general manager of Weston Woods, and Paul Gagne, the director of production, who has been with the studio since 1978. Lee and Gagne began or have spent a large portion of their careers in a variety of positions at Weston Woods, learning the workings and the unique ethos of the company over a number of years. Most important, the two have formed—through their complementary talents, mutual respect for each other, and ensemble spirit—a highly productive team that has been in place at the studio since Schindel passed the torch to them. Their long-term, often multifaceted working relationship with the studio and with Schindel steeped Lee and Gagne in Weston Woods' core values. Lee summarized part of the learning curve for herself and her colleagues this way: "With each new production [Mort] taught us to evaluate our approach, and ask, 'Is this going to result in something better for kids?' We were taught to improve and remake whatever we [were] working on, until we [could] answer his question, 'Yes.' Following these lessons keeps us passionately connected to what we do. I firmly believe this passion is what sets us apart. It's the basis of what many people have called 'the Weston Woods mystique.'"[2]

Robinson recognized this unique energy among the tightly knit core of the studio, noting that Schindel "found a group of people to carry on what he is doing, and they still work in his image, with their own impressions and style."[3] Robinson valued Lee and Gagne's expertise and proven chemistry, and when Schindel stepped down, Scholastic agreed to continue running the Weston Woods studio with this capable group. Schindel stayed on in an advisory capacity for another three years, and then ended his active association with the studio (though not his emeritus status or his self-described role as its ex-officio "conscience") in order to work full-time on the Weston Woods Institute. Retirement seems not to be in Schindel's makeup, as is evidenced by his frequent visits to the studio. He keeps in regular touch with Lee and Gagne—but he has left the running of the company in their hands. The projects that

Weston Woods has undertaken in the last dozen years are the choices of the current leadership team, and Lee notes that since becoming a part of Scholastic, "our production team continues to have complete creative license.... Weston Woods really isn't so different today than it was fifty years ago. We basically follow the same guiding principles of finding the best children's literature and adapting it in such a way that it's as true to the book as possible."[4]

As we have seen, what had changed during the half century of the studio's life was its continuing transitions into the latest technologies. Starting with the iconographic film, the product line was expanded to include filmstrips, then filmstrips with an LP record or audiocassette for its soundtrack, and then fully animated films. With the arrival of videocassettes in 1985, the studio kept pace with technological advances through its Children's Circle line of videotapes for an expanding national and international home-media market. Schindel highlighted the Children's Circle in the 1991 Weston Woods catalog: "Since the fall of 1985…our audience has been growing all over the world. In fact, Curious George has pedaled his bicycle all the way from Canada to Brazil and is now on his way through Europe, Scandinavia, England, France, and Italy—heading for Japan, Taiwan, and Australia!"[5] The catalog also offered a new line of innovative curriculum-related packages for teachers in its Literature to Think About series; these materials "provide ways to develop 'story-literate' children who are able to interpret and interact with a story." The series included media guides such as *Metacognition: Analyzing Thought Processes*, which incorporated Robert McCloskey's picture book about a hardworking Maine fisherman, *Burt Dow: Deep-Water Man* (1963, 1983 film) and *Observation* based on Pat Hutchins's constantly threatened, but seemingly oblivious, strolling barnyard hen in *Rosie's Walk* (1968, 1970 film). Yet as one technology replaced another, and as the studio explored different strategies for making its materials useful to the classroom teacher, Weston Woods continued to remember its base constituents: school and public libraries. The studio remained constant in its mission to support the work of these cherished (but often beleaguered) institutions and to make available its products in older formats, as many libraries could not afford updated equipment. As late as 1991, the output of Weston Woods included videocassettes and 16-mm films.

Today the Weston Woods catalog brims over with a variety of media formats for the products that are generated by the studio or other Scholastic entities. Along with videos and DVDs (which now include a new Read-Along function that highlights words on screen as they are being spoken, plus author interviews), audiocassettes, and Playaway audio devices, there are book and CD packages for early readers and the

Scholastic Audio series, including a line of unabridged audiobooks for middle-school audiences. Adding to this spectrum of materials are DVDs of the I Spy and Clifford the Big Red Dog series. The list seems to grow with each new catalog. These products are currently being expanded to include digital spin-offs such as MP3s, podcasts, and other downloadable formats.

But the signature dimension of the Weston Woods catalog remains its adaptations of highly regarded picture books. Today, the process for selecting the titles can be defined by three basic principles: desirability, adaptability, and availability. From the beginning, Schindel carefully screened the books he was interested in adapting, drawing on those that had won a number of the conventional seals of approval, beginning with the Caldecott Medal. In the early years, Schindel had even gone so far as to draw graphs charting the positive reviews that books had received to gauge their success, and thus their desirability. This aspect of the selection process is exemplified in the 2007 films based on such recent award-winning books as Nikki Giovanni's and Bryan Collier's *Rosa* (2005, 2007 film) and Ed Young's *Seven Blind Mice* (1992, 2007 film), both of which were named Caldecott Honor Books; Lane Smith's *John, Paul, George, and Ben* (2006, 2007 film), which was designated a *New York Times* Best Illustrated Book of the Year; and Kate Banks and Boris Kulikov's *Max's Words* (2006, 2007 film), which received the *School Library Journal* Best Book of the Year Award.

The second criteria, adaptability, is largely an aesthetic consideration to determine if the book can be translated into the medium of film. This principle is open to a wide array of illustrative styles—from the stylized watercolors in Tomie dePaola's *Strega Nona* (1975, 1978 film) and Simms Taback's folk art forms in *There Was an Old Lady Who Swallowed a Fly* (1997, 2002 film) to the solid shapes and unmodulated colors of Frank Asch's *Happy Birthday, Moon* (1982, 1985 film) and the mixed-media approach of Mo Willems's *Knuffle Bunny* (2004, 2006 film). Despite their stylistic differences, all of these titles are picture books and thus potentially adaptable. Other works are not so malleable. For example, alphabet and other concept books (books that explain in concrete terms basic, abstract ideas such as numbers, colors, shapes, or directions) are generally short on drama and tend to disqualify themselves from film adaptations; additionally, pop-up and novelty books cannot usually be duplicated two-dimensionally. Early readers and novels present other problems for highly visual forms like animation—that is, if one wants to be faithful to the original. Thus, the studio passed on William Steig's novella *Shrek!* (1990, 2001 film) because it was text-heavy, adult-oriented, and did not seem to have the necessary visual elements to

Model sketches for characters in the adaptation of *Knuffle Bunny: A Cautionary Tale* by Mo Willems give animators vital information on scale, character movements, and other visual keys.

support a film of the kind that Weston Woods would make. It would be years before the digital revolution and CGI (computer-generated images) would make it possible to take on a project like *Shrek!*, and the book lay dormant for nearly a decade until DreamWorks Animation developed it into a feature-length animated film in 2001.

Unlike the easy availability of works in the early years of Weston Woods, today publishers, authors, and artists are keenly aware of the lucrative potential of subsidiary rights to their titles; this reality, ironically, is due in large part to the attention that Schindel gave to these rights from the beginning of the studio's productions. Schindel's film rights contracts, with royalties assigned to both the authors and the artists, were among the first in the industry. In the ensuing years, Schindel was instrumental in helping to establish a general adaptation-rights protocol, one that sought to standardize the contractual process. The growing media market and the commensurate competition for adaptation rights today is significantly different from what it was in the 1950s and 1960s, or even the 1980s; and it continues to increase in intensity with every highly visible and lucrative translation of a book into some other medium. Much like the dramatic change that the advent of *The Antiques Road Show* has brought to the world of collectibles, so, too, is contemporary children's book publishing only rarely a place where bargains can be found. The few hundred dollars that Schindel paid for adaptation rights in the 1950s have multiplied into the thousands, if not the tens of thousands, of dollars today. Moreover, the media market for children and families is no longer a small, isolated one. Rather, it bears the impact and often the imprint of the rapidly expanding cable-television industry and of the various other outlets for "edutainment," as well as of successful feature-length films based on picture books—as seen in the high-octane Hollywood treatments of Chris Van Allsburg's books *Jumanji* (1981, 1995 film) and *The Polar Express* (1985, 2004 film). It's not surprising, then, to find an ever-growing contest each year to acquire the adaptation rights for the most prized picture books and novels. In such a frenzied, high-stakes market, a book like Sendak's *Where the Wild Things Are* (1963, 1975 and 1988 film) will not remain a picture book that becomes a short animated film or a one-act opera; with a great deal of added backstory and revved-up special effects, it has now been transformed into a highly anticipated (if often delayed) feature film.

As in the early years of the studio, satisfying the three criteria for selecting books to adapt into films is the threshold for any work that Weston Woods decides to produce. It is understood that, along with a specific budget, the studio has a target goal of profitability each year. But aside from these basic terms, the production team is free

Opposite: Storyboard page for Jules Feiffer's *I Lost My Bear*, a film by Gene Deitch for Weston Woods. Feiffer's daughter, Halley, narrated the film.

Sudden ZOOM IN

But I know it's gone.........forever !

She turns as BG color fades in fast

(sound of door knob and door opening)

CUT as door opens and sister shoults

2

(sister) "If you close your eyes...."

....and reveal the little girl, hearing that revelation!

sometimes it lands in the same place!"

CUT to CU girl, as she takes it in.

3

"WOW!"

She turns to camera, aghast!

"If I throw one of my favorites, what if I lose that one too?"

CUT snd PAN across stuffed animal closet

So I'd better throw a stuffed animal i don't care about...

to choose its own projects from among the thousands of new picture books that are published each year and to take the time necessary to create an adaptation worthy of the Weston Woods name. Lee and Gagne have worked together so long that the process of selecting films is not problematic. And though each has absolute veto power, especially if one feels a work is inappropriate for the studio, the selection process is, in practice, one of reaching consensus through support, debate, and compromise.

The output for Weston Woods has ranged between ten and fifteen films each year, and it continues at that level today. As has been the case since the 1960s, the actual animation of the films has been done in the studio of whoever happens to be a particular film's director, whether in the United States or abroad. Many of the same animators have provided films for Weston Woods on a continual basis—most notably, Gene Deitch, Michael Sporn, Virginia Wilkos, and Gary McGivney. After a hiatus from directing films for Weston Woods during the 1990s to work on some of his own projects, Deitch has returned to making films for the studio once again, among them adaptations of books by Jules Feiffer, including film versions of Feiffer's *Bark, George* (1999, 2003 film) and *I Lost My Bear* (1998, 2004 film). Deitch has also animated a string of the award-winning books from

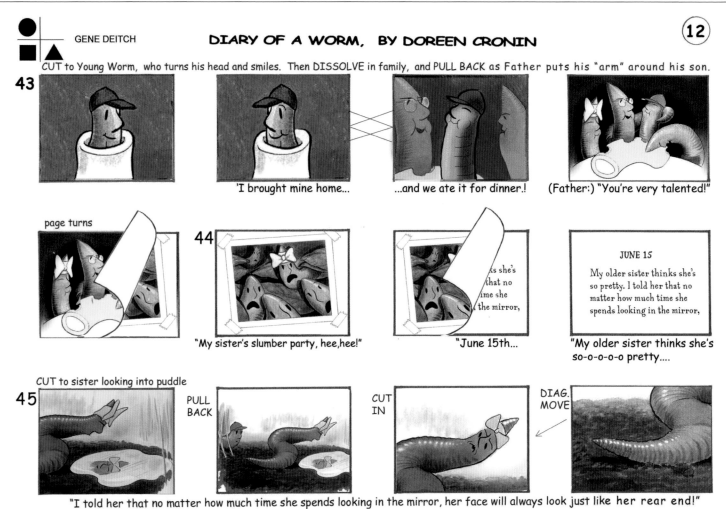

DIARY OF A WORM, BY DOREEN CRONIN

CUT to Young Worm, who turns his head and smiles. Then DISSOLVE in family, and PULL BACK as Father puts his "arm" around his son.

43

'I brought mine home...   ...and we ate it for dinner.!   (Father:) "You're very talented!"

page turns

44

"My sister's slumber party, hee, hee!"   "June 15th...   "My older sister thinks she's so-o-o-o-o pretty...."

JUNE 15

My older sister thinks she's so pretty. I told her that no matter how much time she spends looking in the mirror,

CUT to sister looking into puddle

45   PULL BACK   CUT IN   DIAG. MOVE

"I told her that no matter how much time she spends looking in the mirror, her face will always look just like her rear end!"

Top: A storyboard from Deitch's adaptation of Doreen Cronin's clever send-up of the journal form as narrative, *Diary of a Worm*, illustrated by Harry Bliss. Cronin and Bliss created other variations on this theme, *Diary of a Spider* and *Diary of a Fly*, which have also become Weston Woods films.

Right: A character study for the narrator in Cronin's *Diary of a Worm*. The character was voiced by the young actor Alexander Gould.

A study of Cronin's *Diary of a Worm* shows the relative scale of the main character to his environment. In the adapation, Deitch used visual cues like this to remind viewers that the story's larger-than-life protagonist is only a few inches long.

the Diary series of writer Doreen Cronin and illustrator Harry Bliss—*Diary of a Worm* (2003, 2004 film), *Diary of a Spider* (2005, 2006 film), and *Diary of a Fly* (2007, 2008 film)—which incorporate biological facts into a comedic, first-person story line. Deitch has completed one of his most ambitious projects for Weston Woods, the nineteen-minute trilogy of Rosemary Wells stories, narrated by Maggie Gyllenhaal, about finding a place of peace amid life's stresses—the sweet lullaby that is *Voyage to the Bunny Planet* (1992, 2008 film).

From the 1980s on, Michael Sporn has also continued to animate films for Weston Woods. After receiving an Academy Award nomination for his adaptation of William Steig's *Doctor De Soto* (1982, 1984 film), Sporn has adapted more than a dozen films for Weston Woods, including Stephen Kellogg's *The Mysterious Tadpole* (1977, 1986 film), James Stevenson's *What's Under My Bed?* (1983, 1990 film), Robert Kraus and Jose Aruego's *Leo the Late Bloomer* (1971, 1999 film), Fred Marcellino's *I, Crocodile* (1999, 2001 film), and Rosemary Wells's *Read to Your Bunny* (1998, 2006 film). But the pièce de résistance of Sporn's work for the studio, as mentioned earlier, remains the moving, unforgettable *The Man Who Walked Between the Towers* (2003, 2005 film), which was shortlisted for an Academy Award nomination and a recipient of the Andrew Carnegie Medal for Excellence in Children's Video. By the Caldecott Award–winning Mordicai Gerstein, *The Man Who Walked Between the Towers* tells the story of Philippe Petit, the high-wire performer who undertook the spectacular feat of walking between New York City's Twin Towers. Melissa Reilly, the coproducer on this project, credits the emergence of this great film to a "perfect storm" of elements: the right book, the right narrator (actor Jake Gyllenhaal), the right animator (Michael Sporn), the right music (by Michael Bacon), and the right moment (four years after

A sketch from Mordicai Gerstein's *The Man Who Walked Between the Towers* helped animators plan to render a juggling scene by the street performer and aerialist Philippe Petit.

the September 11th catastrophe).[6] Though it ultimately was not nominated for an Oscar, the film has been celebrated with more than a dozen national and international awards. This work has become the quintessential work of all the contemporary Weston Woods productions, one through which the tradition of the studio advances into the future.

Many of the studio's other projects have been outsourced to a large group of talented animation shops like those of Maciek Albrecht, whose MaGiK Studio has done such films for Weston Woods as Cronin and Betsy Lewin's Caldecott Honor–winning *Click, Clack, Moo* (2000, 2001 film), Jane Yolen and Mark Teague's *How Do Dinosaurs Get Well Soon?* (2003, 2005 film), and Mo Willems's Caldecott Honor book, *Knuffle Bunny* (2004, 2006 film). The credits for Daniel Ivanik, another animator for the studio, include Laurie Keller's *Arnie, the Doughnut* (2003, 2005 film), Andrea Zimmerman, David Clemesha, and Dan Yaccarino's *Trashy Town* (1999, 2001 film), and Cari Best and Giselle Potter's *Three Cheers for Catherine the Great!* (1999, 2001 film). In the past, Virginia Wilkos has adapted *Musical Max* (1990, 1993 film) by Robert Kraus, with illustrations by Jose Aruego and Ariane Dewey; *Chrysanthemum* (1996, 1998 film) by Kevin Henkes; *Miss Nelson Has a Field Day* (1985, 1999 film) by Harry Allard, with illustrations by James Marshall; and *Chicka Chicka Boom Boom* (1989, 1999 film) by Bill Martin, Jr. and John Archambault, with illustrations by Lois Ehlert. Another animator who has done a number of films for the studio is Galen Fott, whose Bigfott Studios adapted Nina Laden's *Roberto the Insect Architect* (2000, 2005 film), Kate Banks and Boris Kulikov's *Max's Words* (2006, 2007 film), Mike Thaler and Jared Lee's *The Librarian from the Black Lagoon* (1997, 2007 film), and Laurie Keller's *Do Unto Otters* (2007, 2008 film). The films of these animators, as well as others who produce films for Weston Woods, continue to win awards, not only for their faithful adaptations of their source material, but also for the fresh animations (like those for *Knuffle Bunny* and *Max's Words*) that reflect the styles and tones of the original books.

One continuing concern of the Weston Woods studio is its dedication to a diverse, international range of film adaptations. "The real difference today," Linda Lee observes, "is that the world is so much more multicultural. We have to find literature that speaks to that broader audience."[7] This openness to works from other cultures has been a hallmark of Weston Woods from its earliest books—when, to recapitulate, it took us to China with *The Story about Ping* (1933, 1955 film) and through France and Africa in *Alexander and the Car with a Missing Headlight* (1967, film 1967); stayed in Africa with Gail E. Haley's *A Story, A Story* (1970, 1973 film),

Four panels from Michael Sporn's storyboard for Gerstein's *The Man Who Walked Between the Towers* show the radically different points of view the animators planned to use in depicting the spectacle. The result for the viewer is a visceral sense of both the intimacy and grandeur of the event.

These two frames from the storyboard for *The Man Who Walked Between the Towers* show Petit's triumphant final gesture and the mixed reactions of the waiting policemen.

Margaret Musgrove and Leo and Diane Dillon's *Ashanti to Zulu* (1976, 1977 film-strip), and John Steptoe's *Mufaro's Beautiful Daughters* (1987, 1989 film); and guided us in other books to cultures as varied as their geographical areas—from Eastern European Yiddish tales to the myths of Native Americans, from the haikus of Japan to the life of a famous Mexican potter. One can see this international interest celebrated today in such Weston Woods films as Sheila Hamanaka's *All the Colors of the Earth* (1994, 1997 film); Gary Soto's books about Chato the cat, *Chato and the Party Animals* (2000, 2003 film) and *Chato's Kitchen* (1995, 1999 film), both illustrated by Susan Guevara; and *Elizabeti's Doll* (1998, 2000 film) by Stephanie Stuve-Bodeen, with illustrations by Christy Hale.

African-American authors and artists are also represented in numerous films that the studio has produced. Among these adaptations from celebrated books, one finds the Caldecott Medal–winning *Why Mosquitoes Buzz in People's Ears* (1975, 1984 film) by Verna Aardema, with illustrations by Leo and Diane Dillon. The Caldecott Medal Honor Books include: *Duke Ellington* (1998, 2000 film) by Andrea Davis Pinkney, with illustrations by Brian Pinkney; *John Henry* (1994, 1998 film) by Julius Lester, with illustrations by Jerry Pinkney; *Martin's Big Words* (2001, 2002 film) by Doreen Rappaport, with illustrations by Bryan Collier; *Mufaro's Beautiful Daughters*, by Steptoe; *Rosa* (2005, 2007 film) by Nikki Giovanni, with illustrations by Bryan Collier; and *March On!* (2008, 2008 film) by Dr. Christine King Farris, with illustrations by London Ladd. Yet other examples of lauded books that reflect similar social or cultural concerns are reflected in such films as Shange's *Ellington Was Not a Street* (2004, 2005 film), with Nelson's illustrations; and Patricia McKissack's

Flossie and the Fox (1986, 1991 film). And then there are works like Chris Raschka's *Yo! Yes?* (1993, 2000 film) and Nelson's *He's Got the Whole World in His Hands*, whose thematic attentions suggest the simple and subtle ways that stories or songs can encourage racial harmony.

Other areas that the studio has cultivated in recent years are films that look at American history and the political process, often from an unusual, slightly quirky perspective. In 2007 alone, for example, the studio released *The Journey of the One and Only Declaration of Independence* (2005, 2007 film) by Judith St. George, with illustrations by Will Hillenbrand, one of several films based on books that are meant to make the subjects of history and politics accessible to a contemporary young audience. Other authors are adding to the growing emphasis on books with American themes (just right for social studies classes); these include Woody Guthrie's classic *This Land Is Your Land* (1998, 2000 film), with illustrations by Kathy Jakobsen, who also provided the pictures for Reeve Lindbergh's *Johnny Appleseed* (1993, 2000 film), a verse retelling of the legend of one of America's folk heroes.

In the end, though, the films of Weston Woods Studios will continue to rely on the quality of the books that they are able to select and adapt in an increasingly competitive media market. Just a quick glance at a Weston Woods catalog indicates the number of other studios that are currently making films in genres (like the author or artist documentary) that in previous decades were nearly the exclusive province of Weston Woods. To its credit, Weston Woods has remained the distributor for a number of these productions from other studios, and by listing these films in their catalogs, Weston Woods has publicized works that might otherwise have been overlooked. In its releases for 2007 and 2008, for example, Weston Woods offers highly regarded documentaries about the children's book author/illustrators Tasha Tudor in *Take Joy! The Magical World of Tasha Tudor* (1996) and Virginia Lee Burton in *Virginia Lee Burton: A Sense of Place* (2008). This would be a heretical move in most companies—giving valuable marketing space to the work of one's competitors—and yet Weston Woods' approach has been, from the start, one of inclusiveness. Obviously, the financial goal of the studio is to be profitable, and the distribution of the works of other studios ultimately serves that end—as it has for Scholastic, which for decades has distributed the books of other publishers. But in a larger sense, as Lee puts it, the mission of the studio is about something more than the bottom line. In the end, Weston Woods asks that bedrock question that defines the founding principles of the studio: "Is this going to result in something better for kids?"[8]

Chapter 10

The highlights of my life have been innumerable. Hard to choose among them.
But I think the real highlight is the persistent feeling that the best is yet to come.

—Mort Schindel

A view of the entrance hallway to the gallery building of the Weston Woods Museum, with a display of the studio's products and plush toys based on characters in Weston Woods films.

At the turn of the new millennium, Mort Schindel revised his vision statement for perhaps his final and continuing endeavor, the Weston Woods Institute. Elaborating on its mission—to create innovative educational and cultural communications to enrich the lives of children—the vision statement described the institute as an organization that would concentrate on the ever-expanding domain of children's media in order to "develop and initiate activities that would be disseminated in the field through the use of electronic media...and traveling classrooms." Schindel envisioned the organization as a part of a much larger network of interrelated centers of activity, in which, as "a home for activities related to quality children's media," it had "the potential to become a key destination on a children's literature trail." This network could be developed and would include, in future years, significant additions to the scene such as the Eric Carle Museum of Picture Book Art in Amherst, Massachusetts. In both the real and the abstract, Schindel saw a vibrant, fluid nexus of discussion and action that would both "adapt itself to a changing society [and] serve the needs of the local community, the state, and the world at large."[1]

The Weston Woods Institute was meant to seek ways to translate concepts into reality. The institute has explored such varied subjects as the development of television programs; the establishment of regular contracts for media rights and royalty distribution between authors, artists, and publishers; and the creation of the Children's Media Trust—a project designed to foster amicable relations between publishers and media producers, writers and artists. In addition, it has promoted and administered such innovative projects as Schindel's media mobiles, the development of arts-and-humanities-based curricula for schools, as well as other ventures that did not fit,

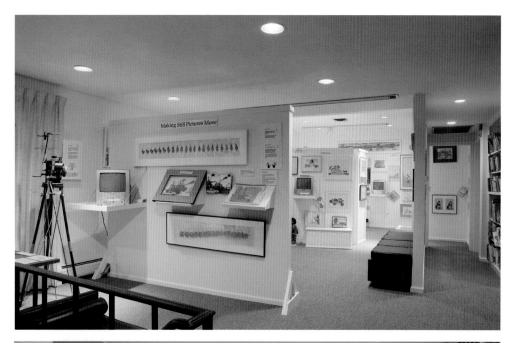

strictly speaking, into the focused purpose of the film studio.

Although Schindel played a key role in its establishment—conceiving of its mission, providing financial support, and offering ten acres of land and the four original studio buildings on the Weston Woods grounds—the institute has been led by a board of directors and an advisory board that drew its rotating membership from the library, literary, media, publishing, and academic communities. The Board of Directors continues to be composed of distinguished people drawn principally from the fields of education and literature for children.

After Weston Woods was sold to Scholastic, Richard Robinson pledged to help support the work of the institute once it was fully established in Weston.[2] By 2007, the institute had fashioned a new branch of activity—the Weston Woods Museum and Library. This profile serves to redefine the institute's goals, which most certainly include more exhibitions based on original Weston Woods material. And since so much of what Robinson has described as the "treasure trove" of animation art that is in the institute's archives is quite fragile, the Weston Woods Museum and Library will likely make use of digital technology through a series of online exhibitions, which would provide a venue for some of the museum's rarer holdings.

With the 1985 purchase of Dromkeen Children's Literature Collection in Australia, and more recently, of Weston Woods, Robinson is anticipating a global constellation of retreats where people involved with children's books and media can

Top: Schindel's collection of magic-lantern projectors, a precurser to the modern motion picture projector, is housed in the former studio building at the Weston Woods Museum.

Bottom: The Eric Carle Museum of Picture Book Art in Amherst, Massachusetts, opened in 2002.

Opposite top: One of the galleries in the Weston Woods Museum demonstrates the basic principles of animation, with hands-on displays that allow visitors to examine the layers of images used in traditional cel animation.

Opposite bottom: One of the smaller viewing areas in the gallery is used for more focused discussions of specific films. This space is devoted to *Alexander and the Car with a Missing Headlight*; on the other side of the wall is a larger room that features storyboards and other graphic materials related to Maurice Sendak's *Where the Wild Things Are.*

find a haven to think about their work and meet with others who are engaged in the field. In these shared musings, Robinson and Schindel are fellow travelers who are dreaming the same dream. The lengthy process of achieving these goals has required that Schindel and Robinson remain patient and unflaggingly hopeful that the Weston Woods Museum will soon become a place of tranquil seclusion, as well as a place where new ideas and creative plans can be dreamed, discussed, and set in motion. After all, a museum is the namesake of and a place sacred to the Muses.

Meanwhile, Schindel continues to imagine the possibilities for the museum. Along with exhibitions, real and virtual, there will be the opportunity to introduce a large—indeed, international—audience to the work of Weston Woods, and to the art form of animation, through a sophisticated web-based hub of information offering documentaries of Weston Woods subjects and other interconnected areas of interest. Such an online presence would also provide a site for young filmmakers; Schindel has in mind an innovative, international YouTube-style setting for aspiring animators that might involve a web-based film festival, complete with awards.

With the recent public recognition of the limits of the so-called "back to basics" movement—defining and evaluating teaching methods in terms of whether children pass standardized tests—and its irrelevance to a well-rounded education, Schindel has begun to think about his earlier plans to help rejuvenate the elementary-school curriculum in the context of the collection of the Weston Woods Museum. He would like to provide online or televised courses in children's literature that would make

A view of the Dromkeen Children's Literature Collection near Melbourne, Australia. The collection's holdings are devoted to Australian artists and writers of children's picture books.

extensive use of the studio's film and documentary archives, furthering his principle that the arts lie at the center of creative and intellectual thinking. Thus, whether in physical or virtual reality, the Weston Woods Museum has been envisioned as a portal for national and international audiences and as an entrance to projects that Schindel believes are essential for promoting greater understanding, creativity, and knowledge.

At the age of ninety-one, Schindel continues to receive awards and accolades—most recently from Purdue University, which conferred an honorary doctorate of education on him in May 2008. In 2006 Schindel received one of the first Carle Honors Awards from the Eric Carle Museum, which cited Schindel as "both an innovator and a visionary for his work in giving treasured picture books new life on the screen, while remaining faithful to the originals." Other acknowledgments of Schindel's eminence are registered in the frequent articles and testimonials that appear about him and his work. Joseph Yranski, for example, the senior film and video historian at the New York Public Library, has referred to Schindel as "a living national treasure." An article about Schindel in the *School Library Journal* was more casual, giving him the hip moniker "the king of kids' flicks." And in *Westport Magazine,* Stephanie Izarek titled her celebratory portrait of Schindel "The Immortal Mort." Indeed, all are befitting appellations.

Each morning, as he has done for more than fifty years, Schindel steps over the threshold of his office door and enters into the daily life of Weston Woods. He still gives tours of the studio grounds, though not as prolonged or as frequent as in previous years. He stays in touch by phone or e-mail with a large group of friends, associates, and correspondents from all over the world. Half jokingly, he ascribes his success to the way he internalized his mother's ability to spend long hours on the phone, continually building networks or fortifying existing ones. He still drives, confidently and at the top of the speed limit. He still has a hearty appetite—for dessert, people, conversation, and ideas, although not necessarily in that order. New technologies do not seem to fluster him; he's taking lessons from his younger cognoscenti on how to manipulate digital images, instead of remaining frustrated by the powers of his new computer.

Schindel does not speak about his own health, which has had its ups and downs over the years. If you ask him how he feels, he'll just smile, say he's fine, and move on. And in some fundamental way, he *is* fine. He has found, as his doctor prescribed in 1939, something to be engaged in that did not feel like work. In that quest, Mort Schindel has discovered what he totally, completely, tirelessly loves to do.

Schindel in the living room of the main house
at Weston Woods, surrounded by the many
characters who have been featured in Weston
Woods films over the years.

Notes

Unless otherwise noted, all quotes from Morton Schindel are from interviews with the author conducted on 2 August, 28 September, 23 October, and 1 November 2007.

Foreword

"Into the Woods" is a substantially revised version of an interview with Maurice Sendak conducted by Paul Gagne on February 12, 2003. A recording of the interview is in the archive of Weston Woods Studios.

Introduction

1. Schindel refers to his "luck" frequently, including in his acceptance speech for the Regina Medal in which he stated, ". . . I'm convinced that the secret ingredient in what I've been doing all these years is luck. My first big break came when I contracted tuberculosis. . . ." Morton Schindel, transcript of acceptance speech for the Regina Medal (Weston Woods Institute and Museum Archive, 17 April 1979), 3–4.

2. Gene Deitch, "Make Luck Happen," in *How to Succeed in Animation*, http://genedeitch.awn.com, 2001.

3. Schindel identified "his pattern" in a case study included in *The Power of Form: A Psychoanalytic Approach to Aesthetic Form* by Gilbert J. Rose (New York: International Universities Press, 1980), 53.

4. For the first mention of Keats's concept of "negative capability," see John Keats, *The Letters of John Keats*, ed. Maurice Buxton Forman (New York: Oxford University Press, 1952), 71.

5. Paul Gagne, interview by the author, Norwalk, CT, 10 December 2007.

Chapter I

1. With the exception of the Carnegie Medal, Schindel further notes, "There are so many of them [awards], and there is so little competition in the children's category, which I rather regret. We are reasonably assured of getting an award almost every time that we submit a film. I think that really is unfortunate, because it tends to lower the standard, the quality of films for children." Morton Schindel, "Tour Tape of the Buildings at Weston Woods That is My Home" (unpublished audio recording documenting the contents of the original Weston Woods Studios, Weston Woods Institute and Museum Archives, 2003), tape 2, sides 1–2.

Chapter 2

1. Morton Schindel, "Notes Pertaining to Weston Woods Mystique" (Weston Woods Institute and Museum Archives, n.d.), 15.

2. Schindel, interview by Leonard Marcus (Weston Woods Institute and Museum Archives, 2003), tape recording, tape 3.

3. Schindel, transcript of acceptance speech for the Regina Medal, op cit., 4.

4. Schindel, "Background and Development of Weston Woods" (Weston Woods Institute and Museum Archives, n.d.), 3.

5. Margalit Fox, obituary for Sid Davis in the *New York Times*, 9 November 2006.

6. Schindel, "Background and Development of Weston Woods," op. cit., 7.

7. *The Outlivers: Two Hundred Years in Weston 1787–1987*, prod. Morton Schindel, Nancy Hammerslough, and Barbara Wagner and dir. Harvey Bellin, 37 min., The Weston Historical Society, Weston, CT, 1987, videocassette.

8. Ibid.

9. Morton Schindel, "Notes on Weston Woods Buildings and Grounds" (Weston Woods Institute and Museum Archives, n.d.), 46.

Chapter 3

1. Schindel, "Notes Pertaining to the Weston Woods Mystique," op. cit., 20.

2. Schindel, *Morton Schindel: From Page to Screen*, op. cit.

3. Schindel, "Background and Development of Weston Woods," op. cit., 10.

4. Ibid.

5. Ibid, 12.

6. Ibid.

7. Morton Schindel, unpublished agreement between Schindel and James Daugherty (Weston Woods Institute and Museum Archives, 13 October 1954), 1.

8. Schindel, "Background and Development of Weston Woods," op. cit., 13–16.

9. Schindel, transcript of acceptance speech for the Regina Medal, op. cit., 12.

10. Morton Schindel, "Augusta Baker Tribute" (Weston Woods Institute and Museum Archives, 2005), 4.

11. The musical aesthetic of Weston Woods films is discussed by Schindel in *From Page to Screen*, op. cit. This phrase is also quoted in Carol L. Birch's "Weston Woods: A Commitment to Excellence" in *Top of the News* (Summer 1985) in order to characterize the deliberately understated, minimalist musical scoring of the studio's early films.

12. Schindel, "Notes Pertaining to the Weston Woods Mystique," op. cit., 21.

13. Morton Schindel, "The Story of Weston Woods: Background Documentation" (unpublished, compiled by Gitta Selva, Weston Woods Institute and Museum Archives, 2006). This reference resource consists of article excerpts, interviews, quotations, and biographical and studio data. It will henceforth be referred to as "Background Documentation." Schindel further describes the challenges he faced with *The Story about Ping*: "It has only 27 illustrations, however, and I needed about a hundred pictures to illustrate the story. . . . I took the liberty of using the last picture first and again at the end

of the film. . . . no one ever complained . . . my job was to tell the story in the best way I knew for the medium in which I was working. . . ." Schindel, "Working With Picture Book Artists in Adapting Their Work" (Weston Woods Institute and Museum Archives, n.d.), 1–2.

14. Morton Schindel, "From Books to Films to Kangaroo," *Rushes* (17 December 1956), 53.

15. Unsigned, "Picture Books to Live on TV," review of The Picture Book Parade, *New York Times*, 9 January 1956, 22.

16. Deitch, "The Terry-fying Challenge," in *How to Succeed in Animation*, op. cit.

17. Morton Schindel, "The Birth of Weston Woods and First Films: The Seven Films" in Background Documentation, op. cit., 59.

Chapter 4

1. Schindel, "From Books to Films to Kangaroo," op. cit. The number of viewers is reiterated in "What's Good for Them," *Newsweek* 54 (10 September 1956): 54.

2. Frances Lander Spain in Cecile Starr, "16-mm for Children," *The Saturday Review of Literature* 41 (10 May 1958): 46.

3. Unsigned, "What's Good for Them," *Newsweek* 54 (10 September 1956): 54.

4. Paul Nathan, "Rights and Permissions," *Publishers Weekly* 194 (9 September 1968): 51.

5. Promotional literature for Picture Book Parade, Weston Woods Institute and Museum Archives, 1957.

6. Ibid.

7. Nathan, *Publishers Weekly*, op. cit.

8. Promotional literature for Picture Book Parade, op. cit.

9. Morton Schindel, "Questions and Answers," interview by Jill May ("The Birth of Weston Woods and First Films," in Background Documentation, op cit., 2002), 4.

10. Howard Thompson, "A Satire on Mechanization is Filmed for Children; Filmmaker Uses Children's Books: Studio in Connecticut Bases Shorts on Literary Merit," *New York Times*, 12 November 1963, 43.

11. Morton Schindel, *From Page to Screen: Celebrating Fifty Years of Bringing Books to Life*, prod. and dir. Richard A. Carey, Leigh Corra, Paul R. Gagne, Kim Hayes, and Melissa Reilly, 21:06 min., Weston Woods Studios, Weston, CT, 2003, videocassette.

12. Robert McCloskey, acceptance speech for the Caldecott Award for *Time of Wonder* ("The Creative Process of Making Movies and Working with Authors" in Background Documentation, op. cit., 1958), 1.

13. Schindel, transcript of acceptance speech for the Regina Medal op. cit., 12–13.

14. Terri Payne Butler, "Moving Pictures: Morton Schindel Revisited," *The Horn Book* 74 (September/October 1998): 564.

15. Morton Schindel, "The Books that Weston Woods has Adapted over the Years" (Weston Woods Institute and Museum Archives, 1978), 59.

16.–19. Ibid.

20. Schindel, "Augusta Baker Tribute" (quoted in "Storytelling and the Evolving Mission of Weston Woods" in Background Documentation, op. cit.), 91.

Chapter 5

1. Schindel, "Notes Pertaining to the Weston Woods Mystique," op. cit., 43.

2. Ibid., 44.

3. Morton Schindel, "Status Report 1985" (Weston Woods Institute and Museum Archives, 1985), 9.

4. Schindel, "Notes on Weston Woods Buildings and Grounds," op. cit., 18.

5. Schindel, "Questions and Answers," interview by May, op. cit.

6. Schindel, "The Books that Weston Woods has Adapted over the Years" op. cit., 82.

7. Ibid., 82–83.

8. Gene Deitch, "Storytelling and the Evolving Mission of Weston Woods" in Background Documentation, op. cit., 82.

9. Deitch gives an extensive account of his move to Prague in *For the Love of Prague: The True Story of the Only Free American In Prague During Thirty Years of Communism* (Prague: Baset Books, 1997).

10. Schindel, interview by Marcus, op. cit., tape 11.

11. Schindel, "Notes Pertaining to the Weston Woods Mystique," op. cit., 32–33.

12. Schindel, interview by Marcus, op. cit., tape 11.

13. Deitch, "Storytelling and the Evolving Mission of Weston Woods: TV Efforts" in Background Documentation, op. cit., 103.

14. Deitch, *Gene Deitch: The Picture Book Animated*, prod. Morton Schindel and dir. Gene Deitch, 26 min, Weston Woods Studios, Weston, CT, 1977.

15. Schindel, "Background and Development of Weston Woods," op. cit., 19.

16. Schindel, "Personal Recollections" (Weston Woods Institute and Museum Archives, n.d.), 95. Schindel has repeated his praise of Deitch in other places, including interviews with Leonard Marcus (op. cit., tape 11) and in an interview with the author 23 October 2007.

17. Deitch, *Gene Deitch: The Picture Book Animated*, op. cit.

18. Ibid.

19. Gene Deitch, "The Creative Process of Making Movies and Working with Authors" in Background Documentation, op. cit., 153.

20. Ibid., 154.

21.–22. Ibid., 153.

23. Ibid., 153–154.

24. Meg Angus-Smith, "Out of the Weston Woods," *News-Times* (Danbury, CT), 29 January 1989, Living section, 1–3.

25. For a description of the creative differences surrounding the music for *Sylvester and the Magic Pebble*, see Deitch, "In and Out of the Woods," in *How to Succeed in Animation*, op. cit.

26. Butler, op. cit., 561–562.

Chapter 6

1. Rex Lardner, "In Defense of Print Heads," *New York Times Book Review*, 12 October 1969, 8, 53.

2. Ibid., 8.

3. Schindel, "The Books That Weston Woods has Adapted Over the Years," op. cit., 32B.

4. Schindel, "Notes Pertaining to the Weston Woods Mystique," op. cit., 37.

5. Ibid., 38.

6. International Storytelling Center Lifetime Achievement Award commemorative plaque, Weston Woods Institute and Museum Archives.

7. Scott Alarik, "John Langstaff: A Man for All Seasons," *Sing Out!* (January 2005).

8. Ruth Hill Viguers, "An Anniversary," *The Horn Book* 40 (October 1964): 457.

9. *Gene Deitch: The Picture Book Animated*, op. cit.

Chapter 7

1. Walter Benjamin, *Illuminations*, trans. Harry Zohn (New York: Shocken Books, 1973), 91.

2. Schindel, "Tour Tape of the Buildings at Weston Woods That is My Home," op. cit., tape 2, side 1.

3. Ibid.

4. Promotional literature for SIM Productions, Weston Woods Institute and Museum Archives, 1973.

5. Ibid.

6. Lisl Weil, promotional literature for *The Sorcerer's Apprentice* (Weston Woods Institute and Museum Archives, n.d.), 2.

7. Lee Kingman, *Children's Books and Their Creators*, ed. Anita Silvey (Boston, New York: Houghton Mifflin Company, 1995), 672.

8. Schindel, "The Books that Weston Woods has Adapted over the Years," op. cit., 69.

9. Ibid., 71.

10. Ibid., 72.

11. Promotional literature for Poetry Parade, Weston Woods Institute and Museum Archive, 1967.

12. Schindel, "The Books that Weston Woods has Adapted over the Years," op. cit., 91.

13. Gene Deitch, "Filming *Zlateh the Goat*" (promotional literature, Weston Woods Institute and Museum Archives, 1975), 4.

14. Ibid., 5.

15. Schindel, "The Books that Weston Woods has Adapted over the Years," op. cit., 93–94.

16. Deitch, "Filming *Zlateh the Goat*," op. cit., 9.

17. Schindel in Deitch, ibid., 4.

Chapter 8

1. Peggy Mann and John Poignand, "Curtain of Illusion: The Odyssey of the Children's Caravan," *School Library Journal* (February 1967), 1.

2. Betty Tyler, "Weston's Mort Schindel to Raise Curtain on Mobile Art Cinema for Children," *Bridgeport Sunday Post*, 22 December 1963, C2.

3. Ibid., C1.

4. Mann and Poignand, op. cit., 1.

5. Ibid.

6. Adrienne Schure, "Tune in and Watch a Good Book," http://www.aarp.org/about_aarp/nrta/livelearn/archive/a2003-08-13-schindel.html, 13 August 2003.

7. Ibid.

8. Morton Schindel, "Report from Iran," *The Horn Book* 43 (December 1967): 726–727.

9. Morton Schindel, "Films: The Key to Worldwide Dissemination of Literature for Children" (Weston Woods Museum and Institute Archives, ca. 1978), documentation 2, 910.

10. Summary of "Status Report 1985" ("Storytelling and the Evolving Mission of Weston Woods" in Background Documentation, op. cit.), 121.

11. Schindel ("Storytelling and the Evolving Mission of Weston Woods: TV Efforts" in Background Documentation, op. cit.), 3.

12. Ibid.

13. Schindel, proposal to the Corporation for Public Broadcasting ("Storytelling and the Evolving Mission of Weston Woods" in Background Documentation, op. cit., 1968), 133.

14. C. A. Waite, "No Frontiers For Picture Books," *Bookbird* 6, no. 1 (January 1968): 8.

Chapter 9

1. Schindel, "Q & A" ("Info on Scholastic Sale" in Background Documentation, op. cit., 2002).

2. Linda Lee, "Lessons Learned from Mort" ("The Weston Woods Mystique: Relationship With Staff" in Background Documentation, op. cit.).

3. Richard Robinson ("Info on Scholastic Sale: Weston Woods Legacy" in Background Documentation, op. cit.)

4. Linda Lee, "Lessons Learned from Mort" ("The Weston Woods Mystique: Relationship with Staff" op. cit.)

5. "Children's Circle: Where Books Come Alive!" (catalog, Weston Woods Institute and Museum Archives, 1991).

6. Melissa Reilly, interview by the author, Norwalk, CT, 6 December 2007.

7. Linda Lee, "Lessons Learned from Mort" ("The Weston Woods Mystique: Relationship with Staff" op. cit.)

8. Linda Lee, interview by the author, Norwalk, CT, 6 December 2007.

Chapter 10

1. Schindel, "Weston Woods Institute Background" (prepared for Town of Weston Planning and Zoning Board, Weston Woods Institute and Museum Archives, 2000, revised 2005).

2. Richard Robinson, telephone interview by the author, 17 March 2008.

Notes on the text

We have cited the earliest recorded release date of a film adaptation according to the records at Weston Woods Studios. Please note that subsequent versions of some films have been released in different formats and/or with different elements, such as sound tracks. For book publication dates, we have cited the first English language/US edition. We have retained the original grammar in previously published quotes.

Notes on the filmography

The information in the filmography is compiled from records at Weston Woods Studios. Only motion pictures (iconographic, animated, and live-action) are included here; filmstrips, audio recordings, and other formats are excluded. Films distributed (but not produced) by Weston Woods and re-releases are likewise not included. "ALA" is the acronym for the American Library Association.

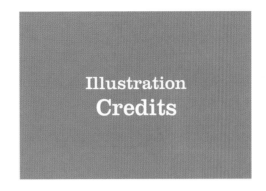

Illustration Credits

T=top; B=bottom; L=left; R=right; WWI=Weston Woods Institute; WWS=Weston Woods Studio; a page number not followed by a directional refers to all images on page.

© Academy of Motion Pictures Arts and Sciences®/Courtesy WWI: 89TL; © Aladdin Paperbacks, an imprint of Simon and Schuster/Greg Griffin Photography: 71TL; © Robert Benson Photography: 147; © 2003 The Eric Carle Museum of Picture Book Art/Paul Shoul: 145B; From *The Snowy Day* by Ezra Jack Keats, © 1962 by Ezra Jack Keats, renewed © 1990 by Martin Pope, Executor, used by permission of www.penguin.com, all rights reserved: 1; From *Lentil* by Robert McCloskey, © 1940, renewed © 1968 by Robert McCloskey, used by permission of www.penguin.com, all rights reserved/Greg Griffin Photography: 49R, 102R; Courtesy Morton Schindel: 11L, 25–26, 29–31; Courtesy Morton Schindel/Greg Griffin Photography: 10, 11R; © 1963, 1991 Maurice Sendak, reprinted by permission of HarperCollins Publishers: 8L; Previously unpublished drawings by Maurice Sendak, copyright © 2009 by Maurice Sendak, are reproduced by his permission: 79, 127T; Courtesy The Trudeau Institute Archives: 27; Special permission granted by *Weekly Reader*, published and copyrighted by Weekly Reader Corporation, all rights reserved/Greg Griffin Photography: 119T; Courtesy Dennis Wisken: 146; Courtesy WWI: 14, 43, 45, 47, 154–155; Courtesy WWI/Greg Griffin Photography: 12, 143–145T; © WWS/Greg Griffin Photography: 5, 16B, 24L, 24R, 32, 37–40, 41B, 46, 48, 50, 52, 58–59, 60T, 60R, 66–67, 69–70, 71TR, 72–73, 74R–75T, 76, 78R, 80–87, 89TR, 90L, 97, 100–101, 102T, 102L, 107–108, 110–113, 116, 120L, 123 (cels), 124–125T, 128T, 142, 176; © WWS/Courtesy WWI: 4, 7, 8T, 8R, 9, 16T, 16L, 17–22, 24T, 33, 35–36, 41T, 45L, 49L, 51, 53, 55–56, 71B, 74L, 75B, 77, 78L, 90R, 92, 94–95, 104, 106, 118, 119B, 120R, 121, 123 (photo), 125B–126, 127B, 128R, 130–140, 153; © WWS/Photo Kratký Films: 63–64, 114; © WWS/Courtesy Michael Sporn Animation: 60B, 88, 89R.

FRONT JACKET (clockwise from top left): Reprinted with the permission of Simon & Schuster Books for Young Readers, an imprint of Simon & Schuster Children's Publishing Division from *Happy Birthday, Moon* by Frank Asch, copyright © 1982 Frank Asch; From *Owl Moon* by Jane Yolen, illustrated by John Schoenherr, © 1987 by John Schoenherr (illustrations), used by permission of www.penguin.com, all rights reserved; From *Goldilocks and the Three Bears* by James Marshall, ©1988 by James Marshall, used by permission of www.penguin.com, all rights reserved; From *Where the Wild Things Are* © 1963, 1991 Maurice Sendak, reprinted by permission of HarperCollins Publishers; From *The Island of the Skog* by Steven Kellogg, © 1973, renewed 2001 by Steven Kellogg, used by permission of www.penguin.com, all rights reserved; From *Noisy Nora* (with all new illustrations) by Rosemary Wells, © 1973 by Rosemary Wells (text), © 1997 by Rosemary Wells (illustrations), used by permission of www.penguin.com, all rights reserved; From *Max's Christmas* by Rosemary Wells, © 1986 by Rosemary Wells, used by permission of www.penguin.com, all rights reserved; From *The Snowy Day* by Ezra Jack Keats, © 1962 by Ezra Jack Keats, renewed © 1990 by Martin Pope, Executor, used by permission of www.penguin.com, all rights reserved; Reprinted with the permission of Atheneum Books for Young Readers, an imprint of Simon & Schuster Children's Publishing Division from *A Story, A Story* by Gail E. Haley, copyright © 1970 Gail E. Haley; From *Make Way for Ducklings* by Robert McCloskey, © 1941, renewed © 1969 by Robert McCloskey, used by permission of www.penguin.com, all rights reserved; From *The Day Jimmy's Boa Ate the Wash* by Trinka Hakes Noble, pictures by Steven Kellogg, © 1980 by Steven Kellogg (pictures), used by permission of www.penguin.com, all rights reserved; From *Goldilocks and the Three Bears* by James Marshall, ©1988 by James Marshall, used by permission of www.penguin.com, all rights reserved; Reprinted by permission of Farrar, Straus and Giroux, LLC: From *The Amazing Bone* by William Steig, copyright © 1976 by William Steig; From *Smile for Auntie* by Diane Paterson, © 1976 by Diane Paterson, used by permission of www.penguin.com, all rights reserved; From *Whistle for Willie* by Ezra Jack Keats, © 1964 by Ezra Jack Keats, renewed © 1992 by Martin Pope, Executor, used by permission of www.penguin.com, all rights reserved.

BACK JACKET (clockwise from top left): From *Morris's Disappearing Bag* by Rosemary Wells, © 1975 by Rosemary Wells, used by permission of www.penguin.com, all rights reserved; Reprinted with the permission of Simon & Schuster Books for Young Readers, an imprint of Simon & Schuster Children's Publishing Division from *Sylvester and the Magic Pebble* by William Steig, copyright © 1969 William Steig; Reprinted with the permission of Simon & Schuster Books for Young Readers, an imprint of Simon & Schuster Children's Publishing Division from *Strega Nona* by Tomie dePaola, copyright © 1975 Tomie dePaola; Reprinted by permission of Farrar, Straus and Giroux, LLC: From *Doctor De Soto* by William Steig, copyright © 1982 by William Steig.

Acknowledgments

This book was inspired by three decades of visiting the Weston Woods Studios and by the lifetime that Mort Schindel has devoted to building this unique, creative environment. I am profoundly grateful to Mort for his generous participation, his indefatigable hospitality, his astonishing memory, and his unflagging good spirits.

Through her lively wit and creative acumen, Cari Best helped me navigate the intricate history of the studio. Andrea Davis Pinkney, who edited this volume, will always have my abiding gratitude for her sustaining energy and patience which have steered this book to its safe harbor. My deep thanks to Richard Robinson for urging me to write a book about Mort and the studio that would do justice to both of their remarkable histories. My hope is to have done that.

To the highly talented production team at today's Weston Woods Studios, I am especially grateful. Linda Lee graciously opened its doors and shared its continuing vision. Paul Gagne offered valuable insights gained from his long and widely recognized role as a director and producer; he also provided the comprehensive filmography which completes this study. Melissa Reilly expanded my understanding of the responsibilities of an award-winning producer. And Christine Flaherty has cordially answered our myriad requests for images. At Sideshow Media, Dan Tucker and Elizabeth Zechella took mountains of images and words and, like alchemists, transformed them into the *ultima materia* that flow through these pages.

Gene Deitch, who has elevated the storyboard to an art form, has been a generous source of information. I am exceedingly grateful to him for his astonishing presence throughout this book. My thanks also goes to Michael Sporn who supplied images of his masterly animations. And to the distinguished artists and authors whose illustrations and words are the spirit of Weston Woods as well as an inspiration for this book, I also offer my lasting gratitude.

Gitta Selva assembled the indispensable file of background documentation on the studio's complex history, and Greg Griffin and Robert Benson contributed their fine photographs. There are others to whom I am very grateful for their kind words of encouragement and reflections on Weston Woods, among them Nicole Dreiske, Ken Jolly, Sally McCloskey, Susan Raab, Andrew Schindel, Sim Schindel, Anita Silvey, Peter Sís, and Linda Gramatky Smith. My sincere thanks to Ramona Caponegro and Kathy Carroll for "reframing" parts of this book, and to Lorna and Mel Rubin and Lola Haskins whose weekly inquiries buoyed my spirits.

I send my loving gratitude to Koren Stembridge, my daughter, who brought a discerning eye to the process of image selection; to her husband, Joel, who asked pertinent questions; and to their son, Jage, who gave the research a joyful bounce.

First, last, always, I must thank my wife, my dearest Eve. She helped me imagine this book into existence and read the manuscript in its earliest stages. In so many ways, this book is due to her steady stride, her love of the woods, her passion for things well written and filmed, and her sublime influence on my often peripatetic, easily bemused nature. —John Cech

A note from Mort Schindel:

Filmmaking is complicated. More than two hundred different skills or talents are employed in the production of a feature movie. Weston Woods films are simpler, but still very exacting because their intended audience is the most discerning of all: children.

At last count, there were over six hundred names in my address book—people who in one way or another played a part in the work that has been central to my life. Without the many who gave so generously of themselves, Weston Woods and its productions would not have flourished.

To family, friends, colleagues, authors, illustrators, publishers, librarians, teachers, and caregivers, and to all who have cared enough about our work to share it with children, I give my heartfelt thanks and abiding affection.

Visual
Identity

weston woods

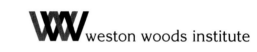

weston woods institute

Beginning in the 1950s, the studio was in search of a visual identity that encapsulated the world of children's books, the Weston Woods name, and the concept of woodsy surroundings. The graphic design firm Trinkaus, Aron, and Wayman conceived of a simple row of evergreen trees, establishing what has been deemed "the most recognizable identity in the field of education."

In a humorous take on the masks of classical drama, George Zariff of Trinkaus, Aron, and Wayman reversed the order of comedy and tragedy (leaving the symbols, and audiences, smiling) for the logo of the Children's Caravan media mobile. The logo, developed in the 1980s, represented the range of activities that took place in this unique vehicle and was judged Best of Show in Any Category by the Connecticut Advertising Association.

When the Weston Woods Institute, the non-profit arm of Weston Woods, was launched in the 1980s, the studio began to grasp the role it could play in the interrelated fields of children's literature, media, and education in a global cultural context. The overlapping Ws are used to visualize this broader perspective.

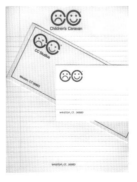

1953–2008
Weston Woods Chronology

Morton Schindel

1953

Morton Schindel, founder of Weston Woods, sets up shop in the wilderness of Weston, CT

1954

Contract for the first production, **Andy and the Lion** based on the Caldecott Honor Book by James Daugherty, is signed

1956

First public screening of Weston Woods films at the Museum of Modern Art in New York, NY

1956

TV Broadcast Premiere of Weston Woods productions on CBS's *Captain Kangaroo*

Ezra Jack Keats

1963

Weston Woods releases its first animated production, **The Snowy Day**, based on the Caldecott Medal Book by Ezra Jack Keats

1964

Weston Woods produces documentary for the American Library Association: *The Lively Art of Picture Books*

1964

Weston Woods produces the country's first live-action film based on a children's book: **The Doughnuts** (from *Homer Price*) by Robert McCloskey

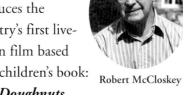

Robert McCloskey

1968

Weston Woods begins collaboration with principal animator Gene Deitch,  who directed **Drummer Hoff**, based on the Caldecott Medal Book by Barbara & Ed Emberley, in his studio in Czechoslovakia with wife, Zdenka Deitchová

1972

Weston Woods opens its first international office—Henley-on-Thames, UK

1975

Weston Woods opens Canadian office. Manager Betty Janes was frequently assisted by husband, Allen Janes

1977

Weston Woods opens Australian office

1985

First Weston Woods titles released to the home video market under the name *Children's Circle*©

1986

Doctor De Soto, based on the Newbery Honor Book by William Steig, nominated for an Academy Award

William Steig

1988

Morton Schindel and Weston Woods inducted into the Action for Children's Television Hall of Fame for "using TV and home video to lead children to the magic world of books"

1996

Paul Gagne, director of production, is awarded the Carnegie Medal for Excellence in Children's Video by the American Library Services for Children Division of the American Library Association for **Owen**, based on the Caldecott Honor Book by Kevin Henkes

Paul Gagne

1996

Weston Woods purchased by Scholastic Inc.

⋀⋁⋀ SCHOLASTIC

Richard Robinson (left), CEO of Scholastic Inc., and Morton Schindel (right), founder of Weston Woods

1999

Paul Gagne wins second *Carnegie* Medal for **Miss Nelson Has a Field Day**, based on the book by James Marshall

2000

Paul Gagne wins third Carnegie Medal for **Antarctic Antics**, based on the book by Judy Sierra, illustrated by Jose Aruego & Ariane Dewey

2001

Weston Woods moves into new headquarters in Norwalk, CT

2002

The Scholastic Video Collection™ produced by Weston Woods is released to the home market

"...wonderful storytelling with excellent integration of music, story and video."
—*Children's Video Report*

"...This beautiful animated version of three Sendak classics is one of the finest made-for-video children's titles ever produced."
—*Child Magazine*

2003

Paul Gagne wins his fourth Carnegie Medal along with Melissa Reilly, producer, for **So You Want to Be President?**, based on the Caldecott Medal Book by Judith St. George, illustrated by David Small

Paul Gagne and Melissa Reilly

2005

The Man Who Walked Between the Towers, based on the book by Mordicai Gerstein, receives the Carnegie Medal and is shortlisted for an Academy Award

2007

Weston Woods expands product line to include the handheld Playaway® series, and bilingual DVDs in Spanish and Mandarin

2008

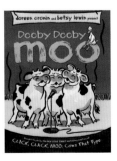

Weston Woods receives an Odyssey Honor Award for the adaptation of Doreen Cronin's **Dooby Dooby Moo**

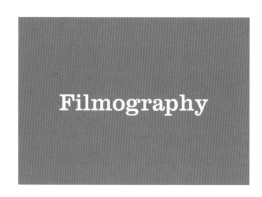

Filmography

1955

Make Way for Ducklings
AUTHOR: Robert McCloskey
ILLUSTRATOR: Robert McCloskey
DIRECTOR: Morton Schindel
NARRATOR: Owen Jordan
MUSIC: Arthur Kleiner
TYPE: Iconographic

Millions of Cats
AUTHOR: Wanda Gág
ILLUSTRATOR: Wanda Gág
DIRECTOR: Morton Schindel
NARRATOR: Owen Jordan
MUSIC: Arthur Kleiner
TYPE: Iconographic

Stone Soup
AUTHOR: Marcia Brown
ILLUSTRATOR: Marcia Brown
DIRECTOR: Morton Schindel
NARRATOR: Marcia Brown
MUSIC: Arthur Kleiner
TYPE: Iconographic
AWARDS: Award of Merit, Columbus International Film Festival

The Little Red Lighthouse and the Great Gray Bridge
AUTHOR: Hildegarde Swift
ILLUSTRATOR: Lynd Ward
DIRECTOR: Morton Schindel
NARRATOR: Owen Jordan
MUSIC: Arthur Kleiner
TYPE: Iconographic

The Red Carpet
AUTHOR: Rex Parkin
ILLUSTRATOR: Rex Parkin
DIRECTOR: Morton Schindel
NARRATOR: Owen Jordan
MUSIC: Arthur Kleiner
TYPE: Iconographic

The Story About Ping
AUTHOR: Marjorie Flack
ILLUSTRATOR: Kurt Wiese
DIRECTOR: Morton Schindel
NARRATOR: Beman Lord
MUSIC: Arthur Kleiner
TYPE: Iconographic
AWARDS: Award of Merit, Columbus International Film Festival

1956

Georgie
AUTHOR: Robert Bright
ILLUSTRATOR: Robert Bright
DIRECTOR: Morton Schindel
NARRATOR: Owen Jordan
MUSIC: Arthur Kleiner
TYPE: Iconographic
AWARDS: 1st Prize, American Film Festival

Hercules
AUTHOR: Hardie Gramatky
ILLUSTRATOR: Hardie Gramatky
DIRECTOR: Morton Schindel
NARRATOR: Owen Jordan
MUSIC: Arthur Kleiner
TYPE: Iconographic

Jenny's Birthday Book
AUTHOR: Esther Averill
ILLUSTRATOR: Esther Averill
DIRECTOR: Morton Schindel
NARRATOR: Owen Jordan
TYPE: Iconographic

Lentil
AUTHOR: Robert McCloskey
ILLUSTRATOR: Robert McCloskey
DIRECTOR: Morton Schindel

NARRATOR: Owen Jordan
MUSIC: Folk tunes played by Robert McCloskey & Arthur Kleiner
TYPE: Iconographic
AWARDS: The Chris Award, Columbus International Film Festival

Mike Mulligan and His Steam Shovel
AUTHOR: Virginia Lee Burton
ILLUSTRATOR: Virginia Lee Burton
DIRECTOR: Morton Schindel
NARRATOR: Owen Jordan
MUSIC: Arthur Kleiner
TYPE: Iconographic
AWARDS: Short Film Award, Kids First!

The Circus Baby
AUTHOR: Maud & Miska Petersham
ILLUSTRATOR: Maud & Miska Petersham
DIRECTOR: Morton Schindel
NARRATOR: Owen Jordan
MUSIC: Arthur Kleiner
TYPE: Iconographic

1957

The Camel Who Took a Walk
AUTHOR: Jack Tworkov
ILLUSTRATOR: Roger Duvoisin
DIRECTOR: Morton Schindel
NARRATOR: Owen Jordan
MUSIC: Arthur Kleiner
TYPE: Iconographic
AWARDS: 1st Prize, American Film Festival

1958

Curious George Rides a Bike
AUTHOR: H. A. Rey
ILLUSTRATOR: H. A. Rey
DIRECTOR: Morton Schindel
NARRATOR: Owen Jordan
MUSIC: Arthur Kleiner
TYPE: Iconographic
AWARDS: Bronze Plaque, Columbus International Film Festival; 2nd Place, National Educational Film & Video Festival

The Five Chinese Brothers
AUTHOR: Claire Huchet Bishop
ILLUSTRATOR: Kurt Wiese
DIRECTOR: Morton Schindel
NARRATOR: Owen Jordan
MUSIC: Arthur Kleiner
TYPE: Iconographic

1960

Caps for Sale
AUTHOR: Esphyr Slobodkina
ILLUSTRATOR: Esphyr Slobodkina
DIRECTOR: Morton Schindel
NARRATOR: Owen Jordan
MUSIC: Arthur Kleiner
TYPE: Iconographic

Pancho
AUTHOR: Berta & Elmer Hader
ILLUSTRATOR: Berta & Elmer Hader
NARRATOR: Owen Jordan
TYPE: Iconographic

1961

Frog Went A-Courtin'
AUTHOR: John Langstaff
ILLUSTRATOR: Feodor Rojankovsky
DIRECTOR: Morton Schindel
NARRATOR: John Langstaff (performed)
MUSIC: Arthur Kleiner (arranged)
TYPE: Iconographic

Time of Wonder
AUTHOR: Robert McCloskey
ILLUSTRATOR: Robert McCloskey
DIRECTOR: Morton Schindel
NARRATOR: Ted Hoskins
MUSIC: Arthur Kleiner
TYPE: Iconographic

1962

This Is New York
AUTHOR: Miroslav Sasek
ILLUSTRATOR: Miroslav Sasek
DIRECTOR: Morton Schindel
NARRATOR: Benjamin Bergery
MUSIC: Arthur Kleiner
TYPE: Iconographic

1963

The Doughnuts
(from Homer Price)
AUTHOR: Robert McCloskey
ILLUSTRATOR: Robert McCloskey
DIRECTOR: Beth Sanford in association with Edward English
NARRATOR: Owen Jordan
MUSIC: Loren Glickman
TYPE: Live-action

The Sorcerer's Apprentice
AUTHOR: Lisl Weil
ILLUSTRATOR: Lisl Weil
DIRECTOR: Edward English
MUSIC: Paul Dukas (composed),
Columbia Special Products (recorded),
Jay Fredericks (performed)
TYPE: Live-action

1964

Robert McCloskey
DIRECTOR: Morton Schindel
TYPE: Live-action

The Lively Art of Picture Books
DIRECTOR: Joanna Foster Dougherty
TYPE: Live-action

The Snowy Day
AUTHOR: Ezra Jack Keats
ILLUSTRATOR: Ezra Jack Keats
DIRECTOR: Mal Wittman
NARRATOR: Jane Harvey
MUSIC: Barry Galbraith (composed/
performed)
TYPE: Animated
AWARDS: Best Children's Film, Venice
Film Festival

The Tale of Custard the Dragon
AUTHOR: Ogden Nash
ILLUSTRATOR: Linell Nash Smith
DIRECTOR: Peter Rubin (adapted/directed)
NARRATOR: Marilyn Reynolds
MUSIC: Jay Frederick
TYPE: Live-action

1965

Maurice Sendak
DIRECTOR: Joanna Foster
TYPE: Live-action

Whistle for Willie
AUTHOR: Ezra Jack Keats
ILLUSTRATOR: Ezra Jack Keats
DIRECTOR: Mal Wittman
NARRATOR: Jane Harvey
MUSIC: Barry Galbraith
TYPE: Animated

1967

*Alexander and the Car with a
Missing Headlight*
AUTHOR: Peter Fleischmann,
Morton Schindel

ILLUSTRATOR: French & German
schoolchildren
DIRECTOR: Peter Fleischmann,
Cynthia Freitag (English version)
NARRATOR: Children from Weston, CT
TYPE: Animated
AWARDS: Award of St. Mark, Venice
Film Festival

Blueberries for Sal
AUTHOR: Robert McCloskey
ILLUSTRATOR: Robert McCloskey
DIRECTOR: Cynthia Freitag
NARRATOR: Owen Jordan
MUSIC: Daniel Sable
TYPE: Iconographic

1968

In a Spring Garden
AUTHOR: Richard Lewis
DIRECTOR: Cynthia Freitag
TYPE: Iconographic

Over in the Meadow
AUTHOR: John Langstaff
ILLUSTRATOR: Feodor Rojankovsky
DIRECTOR: Cynthia Freitag
NARRATOR: John Langstaff (perfomed)
MUSIC: John Langstaff (arranged)
TYPE: Iconographic
AWARDS: Notable Video, ALA

1969

Drummer Hoff
AUTHOR: Barbara Emberley
ILLUSTRATOR: Ed Emberley
DIRECTOR: Gene Deitch (adapted/directed)
ANIMATOR: Krátký Film Praha
NARRATOR: John Cunningham
MUSIC: František Belfín
TYPE: Animated
AWARDS: Golden Plaque, Teheran
International Festival of Films for
Children

Harold and the Purple Crayon
AUTHOR: Crockett Johnson
ILLUSTRATOR: Crockett Johnson
DIRECTOR: David Piel
NARRATOR: Norman Rose
MUSIC: Jimmy Carroll
TYPE: Animated
AWARDS: 1st Place, Audience Award,
Film Fest New Haven

The Happy Owls
AUTHOR: Oral tradition
ILLUSTRATOR: Celestino Piatti
DIRECTOR: Gene Deitch (adapted/directed)
ANIMATOR: Krátký Film Praha
NARRATOR: Pauline Brailsford
MUSIC: Peter Eben
TYPE: Animated
AWARDS: Honors Certificate, American
Film Festival; Golden Eagle, CINE

Wheel on the Chimney
AUTHOR: Margaret Wise Brown
ILLUSTRATOR: Tibor Gergely
DIRECTOR: Cynthia Freitag
NARRATOR: John Cunningham
MUSIC: Ruth Anderson
TYPE: Iconographic

1970

A Letter to Amy
AUTHOR: Ezra Jack Keats
ILLUSTRATOR: Ezra Jack Keats
DIRECTOR: Cynthia Freitag
NARRATOR: Loretta Long
MUSIC: Robert M. Freedman
TYPE: Iconographic

Ezra Jack Keats
DIRECTOR: Cynthia Freitag
TYPE: Live-action

Rosie's Walk
AUTHOR: Pat Hutchins
ILLUSTRATOR: Pat Hutchins
DIRECTOR: Gene Deitch
ANIMATOR: Krátký Film Praha
NARRATOR: Gene Deitch
MUSIC: American Folk Tune: "Turkey in
the Straw" played by The Greenhorns
(Czechoslovakia)
TYPE: Animated
AWARDS: Golden Eagle, CINE;
Blue Ribbon, American Film Festival;
The Chris Award, Columbus
International Film Festival

*The Cow Who Fell
in the Canal*
AUTHOR: Phyllis Krasilovsky
ILLUSTRATOR: Peter Spier
DIRECTOR: Cynthia Frietag
NARRATOR: Owen Jordan
MUSIC: Howard Rovics
TYPE: Iconographic

*The Fisherman and
His Wife*
DIRECTOR: Gisela Frisen, Per Ekholm
(designed/directed)
MUSIC: Leo Rosenbluth
TYPE: Animated

1971

A Picture for Harold's Room
AUTHOR: Crockett Johnson
ILLUSTRATOR: Crockett Johnson
DIRECTOR: Gene Deitch
ANIMATOR: Krátký Film Praha
NARRATOR: Charles Cioffi
MUSIC: Leopold Kozeluh
(String Quartet in B-minor),
Prague Janáček Quartet (performed)
TYPE: Animated

Crow Boy
AUTHOR: Taro Yashima
ILLUSTRATOR: Taro Yashima
DIRECTOR: Cynthia Freitag
NARRATOR: Ned Hoopes
MUSIC: František Belfín
TYPE: Iconographic

*Leopold the See-Through
Crumbpicker*
AUTHOR: James Flora
ILLUSTRATOR: James Flora
DIRECTOR: Gene Deitch (adapted/
designed/directed)
ANIMATOR: Krátký Film Praha
NARRATOR: Larry Keith
MUSIC: Peter Eben
TYPE: Animated

Norman the Doorman
AUTHOR: Don Freeman
ILLUSTRATOR: Don Freeman
DIRECTOR: Cynthia Freitag
NARRATOR: Owen Jordan
MUSIC: Josef Ceremuga
TYPE: Iconographic

Peter's Chair
AUTHOR: Ezra Jack Keats
ILLUSTRATOR: Ezra Jack Keats
DIRECTOR: Cynthia Freitag
NARRATOR: Loretta Long
MUSIC: Howard Rovics
TYPE: Iconographic

Petunia
AUTHOR: Roger Duvoisin
ILLUSTRATOR: Roger Duvoisin
DIRECTOR: Anthony Larson
NARRATOR: Kevin Watson
MUSIC: Kevin Watson
TYPE: Animated

The Little Drummer Boy
AUTHOR: Katherine Davis, Henry Oronati,
Harry Simeone
ILLUSTRATOR: Ezra Jack Keats
DIRECTOR: Cynthia Freitag
NARRATOR: Katherine Davis (words/music),
Henry Oronati, Harry Simeone
MUSIC: Theodore Marier (directed),
Robert Freedman (arranged/conducted)
TYPE: Iconographic
AWARDS: Notable Video, ALA

The Owl and the Pussy-Cat
AUTHOR: Edward Lear
ILLUSTRATOR: Barbara Cooney
DIRECTOR: Alexander Cochran
NARRATOR: John Cunningham
MUSIC: Mary Lynn Twombly
TYPE: Iconographic

The Selfish Giant
AUTHOR: Oscar Wilde
ILLUSTRATOR: Gertraud & Walter Reiner
DIRECTOR: Walter Reiner
NARRATOR: Charles Cioffi
MUSIC: Karl von Feilitzsch
TYPE: Animated

Wynken, Blynken and Nod
AUTHOR: Eugene Field
ILLUSTRATOR: Barbara Cooney
DIRECTOR: Morton Schindel
NARRATOR: John Cunningham
MUSIC: Mary Lynn Twombly
TYPE: Iconographic

1972

James Daugherty
DIRECTOR: Cynthia Freitag
TYPE: Live-action

Libraries Are Kids' Stuff
DIRECTOR: Alex Hankocy
TYPE: Live-action

One Monday Morning
AUTHOR: Uri Shulevitz
ILLUSTRATOR: Uri Shulevitz
DIRECTOR: Tom Spain, Uri Shulevitz
NARRATOR: Bruce Sparks
MUSIC: Medieval music, František Belfín
(conducted)
TYPE: Iconographic

The Three Robbers
AUTHOR: Tomi Ungerer
ILLUSTRATOR: Tomi Ungerer
DIRECTOR: Gene Deitch (adapted/
voiced/directed)
ANIMATOR: Krátký Film Praha
NARRATOR: Gene Deitch
MUSIC: Gene Deitch (voiced)
TYPE: Animated
AWARDS: Blue Ribbon, American Film
Festival; Emily Award, American Film
Festival; Bronze Award, International
Film & TV Festival of NY

*The Twelve Days
of Christmas*
AUTHOR: Oral tradition
ILLUSTRATOR: Robert Broomfield
DIRECTOR: Q3 Limited
NARRATOR: Jennifer Brown (aka Buffy
Allen) (performed)
MUSIC: Douglas Wood (arranged/
conducted)
TYPE: Iconographic

1973

A Story, A Story
AUTHOR: Gail E. Haley
ILLUSTRATOR: Gail E. Haley
DIRECTOR: Gene Deitch (adapted/directed)
ANIMATOR: Krátký Film Praha
NARRATOR: John Joseph Akar
MUSIC: Václav Kubica
TYPE: Animated

Changes, Changes
AUTHOR: Pat Hutchins
ILLUSTRATOR: Pat Hutchins
DIRECTOR: Gene Deitch (adapted/directed)
ANIMATOR: Krátký Film Praha
MUSIC: František Belfín & His
Wooden Orchestra
TYPE: Animated

Mr. Shepard and Mr. Milne
DIRECTOR: Andrew Holmes
NARRATOR: Christopher Robin
MUSIC: John Scott
TYPE: Live-action

AWARDS: Gold Medal, Atlantic
International Film Festival

Patrick
AUTHOR: Quentin Blake
ILLUSTRATOR: Quentin Blake
DIRECTOR: Gene Deitch (adapted/directed)
ANIMATOR: Krátký Film Praha
MUSIC: Violin Improvisation on a theme
from Antonín Dvořák played by
Bohumil Purger
TYPE: Animated
AWARDS: Gold Medal, Atlanta
International Film Festival; Bronze
Plaque, Columbus International
Film Festival

The Foolish Frog
AUTHOR: Pete Seeger, Charles Seeger
ILLUSTRATOR: Miloslav Jagr
DIRECTOR: Gene Deitch (adapted/directed)
ANIMATOR: Krátký Film Praha
NARRATOR: Pete Seeger (performed)
MUSIC: Charles Seeger, Pete Seeger
TYPE: Animated
AWARDS: Red Ribbon, American Film
Festival; The Chris Award, Columbus
International Film Festival

Zlateh the Goat
AUTHOR: Isaac Bashevis Singer
ILLUSTRATOR: Maurice Sendak
DIRECTOR: Gene Deitch (adapted/directed)
MUSIC: Leoš Janáček (String Quartets
Nos. 1 & 2)
TYPE: Live-action
AWARDS: Gold Medal, Atlanta
International Film Festival; Silver
Award, International Film & TV
Festival of NY; Silver Plaque, Chicago
International Film Festival; Learning
Award as Best Film of the Year
(1974); Bronze Plaque, Columbus
International Film Festival

1974

Attic of the Wind
AUTHOR: Doris Herold Lund
ILLUSTRATOR: Ati Forberg
DIRECTOR: Alexander Cochran
NARRATOR: John Cunningham
MUSIC: Mary Lynn Twombly
TYPE: Iconographic
AWARDS: 2nd Place, Harrisburg
Film Festival

Goggles!
AUTHOR: Ezra Jack Keats
ILLUSTRATOR: Ezra Jack Keats
DIRECTOR: Isa Wickenhagen
NARRATOR: Geoffrey Holder
MUSIC: Harry D. Buch
TYPE: Iconographic

Harold's Fairy Tale
AUTHOR: Crockett Johnson
ILLUSTRATOR: Crockett Johnson
DIRECTOR: Gene Deitch
ANIMATOR: Krátký Film Praha
NARRATOR: John Cunningham
MUSIC: Karel Velebny
TYPE: Animated

The Swineherd
AUTHOR: Hans Christian Andersen
DIRECTOR: Gene Deitch (adapted/directed)
ANIMATOR: Krátký Film Praha
NARRATOR: Pauline Brailsford
MUSIC: Jaroslav Celba, Bent Fabricius-
Bjerre, Prague Symposium Musicum
(performed)
TYPE: Animated
AWARDS: Notable Film, ALA; Gold
Plaque, Chicago International Film
Festival; Silver Mermaid, Fairytale Film
Festival (Denmark)

Tikki Tikki Tembo
AUTHOR: Arlene Mosel
ILLUSTRATOR: Blair Lent
DIRECTOR: Gary Templeton (adapted/
directed)
NARRATOR: Peter Thomas
MUSIC: Howard Rovics
TYPE: Iconographic

1975

The Beast of Monsieur Racine
AUTHOR: Tomi Ungerer
ILLUSTRATOR: Tomi Ungerer
DIRECTOR: Gene Deitch (designed/
directed)
ANIMATOR: Irena Jandová, Milan Klikar,
Vera Kudrnova, Bohumil Šejda
NARRATOR: Charles Duval
MUSIC: František Belfín & His
Ensemble Bestiale
TYPE: Animated
AWARDS: 1st Prize, Children's Category,
International Animation Film Festival;
Red Ribbon, American Film Festival;

Bronze Plaque, Columbus International Film Festival; Bronze Plaque, Chicago International Film Festival

The Star-Spangled Banner
AUTHOR: Francis Scott Key
ILLUSTRATOR: Peter Spier
DIRECTOR: Isa Wickenhagen
MUSIC: Glee Club of the U.S. Military Academy at West Point (performed)
TYPE: Iconographic

The Stonecutter
AUTHOR: Gerald McDermott
ILLUSTRATOR: Gerald McDermott
DIRECTOR: Gerald McDermott (designed/directed)
ANIMATOR: Gerald McDermott
NARRATOR: George Ross
MUSIC: Reiko Kamata
TYPE: Animated

1976

American Songfest
NARRATOR: Robert McCloskey, Pete Seeger, Stephen Kellogg, Robert Quackenbush
TYPE: Live-action

Hush Little Baby
AUTHOR: Oral tradition
ILLUSTRATOR: Aliki Brandenberg
DIRECTOR: Alexander Cochran
NARRATOR: Jennifer Brown (aka Buffy Allen) (performed)
MUSIC: Arne Markussen (arranged)
TYPE: Iconographic

Little Tim and the Brave Sea Captain
AUTHOR: Edward Ardizzone
ILLUSTRATOR: Edward Ardizzone
DIRECTOR: Dan Smith
NARRATOR: Michael Brew
MUSIC: Harry D. Buch (adapted)
TYPE: Iconographic
AWARDS: Notable Video, ALA

The Case of the Cosmic Comic
(from *Homer Price*)
AUTHOR: Robert McCloskey
ILLUSTRATOR: Robert McCloskey
DIRECTOR: Gary Templeton (adapted/directed)
MUSIC: Harry Manfredini
TYPE: Live-action

The Cat and the Collector
AUTHOR: Linda Glovach
ILLUSTRATOR: Linda Glovach
DIRECTOR: Morton Schindel
NARRATOR: Emery Battis
MUSIC: Bruce Chase
TYPE: Iconographic

The Erie Canal
AUTHOR: Oral tradition
ILLUSTRATOR: Peter Spier
DIRECTOR: John B. Schindel
NARRATOR: Devin Terreson (performed)
MUSIC: Thomas S. Allen, H. D. Buch (arranged)
TYPE: Iconographic

The Ugly Duckling
AUTHOR: Hans Christian Andersen
DIRECTOR: Gene Deitch (adapted/directed)
ANIMATOR: Krátký Film Praha
NARRATOR: Pauline Brailsford, Carl Weismann (animated voice)
MUSIC: Carl Maria von Weber (Quintet Op. 34), Bent Fabricus Bjerre (title theme)
TYPE: Animated

Yankee Doodle
AUTHOR: Edward Bangs
ILLUSTRATOR: Steven Kellogg
DIRECTOR: Isa Wickenhagen
NARRATOR: The children of Sacred Heart Academy, Greenwich, CT
MUSIC: R. Tisdale (arranged), Colonial Williamsburg Fife & Drum Corps (performed)
TYPE: Iconographic

1977

Apt. 3
AUTHOR: Ezra Jack Keats
ILLUSTRATOR: Ezra Jack Keats
DIRECTOR: Alexander Cochran
NARRATOR: Charles Turner
MUSIC: Sugar Blue
TYPE: Iconographic
AWARDS: Gold Venus Medallion, Virgin Islands Film Festival

Charlie Needs a Cloak
AUTHOR: Tomie dePaola
ILLUSTRATOR: Tomie dePaola
DIRECTOR: Gene Deitch (adapted/designed/directed)

ANIMATOR: Krátký Film Praha
NARRATOR: Gene Deitch
MUSIC: František Belfín
TYPE: Animated
AWARDS: Notable Video, ALA; Silver Medal, International Film & TV Festival of NY

Gene Deitch: The Picture Book Animated
DIRECTOR: Gene Deitch
TYPE: Live-action

The Giant Devil-Dingo
AUTHOR: Dick Roughsey
ILLUSTRATOR: Dick Roughsey
DIRECTOR: Alexander Cochran
NARRATOR: Brian Syron
MUSIC: Aborigines Woomera
TYPE: Iconographic

1978

Edward Ardizzone
DIRECTOR: John Phillips
TYPE: Live-action

Strega Nona
AUTHOR: Tomie dePaola
ILLUSTRATOR: Tomie dePaola
DIRECTOR: Gene Deitch (adapted/directed)
ANIMATOR: Krátký Film Praha
NARRATOR: Peter Hawkins
MUSIC: František Belfín
TYPE: Animated
AWARDS: Golden Eagle, CINE; Blue Ribbon, American Film Festival; Silver Plaque, Chicago International Film Festival; Silver Award, 21st International Film & TV Festival of NY

1979

Smile for Auntie
AUTHOR: Diane Paterson
ILLUSTRATOR: Diane Paterson
DIRECTOR: Gene Deitch
ANIMATOR: Krátký Film Praha
NARRATOR: Faith Stanfield
TYPE: Animated
AWARDS: Golden Eagle, CINE; Gold Award, International Film & TV Festival of NY; Outstanding Film of the Year, London Film Festival; Best Children's Film, Zagreb International Animation Film Festival

The Rainbow Serpent
AUTHOR: Dick Roughsey
ILLUSTRATOR: Dick Roughsey
DIRECTOR: Alexander Cochran
NARRATOR: David Gulpilil
MUSIC: Andrew Vial
TYPE: Iconographic

1980

Teeny-Tiny and the Witch-Woman
AUTHOR: Barbara K. Walker
ILLUSTRATOR: Michael Foreman
DIRECTOR: Gene Deitch
ANIMATOR: Krátký Film Praha
NARRATOR: Gene Deitch
MUSIC: Jiri Kolafa (music/sound montage)
TYPE: Animated
AWARDS: Notable Video, ALA; Golden Eagle, CINE; Gold Award, International Film & TV Festival of NY

The Island of the Skog
AUTHOR: Steven Kellogg
ILLUSTRATOR: Steven Kellogg
DIRECTOR: John B. Schindel (adapted in consultation with Steven Kellogg)
NARRATOR: Dan Diggles
MUSIC: Bruce Chase
TYPE: Iconographic

The Trip
AUTHOR: Ezra Jack Keats
ILLUSTRATOR: Ezra Jack Keats
DIRECTOR: Alexander Cochran
ANIMATOR: Alexander Cochran
NARRATOR: Charles Turner
MUSIC: Harry D. Buch
TYPE: Animated (limited animation)
AWARDS: Bronze Remi, WorldFest-Houston International Film Festival

1981

Moon Man
AUTHOR: Tomi Ungerer
ILLUSTRATOR: Tomi Ungerer
DIRECTOR: Gene Deitch (adapted/designed/directed)
ANIMATOR: Krátký Film Praha
NARRATOR: Peter Hawkins
MUSIC: Karel Velebny & the Velebny Orchestra (performed)
TYPE: Animated

AWARDS: Silver Award, WorldFest-Houston International Film Festival

Morton Schindel: From Page to Screen
DIRECTOR: Alexander Cochran, John Schindel
MUSIC: Ernest Troost
TYPE: Live-action
AWARDS: Golden Eagle, CINE; Gold Award, WorldFest-Houston International Film Festival

1982

Fourteen Rats and a Rat-Catcher
AUTHOR: James Cressey
ILLUSTRATOR: Tamasin Cole
DIRECTOR: Francesco Tenze & ATA Studios
NARRATOR: Roderick Cook
MUSIC: Roberto Marzi of ATA Studios
TYPE: Animated
AWARDS: Dutch Silver Pencil Award

John Brown, Rose and the Midnight Cat
AUTHOR: Jenny Wagner
ILLUSTRATOR: Ron Brooks
DIRECTOR: Ernest Troost
NARRATOR: Pauline Brailsford
MUSIC: Ernest Troost
TYPE: Iconographic

Morris's Disappearing Bag
AUTHOR: Rosemary Wells
ILLUSTRATOR: Rosemary Wells
DIRECTOR: Michael Sporn
ANIMATOR: Michael Sporn
NARRATOR: Nicole Freshette
MUSIC: Ernest Troost
TYPE: Animated
AWARDS: Notable Film, ALA; Grand Prize, ASIFA (The International Animated Film Society) Film Festival; Grand Prize, Birmingham International Educational Film Festival; Blue Ribbon, American Film Festival; The Learning AV Award

Suho and the White Horse
AUTHOR: Yuzo Otsuka
ILLUSTRATOR: Suekichi Akaba
DIRECTOR: John B. Schindel (adapted/directed)
NARRATOR: Charles Cioffi
MUSIC: Václav Kubica
TYPE: Iconographic

AWARDS: Ruby Slipper Award, International Children's Film Festival

The Clown of God
AUTHOR: Tomie dePaola
ILLUSTRATOR: Tomie dePaola
DIRECTOR: Gary McGivney (adapted/directed)
ANIMATOR: Ball & Chain Studios
NARRATOR: Charles Cioffi
MUSIC: Ernest Troost
TYPE: Animated
AWARDS: Notable Video, ALA; Golden Eagle, CINE

The Hat
AUTHOR: Tomi Ungerer
ILLUSTRATOR: Tomi Ungerer
DIRECTOR: Gene Deitch (adapted/designed/directed)
ANIMATOR: Krátký Film Praha
NARRATOR: Peter Hawkins
MUSIC: Jaroslav Celba
TYPE: Animated

The Quinkins
AUTHOR: Percy Trezise
ILLUSTRATOR: Dick Roughsey
DIRECTOR: Paul R. Gagne (adapted/directed)
NARRATOR: Brian Syron
MUSIC: David Gulpilil
TYPE: Iconographic

The Tomten
AUTHOR: Victor Rydberg; Astrid Lindgren (adapted)
ILLUSTRATOR: Harald Wiberg
DIRECTOR: Paul R. Gagne
NARRATOR: Owen Jordan
MUSIC: Barry Galbraith
TYPE: Iconographic

Tomi Ungerer: Storyteller
DIRECTOR: Gene Deitch
MUSIC: František Belfín & His Ensemble Bestiale
TYPE: Live-action
AWARDS: Golden Eagle, CINE; Silver Award, International Film & TV Festival of NY

1983

A Dark, Dark Tale
AUTHOR: Ruth Brown
ILLUSTRATOR: Ruth Brown

DIRECTOR: Paul R. Gagne (adapted/directed)
NARRATOR: Ian Thomson
MUSIC: Ernest Troost
TYPE: Iconographic

Burt Dow: Deep-Water Man
AUTHOR: Robert McCloskey
ILLUSTRATOR: Robert McCloskey
DIRECTOR: Václav Bedrich (adapted/directed)
ANIMATOR: Olga Siskova, Vera Michlova, Oldrich Haberle, Jaroslav Zlesakova
NARRATOR: Tim Sample
MUSIC: Petr Skoumal
TYPE: Animated
AWARDS: Bronze Plaque, Columbus International Film Festival

1984

Corduroy
AUTHOR: Don Freeman
ILLUSTRATOR: Don Freeman
DIRECTOR: Gary Templeton (written/directed)
MUSIC: Harry Manfredini
TYPE: Live-action
AWARDS: Notable Video, ALA; Blue Ribbon, American Film Festival; Electra Certificate of Award; Best Early Childhood Film, Birmingham International Educational Film Festival; Golden Eagle, CINE; Bronze Medal, NY International Film & Video Festival; Bronze Plaque, Columbus International Film Festival

Doctor De Soto
AUTHOR: William Steig
ILLUSTRATOR: William Steig
DIRECTOR: Michael Sporn
ANIMATOR: Michael Sporn
NARRATOR: Ian Thomson
MUSIC: Ernest Troost
TYPE: Animated
AWARDS: Academy Award Nominee, Best Animated Short Film; Best Film for Children, Canadian International Animation Festival; Ruby Slipper Award, International Children's Film Festival; Bronze Plaque, Columbus International Film Festival; Golden Eagle, CINE

King of the Cats
AUTHOR: Paul Galdone
ILLUSTRATOR: Paul Galdone
DIRECTOR: Paul R. Gagne (adapted/directed)
NARRATOR: Tim Sample
MUSIC: Ernest Troost
TYPE: Iconographic

Why Mosquitoes Buzz in People's Ears
AUTHOR: Verna Aardema
ILLUSTRATOR: Leo & Diane Dillon
DIRECTOR: Gene Deitch (adapted/directed)
ANIMATOR: Krátký Film Praha
NARRATOR: Gene Deitch
MUSIC: Václav Kubica
TYPE: Animated
AWARDS: Silver Award, NY International Film Festival; Bronze Plaque, Columbus International Film Festival

1985

Happy Birthday, Moon
AUTHOR: Frank Asch
ILLUSTRATOR: Frank Asch
DIRECTOR: Daniel Ivanick
ANIMATOR: Daniel Ivanick
NARRATOR: Melissa Leebaert
MUSIC: Ernest Troost
TYPE: Animated
AWARDS: Notable Video, ALA; Golden Eagle, CINE; Finalist, American Film & Video Festival; Finalist, International Film & TV Festival of NY

The Amazing Bone
AUTHOR: William Steig
ILLUSTRATOR: William Steig
DIRECTOR: Michael Sporn
ANIMATOR: Gary Becker & F-Stop Studios
NARRATOR: John Lithgow
MUSIC: Jeremy Steig, Eddie Gomez
TYPE: Animated
AWARDS: Golden Eagle, CINE; Bronze Plaque, Columbus International Film Festival; Notable Video, ALA; Silver Apple Award, National Educational Film & Video Festival; 2nd Prize, Children's Category, Los Angeles International Film Festival

The Bear and the Fly
AUTHOR: Paula Winters
ILLUSTRATOR: Paula Winters
DIRECTOR: Daniel Ivanick

ANIMATOR: Daniel Ivanick
MUSIC: Ernest Troost
TYPE: Animated
AWARDS: Golden Eagle, CINE; Honorable Mention, Columbus International Film Festival

The Napping House
AUTHOR: Audrey Wood
ILLUSTRATOR: Don Wood
DIRECTOR: Paul R. Gagne (adapted/directed)
NARRATOR: Melissa Leebaert
MUSIC: Ernest Troost
TYPE: Iconographic

The Wizard
AUTHOR: Jack Kent
ILLUSTRATOR: Jack Kent
DIRECTOR: Euan Frizzel
NARRATOR: Ian Thomson
MUSIC: Ernest Troost
TYPE: Animated
AWARDS: Bronze Plaque, Columbus International Film Festival

1986

Andy and the Lion
AUTHOR: James Daugherty
ILLUSTRATOR: James Daugherty
DIRECTOR: Jonathan Van Horn
NARRATOR: Bruce Johnson
MUSIC: Ernest Troost
TYPE: Iconographic
AWARDS: Award of Merit, Columbus International Film Festival

Sendak
DIRECTOR: Nicholas Kuskin
TYPE: Live-action
AWARDS: Golden Eagle, CINE

The Most Wonderful Egg in the World
AUTHOR: Helme Heine
ILLUSTRATOR: Helme Heine
DIRECTOR: Christopher Palesty
ANIMATOR: Christopher Palesty
NARRATOR: Ian Thomson
MUSIC: Ernest Troost
TYPE: Animated
AWARDS: The Chris Award, Columbus International Film Festival; Golden Eagle, CINE

The Mysterious Tadpole
AUTHOR: Steven Kellogg

ILLUSTRATOR: Steven Kellogg
DIRECTOR: Michael Sporn
ANIMATOR: Michael Sporn
NARRATOR: Neil Innes
MUSIC: Ernest Troost
TYPE: Animated
AWARDS: Award Certificate for Early Childhood Films, Birmingham International Educational Film Festival; Youth & Family Prize, Annecy Animation Festival; Golden Eagle, CINE; Early Childhood Winner, Birmingham International Educational Film Festival; Finalist, The American Film & Video Festival

The Silver Cow
AUTHOR: Susan Cooper
ILLUSTRATOR: Warwick Hutton
DIRECTOR: Paul R. Gagne
NARRATOR: Neil Innis
MUSIC: Ernest Troost
TYPE: Iconographic

1987

How a Picture Book Is Made
DIRECTOR: Catherine Urbain
NARRATOR: Steven Kellogg
TYPE: Iconographic

In the Night Kitchen
AUTHOR: Maurice Sendak
ILLUSTRATOR: Maurice Sendak
DIRECTOR: Gene Deitch (adapted/directed)
ANIMATOR: Krátký Film Praha
NARRATOR: Peter Schickele (aka P. D. Q. Bach)
MUSIC: Angelo Michajlov & his Kitchen Sink-o-pators (performed/composed)
TYPE: Animated
AWARDS: Golden Eagle, CINE; Bronze Medal, International Film Festival of NY; Editors' Choice Film, Booklist; Blue Ribbon, American Film & Video Festival

Jean Fritz: Six Revolutionary War Figures
DIRECTOR: Melissa Reilly, Catherine Urbain
TYPE: Iconographic

Jonah and the Great Fish
AUTHOR: Warwick Hutton
ILLUSTRATOR: Warwick Hutton
DIRECTOR: Catherine Urbain

(photographed/edited/directed)
NARRATOR: Neil Innes
MUSIC: Ernest Troost
TYPE: Iconographic

1988

Joey Runs Away
AUTHOR: Jack Kent
ILLUSTRATOR: Jack Kent
DIRECTOR: Daniel Ivanick
ANIMATOR: Daniel Ivanick
NARRATOR: Trish Jones
MUSIC: Susan Winthrop, Nanci Hersh and Audio Antics
TYPE: Animated
AWARDS: Bronze Medal, Best Original Music, International Film & TV Festival of NY; Golden Eagle, CINE

Max's Christmas
AUTHOR: Rosemary Wells
ILLUSTRATOR: Rosemary Wells
DIRECTOR: Michael Sporn
ANIMATOR: Michael Sporn
NARRATOR: Jenny Agutter, Rex Robbins
MUSIC: Barb Luby
TYPE: Animated
AWARDS: Notable Film, ALA; Finalist, Birmingham International Educational Film Festival; Golden Eagle, CINE

Randolph Caldecott: The Man Behind the Medal
DIRECTOR: David R. Paight
NARRATOR: John Tillinger
TYPE: Iconographic

The Caterpillar and the Polliwog
AUTHOR: Jack Kent
ILLUSTRATOR: Jack Kent
DIRECTOR: Daniel Ivanick
ANIMATOR: Daniel Ivanick
NARRATOR: Ruis Woertendyke, Melissa Leebaert
MUSIC: Scott Staton
TYPE: Animated

The Three Little Pigs
AUTHOR: Erik Blegvad
ILLUSTRATOR: Erik Blegvad
DIRECTOR: Jan Mack (photographed/edited/directed)
NARRATOR: Ian Thomson
MUSIC: Ernest Troost
TYPE: Iconographic

Where the Wild Things Are
AUTHOR: Maurice Sendak
ILLUSTRATOR: Maurice Sendak
DIRECTOR: Gene Deitch (adapted/directed)
ANIMATOR: Krátký Film Praha
NARRATOR: Peter Schickele (aka P. D. Q. Bach)
MUSIC: Peter Schickele
TYPE: Animated
AWARDS: Golden Eagle, CINE; Bronze Plaque, Virgin Islands International Film Festival

1989

Brave Irene
AUTHOR: William Steig
ILLUSTRATOR: William Steig
DIRECTOR: Daniel Ivanick
ANIMATOR: Daniel Ivanick, DMI Productions
NARRATOR: Lindsay Crouse
MUSIC: Jeremy Steig and Lee Ann Ledgerwood-Steig
TYPE: Animated

Mufaro's Beautiful Daughters
AUTHOR: John Steptoe
ILLUSTRATOR: John Steptoe
DIRECTOR: David R. Paight (adapted/directed)
NARRATOR: Terry Alexander
MUSIC: Ernest Troost
TYPE: Iconographic
AWARDS: Honorable Mention, Columbus International Film Festival; Silver Apple, National Educational Film & Video Festival

1990

Danny and the Dinosaur
AUTHOR: Syd Hoff
ILLUSTRATOR: Syd Hoff
DIRECTOR: Daniel Ivanick
NARRATOR: Ruis Woertendyke, Peter Prinstein, David Prinstein, Noelle Muro
MUSIC: Carl F. Schurtz
TYPE: Animated
AWARDS: Best Short Film, Kids First!

Hot Hippo
AUTHOR: Mwenye Hadithi
ILLUSTRATOR: Adrienne Kennaway
DIRECTOR: Christopher Palesty

ANIMATOR: Christopher Palesty
NARRATOR: Terry Alexander
MUSIC: Ernest Troost
TYPE: Animated

Owl Moon
AUTHOR: Jane Yolen
ILLUSTRATOR: John Schoenherr
DIRECTOR: Paul R. Gagne
NARRATOR: Jane Yolen
MUSIC: Ernest Troost
TYPE: Iconographic
AWARDS: Silver Apple, National
Educational Film & Video Festival

Picnic
AUTHOR: Emily Arnold McCully
ILLUSTRATOR: Emily Arnold McCully
DIRECTOR: James Bresnahan
ANIMATOR: James Bresnahan
MUSIC: Ernest Troost (composed/
conducted), Kathy Durning (edited)
TYPE: Animated
AWARDS: Notable Video, ALA; Editors'
Choice Film, Booklist

*Shh! We're Writing the
Constitution*
AUTHOR: Jean Fritz
ILLUSTRATOR: Tomie dePaola
DIRECTOR: Chris King
NARRATOR: Jean Fritz
MUSIC: Wayne Abravanel
TYPE: Iconographic

The Emperor's New Clothes
AUTHOR: Nadine Bernard Westcott
ILLUSTRATOR: Nadine Bernard Westcott
DIRECTOR: Gene Deitch (adapted/directed)
ANIMATOR: Krátký Film Praha
NARRATOR: Rex Robbins
MUSIC: Jirí Kadlus & The Prague
Steamboat Stompers
TYPE: Animated
AWARDS: Notable Video, ALA; Bronze
Plaque, Columbus International Film
Festival; Gold Medal, International
Film & TV Festival of NY

The Happy Lion
AUTHOR: Louise Fatio Duvoisin
ILLUSTRATOR: Roger Duvoisin
DIRECTOR: Václav Bedrich
NARRATOR: Rex Robbins
MUSIC: František Belfín
TYPE: Animated

The Pig's Wedding
AUTHOR: Helme Heine
ILLUSTRATOR: Helme Heine
DIRECTOR: Gene Deitch (adapted/directed)
ANIMATOR: Krátký Film Praha
NARRATOR: Rex Robbins
MUSIC: Jaroslav Celba, Gene Deitch
(lyrics ©1989)
TYPE: Animated
AWARDS: 1st Prize, Espinho Portugal
Cinanima Festival; Editors' Choice
Film, Booklist; Bronze Apple, National
Educational Film & Video Festival

The Pilgrims of Plimoth
AUTHOR: Marcia Sewall
ILLUSTRATOR: Marcia Sewall
DIRECTOR: Chris King
NARRATOR: Rex Robbins, Pamela
Payton-Wright, Melissa Leebaert
MUSIC: Arthur Custer
TYPE : Iconographic

*The Village of Round and
Square Houses*
AUTHOR: Ann Grifalconi
ILLUSTRATOR: Ann Grifalconi
DIRECTOR: David R. Paight (adapted/
directed)
NARRATOR: Cheryl Lynn Bruce
MUSIC: Arthur Custer
TYPE: Iconographic
AWARDS: Golden Eagle, CINE; Finalist,
American Film & Video Festival

What's Under My Bed?
AUTHOR: James Stevenson
ILLUSTRATOR: James Stevenson
DIRECTOR: Michael Sporn
ANIMATOR: Michael Sporn
NARRATOR: Barnard Hughes, Melissa
Cayanni, Peter Prinstein
MUSIC: Ernest Troost
TYPE: Animated

1991

Flossie and the Fox
AUTHOR: Patricia C. McKissack
ILLUSTRATOR: Rachel Isadora
DIRECTOR: Roy McDonald
NARRATOR: Patricia C. McKissack
MUSIC: Fred Weinberg
TYPE: Iconographic

Max's Chocolate Chicken
AUTHOR: Rosemary Wells
ILLUSTRATOR: Rosemary Wells
DIRECTOR: Michael Sporn
ANIMATOR: Michael Sporn
NARRATOR: Clayelle Dalferes
MUSIC: Ernest Troost
TYPE: Animated
AWARDS: Notable Video, ALA

Not So Fast, Songololo
AUTHOR: Niki Daly
ILLUSTRATOR: Niki Daly
DIRECTOR: Roy McDonald
ANIMATOR: Roy McDonald
NARRATOR: Gcina Mhlope
MUSIC: Murray Anderson
TYPE: Animated
AWARDS: Golden Eagle, CINE

Pet Show!
AUTHOR: Ezra Jack Keats
ILLUSTRATOR: Ezra Jack Keats
DIRECTOR: Jan Mack
NARRATOR: Terry Alexander
MUSIC: Fred Weinberg, Joe Beck
TYPE: Iconographic

*The Day Jimmy's Boa
Ate the Wash*
AUTHOR: Trinka Hakes Noble
ILLUSTRATOR: Steven Kellogg
DIRECTOR: Michael Sporn
ANIMATOR: Michael Sporn
NARRATOR: Heidi Stallings, Brianna Kittrell
MUSIC: Ernest Troost
TYPE: Animated
AWARDS: Golden Eagle, CINE, Editors'
Choice Film, Booklist

*The Great White
Man-Eating Shark*
AUTHOR: Margaret Mahy
ILLUSTRATOR: Jonathan Allen
DIRECTOR: Euan Frizzell
ANIMATOR: Euan Frizzell, Murray Reece,
Murray Freeth
NARRATOR: Ray Henwood
MUSIC: Ernest Troost
TYPE: Animated
AWARDS: Honorable Mention, Columbus
International Film Festival; Golden
Eagle, CINE; 2nd Prize, Best Animated
Short, Chicago International Film
Festival; 1st Prize, Best Children's Film,
Ottawa Film Festival; Silver Medal,

Language Arts, International Film
& Video Festival of NY

The Little Red Hen
AUTHOR: Paul Galdone
ILLUSTRATOR: Paul Galdone
DIRECTOR: Jan Mack
NARRATOR: Roberta Maxwell
MUSIC: Harry D. Buch
TYPE: Iconographic

The Selkie Girl
AUTHOR: Susan Cooper
ILLUSTRATOR: Warwick Hutton
DIRECTOR: Paul R. Gagne
NARRATOR: Jenny Agutter
MUSIC: Ernest Troost
TYPE: Iconographic

The Three Billy Goats Gruff
AUTHOR: Marcia Brown
ILLUSTRATOR: Marcia Brown
DIRECTOR: Randy Brody
NARRATOR: Rex Robbins
MUSIC: Arthur Custer
TYPE: Iconographic

The Three Little Pigs
AUTHOR: James Marshall
ILLUSTRATOR: James Marshall
DIRECTOR: Virginia Wilkos
ANIMATOR: Virginia Wilkos
NARRATOR: Fritz Weaver
MUSIC: Ernest Troost
TYPE: Animated
AWARDS: Notable Video, ALA; Red
Ribbon, American Film & Video
Festival; Silver Award, Birmingham
International Educational Film Festival;
Bronze Apple, National Educational
Film & Video Festival

*Where Do You Think You Are
Going, Christopher Columbus?*
AUTHOR: Jean Fritz
ILLUSTRATOR: Margot Tomes
DIRECTOR: Chris King
NARRATOR: Jean Fritz
MUSIC: Wayne Abravanel
TYPE: Iconographic
AWARDS: Bronze Plaque, Columbus
International Film Festival

Wings: A Tale of Two Chickens
AUTHOR: James Marshall
ILLUSTRATOR: James Marshall
DIRECTOR: Gene Deitch (adapted/directed)

ANIMATOR: Krátký Film Praha
NARRATOR: Mary Lee Culver, Gene Deitch, Joyce Ebert, James Marshall, Rex Robbins
MUSIC: Zdenek Merta (composed/performed)
TYPE: Animated
AWARDS: Notable Video, ALA; Red Ribbon, American Film & Video Festival

1992

Each Peach Pear Plum
AUTHOR: Janet & Allan Ahlberg
ILLUSTRATOR: Janet & Allan Ahlberg
DIRECTOR: Melissa Reilly
NARRATOR: Jennifer Brown (aka Buffy Allen)
MUSIC: Barb Luby
TYPE: Iconographic

Here Comes the Cat!
AUTHOR: Frank Asch, Vladimir Vagin
ILLUSTRATOR: Frank Asch, Vladimir Vagin
DIRECTOR: Alexander Tatarsky, Igor Kovalev
ANIMATOR: Alekseev Aleksey, Khruskov Oleg, Kolpin Andrey, Kostyuk Irina, Kudryavtsev Oleg, Kuznetsov Andrey, Lisovoy Mikhail, Podkolzin Aleksey, Ratnovsky Alexander, Severtsev Petr, Sherenov Sergey, Stuljev Leonid, Ushakov Svyatoslav, Zaikin Oleg, Zmoire Albert
NARRATOR: Donal Donnelly
MUSIC: Ernest Troost
TYPE: Animated
AWARDS: Notable Video, ALA; Bronze Apple, National Educational Film & Video Festival; Golden Eagle, CINE

Red Riding Hood
AUTHOR: James Marshall
ILLUSTRATOR: James Marshall
DIRECTOR: Virginia Wilkos
ANIMATOR: Virginia Wilkos
NARRATOR: Donal Donnelly
MUSIC: Ernest Troost
TYPE: Animated

1993

Beatrix Potter: Artist, Storyteller, and Countrywoman
AUTHOR: Judy Taylor
DIRECTOR: Cari Best, Paul R. Gagne, Judy Taylor

NARRATOR: Lynn Redgrave
MUSIC: Ernest Troost
TYPE: Iconographic
AWARDS: Gold Apple, National Educational Film & Video Festival

Goldilocks and the Three Bears
AUTHOR: James Marshall
ILLUSTRATOR: James Marshall
DIRECTOR: Milan Klikar
ANIMATOR: Milan Klikar, Vera Hainzová, Anna Habartová
NARRATOR: Joyce Ebert (English version)
MUSIC: Jaroslav Celba
TYPE: Animated

Monty
AUTHOR: James Stevenson
ILLUSTRATOR: James Stevenson
DIRECTOR: Michael Sporn
ANIMATOR: George McClements, Michael Wisniewski, Theresa Smythe, Ray Kosarin
NARRATOR: Marlene Danielle
MUSIC: Caleb Sampson
TYPE: Animated
AWARDS: Best Picture, ASIFA (The International Animated Film Society); Silver Plaque, Chicago International Film Festival

Musical Max
AUTHOR: Robert Kraus
ILLUSTRATOR: Jose Aruego, Ariane Dewey
DIRECTOR: Virginia Wilkos
ANIMATOR: Virginia Wilkos, Ty Varzsegi
NARRATOR: Mary Beth Hurt
MUSIC: Ernest Troost
TYPE: Animated
AWARDS: Notable Video, ALA; Silver Award, Birmingham Film & Video Festival; 1ˢᵗ Prize, Best Animation, ASIFA (The International Animated Film Society); Silver Apple, National Educational Film & Video Festival; 3ʳᵈ Place, Creative Excellence, U.S. International Film & Video Festival

Princess Furball
AUTHOR: Charlotte Huck
ILLUSTRATOR: Anita Lobel
DIRECTOR: Melissa Reilly
NARRATOR: Alice Krige
MUSIC: Neal Hellman, Joe Weed
TYPE: Iconographic

Sylvester and the Magic Pebble
AUTHOR: William Steig
ILLUSTRATOR: William Steig
DIRECTOR: Gene Deitch
ANIMATOR: Anna Habartová, Vera Hainzová, Irena Jandová, Jirí Michl, Ondrej Pecha
NARRATOR: John Lithgow
MUSIC: Jeremy Steig (composed), Eddie Gomez (composed additional music)
TYPE: Animated

What's the Big Idea, Ben Franklin?
AUTHOR: Jean Fritz
ILLUSTRATOR: Margot Tomes
DIRECTOR: Chris King
NARRATOR: Jean Fritz
MUSIC: Wayne Abravanel
TYPE: Iconographic

1994

A Visit with Rosemary Wells
DIRECTOR: Paul R. Gagne
MUSIC: Neal Hellman, Barry Phillips, Joe Weed, Lars Johannesson, Courtesy of Gourd Music
TYPE: Live-action

Amazing Grace
AUTHOR: Mary Hoffman
ILLUSTRATOR: Caroline Binch
DIRECTOR: Paul R. Gagne
NARRATOR: Alfre Woodard
MUSIC: Ernest Troost
TYPE: Iconographic
AWARDS: Golden Eagle, CINE; Certificate of Distinction, Media & Methods Magazine

Cat and Canary
AUTHOR: Michael Foreman
ILLUSTRATOR: Michael Foreman
DIRECTOR: Melissa Reilly
NARRATOR: Rex Robbins
MUSIC: Jeremy Steig
TYPE: Iconographic

In the Month of Kislev
AUTHOR: Nina Jaffe
ILLUSTRATOR: Louise August
DIRECTOR: Jan Northcutt
NARRATOR: Theodore Bikel
MUSIC: Kaila Flexer
TYPE: Iconographic
AWARDS: Golden Eagle, CINE

Noisy Nora
AUTHOR: Rosemary Wells
ILLUSTRATOR: Rosemary Wells
DIRECTOR: Virginia Wilkos
ANIMATOR: Virginia Wilkos, Ty Varszegi
NARRATOR: Mary Beth Hurt
MUSIC: Ernest Troost
TYPE: Animated
AWARDS: Notable Film, ALA; Golden Eagle, CINE; Silver Apple, National Educational Media Network; 3ʳᵈ Prize, ASIFA (The International Animated Film Society)

1995

Getting to Know William Steig
DIRECTOR: Cari Best
MUSIC: Jeremy Steig, Eddie Gomez
TYPE: Live-action

Hiawatha
AUTHOR: Henry Wadsworth Longfellow
ILLUSTRATOR: Susan Jeffers
DIRECTOR: Jan Northcutt
NARRATOR: Maureen Anderman
MUSIC: Fred Weinberg
TYPE: Iconographic
AWARDS: Golden Eagle, CINE

Keeping House
AUTHOR: Margaret Mahy
ILLUSTRATOR: Wendy Smith
DIRECTOR: Euan Frizzell
ANIMATOR: Lily Dell
NARRATOR: Ray Henwood
MUSIC: Peter Haeder
TYPE: Animated

Owen
AUTHOR: Kevin Henkes
ILLUSTRATOR: Kevin Henkes
DIRECTOR: Don Duga, Irra Verbitsky
ANIMATOR: Don Duga
NARRATOR: Sarah Jessica Parker
MUSIC: Ernest Troost
TYPE: Animated
AWARDS: Andrew Carnegie Medal for Excellence in Children's Video; Notable Film, ALA

The Three-Legged Cat
AUTHOR: Margaret Mahy
ILLUSTRATOR: Jonathan Allen
DIRECTOR: Euan Frizzell
ANIMATOR: Murray Freeth, Euan Frizzell,

Andrew Calder, David Gosman
NARRATOR: Ray Henwood
MUSIC: Peter Haeder
TYPE: Animated
AWARDS: 1st Place, Gold Camera Award, US International Film & Video Festival; Gold Plaque, Chicago International Film Festival

Who's in Rabbit's House?
AUTHOR: Verna Aardema
ILLUSTRATOR: Leo & Diane Dillon
DIRECTOR: Virginia Wilkos
ANIMATOR: Virginia Wilkos
NARRATOR: James Earl Jones
MUSIC: Yohuru Ralph Williams
TYPE: Animated

1996

The Cow Who Fell in the Canal
AUTHOR: Peter Spier
ILLUSTRATOR: Peter Spier
DIRECTOR: Gene Deitch Petr Faslonok,
ANIMATOR: Petr Friedl, Vera Hainzova, Irena Jandova, Leos Moravec
TYPE: Animated

1997

All the Colors of the Earth
AUTHOR: Sheila Hamanaka
ILLUSTRATOR: Sheila Hamanaka
DIRECTOR: Paul R. Gagne, Melissa Reilly
NARRATOR: Crystal Taliefero
MUSIC: Crystal Taliefero
TYPE: Iconographic

And Then What Happened, Paul Revere?
AUTHOR: Jean Fritz
ILLUSTRATOR: Margot Tomes
DIRECTOR: Chris King
NARRATOR: Rex Robbins
MUSIC: Jeff Loeb & Musictracks
TYPE: Iconographic

By the Light of the Halloween Moon
AUTHOR: Caroline Stutson
ILLUSTRATOR: Kevin Hawkes
DIRECTOR: Paul R. Gagne, Melissa Reilly
ANIMATOR: Cha-Pow!
NARRATOR: Sherry Stringfield
MUSIC: John Jennings
TYPE: Iconographic

Giving Thanks
AUTHOR: Chief Jake Swamp
ILLUSTRATOR: Erwin Printup, Jr.
DIRECTOR: Daniel Ivanick
ANIMATOR: Daniel Ivanick
NARRATOR: Chief Jake Swamp
MUSIC: Ernest Troost
TYPE: Animated

Harry the Dirty Dog
AUTHOR: Gene Zion
ILLUSTRATOR: Margaret Bloy Graham
DIRECTOR: Virginia Wilkos
ANIMATOR: Virginia Wilkos, Ty Varszegi
NARRATOR: Bruce Johnson
MUSIC: Ernest Troost
TYPE: Animated
AWARDS: 3rd Place, US International Film Festival

Officer Buckle and Gloria
AUTHOR: Peggy Rathmann
ILLUSTRATOR: Peggy Rathmann
DIRECTOR: Chris Larson
ANIMATOR: O'Plenty Animation
NARRATOR: John Lithgow
MUSIC: Ernest Troost
TYPE: Animated
AWARDS: Notable Video, ALA; Best Animated Short, Santa Clarita International Film Festival; 3rd Place, US International Film Festival; Bronze Plaque, Columbus International Film Festival; Golden Eagle, CINE

Seven Candles for Kwanzaa
AUTHOR: Andrea Davis Pinkney
ILLUSTRATOR: Brian Pinkney
DIRECTOR: Melissa Reilly
NARRATOR: Alfre Woodard
MUSIC: Crystal Taliefero
TYPE: Iconographic

The Night Before Christmas
AUTHOR: Clement Clarke Moore
ILLUSTRATOR: Ruth Sanderson
DIRECTOR: Melissa Reilly
NARRATOR: Anthony Edwards
TYPE: Iconographic
AWARDS: Bronze Statuette, Telly Awards

1998

A Weekend with Wendell
AUTHOR: Kevin Henkes
ILLUSTRATOR: Kevin Henkes

DIRECTOR: Virginia Wilkos
ANIMATOR: Virginia Wilkos, Ty Varszegi
NARRATOR: Mary Beth Hurt
MUSIC: Bruce Zimmerman
TYPE: Animated
AWARDS: Golden Eagle, CINE; Bronze Plaque, Columbus International Film Festival

Chicken Little
AUTHOR: Steven Kellogg
ILLUSTRATOR: Steven Kellogg
DIRECTOR: Don Duga, Irra Verbitsky
ANIMATOR: Polestar Animation for Weston Woods Studios
NARRATOR: Helen Hunt, Hank Azaria
MUSIC: Ernest Troost
TYPE: Animated
AWARDS: Bronze Apple, National Education Media Market Competition; Family Award, U.S.A. Film Festival

Chrysanthemum
AUTHOR: Kevin Henkes
ILLUSTRATOR: Kevin Henkes
DIRECTOR: Virginia Wilkos
ANIMATOR: Virginia Wilkos, Ty Varszegi
NARRATOR: Meryl Streep
MUSIC: Ernest Troost
TYPE: Animated
AWARDS: Notable Video, ALA; Gold Medal, The New York Festivals; Golden Eagle, CINE; Gold Award, WorldFest-Flagstaff; Children's Favorite, Aspen Shortsfest; Honor Title, Storytelling World

Good Night, Gorilla
AUTHOR: Peggy Rathmann
ILLUSTRATOR: Peggy Rathmann
DIRECTOR: Don Duga, Irra Verbitsky
ANIMATOR: Don Duga, Irra Verbitsky
NARRATOR: Anthony Edwards
MUSIC: John Jennings
TYPE: Animated
AWARDS: Notable Video, ALA; Silver Statuette, Telly Awards; Honorable Mention, Columbus International Film Festival

John Henry
AUTHOR: Julius Lester
ILLUSTRATOR: Jerry Pinkney
DIRECTOR: Ray Messecar
ANIMATOR: Cha-Pow!
NARRATOR: Samuel L. Jackson
MUSIC: Crystal Taliefero

TYPE: Iconographic
AWARDS: Silver Statuette, Telly Awards; Honor Title, Storytelling World

One Zillion Valentines
AUTHOR: Frank Modell
ILLUSTRATOR: Frank Modell
DIRECTOR: Chris Larson
ANIMATOR: O'Plenty Animation
NARRATOR: Melissa Leebaert, Luke Kelly-Clyne, Scott Terra
MUSIC: Nicholas Hubbell
TYPE: Animated
AWARDS: Bronze Plaque, Columbus International Film Festival

Rapunzel
AUTHOR: Paul O. Zelinsky
ILLUSTRATOR: Paul O. Zelinsky
DIRECTOR: Paul R. Gagne, Melissa Reilly
NARRATOR: Maureen Anderman
MUSIC: Bruce Zimmerman
TYPE: Iconographic
AWARDS: Bronze Statuette, Telly Awards

The Tale of the Mandarin Ducks
AUTHOR: Katherine Paterson
ILLUSTRATOR: Leo & Diane Dillon
DIRECTOR: Paul R. Gagne
ANIMATOR: Paul Apito, Brian Byers
NARRATOR: B. D. Wong
MUSIC: Elizabeth Brown
TYPE: Iconographic

Who's That Stepping on Plymouth Rock?
AUTHOR: Jean Fritz
ILLUSTRATOR: J. B. Handelsman
DIRECTOR: Ray Messecar
NARRATOR: Rex Robbins
MUSIC: Bruce Zimmerman
TYPE: Iconographic

Wilfrid Gordon McDonald Partridge
AUTHOR: Mem Fox
ILLUSTRATOR: Julie Vivas
DIRECTOR: Melissa Reilly
NARRATOR: Mem Fox
MUSIC: Ernest Troost
TYPE: Iconographic

1999

Chato's Kitchen
AUTHOR: Gary Soto
ILLUSTRATOR: Susan Guevara

DIRECTOR: Ray Messecar
NARRATOR: Cheech Marin
MUSIC: Jerry Dale McFadden
TYPE: Iconographic
AWARDS: Notable Video, ALA (English version); Notable Video, ALA (Spanish version)

Chicka Chicka Boom Boom
AUTHOR: Bill Martin, Jr., John Archambault
ILLUSTRATOR: Lois Ehlert
DIRECTOR: Virginia Wilkos
ANIMATOR: Virginia Wilkos, Ty Varszegi
NARRATOR: Crystal Taliefero (performed)
MUSIC: Crystal Talieferos
TYPE: Animated
AWARDS: Notable Video, ALA; Silver Remi, WorldFest-Houston International Film Festival; Bronze Plaque, Columbus International Film Festival; Best Educational Video, Ulysses International Film & TV Festival

Just a Few Words, Mr. Lincoln
AUTHOR: Jean Fritz
ILLUSTRATOR: Charles Robinson
DIRECTOR: Ray Messecar
NARRATOR: Rex Robbins
MUSIC: Bruce Zimmerman
TYPE: Iconographic
AWARDS: Notable Video, ALA

Leo the Late Bloomer
AUTHOR: Robert Kraus
ILLUSTRATOR: Jose Aruego
DIRECTOR: Michael Sporn
ANIMATOR: Michael Sporn, Krista Grasso
NARRATOR: Mary Beth Hurt
MUSIC: Ernest Troost
TYPE: Animated
AWARDS: Gold Remi, WorldFest-Houston International Film Festival; Finalist, The New York Festivals; Honorable Mention, Columbus International Film Festival

Miss Nelson Has a Field Day
AUTHOR: Harry Allard
ILLUSTRATOR: James Marshall
DIRECTOR: Virginia Wilkos, Ty Varszegi
ANIMATOR: Virginia Wilkos, Ty Varszegi
NARRATOR: Diana Canova
MUSIC: Robert Reynolds, Scotty Huff, Jerry Dale McFadden
TYPE: Animated

AWARDS: Andrew Carnegie Medal for Excellence in Children's Video; Notable Video, ALA

Miss Nelson Is Back
AUTHOR: James Marshall
ILLUSTRATOR: Harry Allard
DIRECTOR: Virginia Wilkos
ANIMATOR: Virginia Wilkos, Ty Varszegi
NARRATOR: Diana Canova
MUSIC: Ernest Troost
TYPE: Animated
AWARDS: Golden Eagle, CINE; Gold Award, WorldFest-Flagstaff International Film Festival

Rikki-Tikki-Tavi
AUTHOR: Rudyard Kipling
ILLUSTRATOR: Jerry Pinkney
DIRECTOR: Melissa Reilly
NARRATOR: Michael York
MUSIC: Ernest Troost
TYPE: Iconographic

Sam and the Lucky Money
AUTHOR: Karen Chinn
ILLUSTRATOR: Cornelius Van Wright, Ying-Hwa Hu
DIRECTOR: Ray Messecar
NARRATOR: Ming-Na Wen
MUSIC: Bruce Zimmerman
TYPE: Iconographic

The Rainbabies
AUTHOR: Laura Krauss Melmed
ILLUSTRATOR: Jim LaMarche
DIRECTOR: Paul R. Gagne
NARRATOR: B. J. Ward
MUSIC: John Jennings (composed/arranged/produced)
TYPE: Iconographic

Zin! Zin! Zin! A Violin
AUTHOR: Lloyd Moss
ILLUSTRATOR: Marjorie Priceman
DIRECTOR: Ray Messecar
NARRATOR: Maureen Anderman
MUSIC: Marvin Hamlisch (original music ©1998); Bruce Zimmerman (adapted/arranged)
TYPE: Iconographic

2000

Antarctic Antics
AUTHOR: Judy Sierra
ILLUSTRATOR: Jose Aruego, Ariane Dewey

DIRECTOR: Gary Goldberger, Peter Reynolds
ANIMATOR: FableVision Studios
NARRATOR: Diana Canova, Kristen Hahn, Raul Malo, Peggy Newman, Kimberley Nygren, Jennifer O'Mara, Robert Reynolds, Mae Robertson, Scotty Huff
MUSIC: Robert Reynolds, Scotty Huff
TYPE: Animated
AWARDS: Andrew Carnegie Medal for Excellence in Children's Video; Notable Video, ALA; Gold Award, WorldFest-Flagstaff International Film Festival; Top 10 Poetry Videos, Booklist

Duke Ellington
AUTHOR: Andrea Davis Pinkney
ILLUSTRATOR: Brian Pinkney
DIRECTOR: Ray Messecar
NARRATOR: Forest Whitaker
MUSIC: Duke Ellington & His Orchestra (original music), Joel Goodman, Dan Rosengard
TYPE: Iconographic
AWARDS: Notable Video, ALA; Editors' Choice Film, Booklist; Golden Eagle, CINE

Elizabeti's Doll
AUTHOR: Stephanie Stuve-Bodeen
ILLUSTRATOR: Christy Hale
DIRECTOR: Melissa Reilly
NARRATOR: Lynn Whitfield
MUSIC: Crystal Taliefero
TYPE: Iconographic

George Washington's Mother
AUTHOR: Jean Fritz
ILLUSTRATOR: Dyanne DiSalvo-Ryan
DIRECTOR: Ray Messecar
NARRATOR: B. J. Ward
MUSIC: Bruce Zimmerman
TYPE: Iconographic

How Much Is a Million?
AUTHOR: David M. Schwartz
ILLUSTRATOR: Steven Kellogg
DIRECTOR: Ray Messecar
ANIMATOR: David Berrettini, Andrea Castellani, Elena Castellani, Mattia Laviosa
NARRATOR: Bruce Bayley Johnson
MUSIC: Bruce Zimmerman
TYPE: Animated
AWARDS: Honorable Mention, Columbus International Film Festival

Johnny Appleseed
AUTHOR: Reeve Lindbergh
ILLUSTRATOR: Kathy Jakobsen
DIRECTOR: Paul R. Gagne, Melissa Reilly
NARRATOR: Mary McDonnell
MUSIC: Randy Scruggs
TYPE: Iconographic
AWARDS: Top 10 Poetry Videos, Booklist

Miss Rumphius
AUTHOR: Barbara Cooney
ILLUSTRATOR: Barbara Cooney
DIRECTOR: Paul R. Gagne, Sarah Kerruish
NARRATOR: Claire Danes
MUSIC: John Jennings
TYPE: Iconographic; Live-action
AWARDS: Bronze Plaque, Columbus International Film Festival; UNICEF Prize, Barcelona International Film & Video Festival (Spanish version)

The Paperboy
AUTHOR: Dav Pilkey
ILLUSTRATOR: Dav Pilkey
DIRECTOR: Paul R. Gagne
NARRATOR: Forest Whitaker
MUSIC: Jerry Dale McFadden
TYPE: Iconographic

Pete's a Pizza
AUTHOR: William Steig
ILLUSTRATOR: William Steig
DIRECTOR: Peter Reynolds, Gary Goldberger
ANIMATOR: Gary Goldberger, Noah Jones
NARRATOR: Chevy Chase
MUSIC: Raul Malo
TYPE: Animated
AWARDS: Golden Eagle, CINE; Best Animated Short, Santa Clarita International Film Festival; Honorable Mention, Columbus International Film Festival

The Island of the Skog
AUTHOR: Steven Kellogg
ILLUSTRATOR: Steven Kellogg
DIRECTOR: Paul R. Gagne
ANIMATOR: Don Duga, Irra Verbitsky
NARRATOR: Anthony Edwards with Diana Canova, Steven Kellogg, Mary Beth Hurt
MUSIC: Ernest Troost
TYPE: Animated
AWARDS: Editors' Choice Film, Booklist

The Scrambled States
of America
AUTHOR: Laurie Keller
ILLUSTRATOR: Laurie Keller
DIRECTOR: Daniel Ivanick
ANIMATOR: Daniel Ivanick
NARRATOR: Jon Carroll
MUSIC: Jerry Dale McFadden, Charlie
Monk Music, Curb Songs
TYPE: Animated
AWARDS: Notable Video, ALA; Best Short,
Education Category, Santa Clarita
International Film Festival; Storytelling
World Honor Title; Finalist, CINE;
Finalist, The New York Festivals

This Land Is Your Land
AUTHOR: Woody Guthrie, Nora Guthrie
ILLUSTRATOR: Kathy Jakobsen
DIRECTOR: Ray Messecar
NARRATOR: Nora Guthrie
MUSIC: Arlo Guthrie, Woody Guthrie
TYPE: Iconographic

Yo! Yes?
AUTHOR: Chris Raschka
ILLUSTRATOR: Chris Raschka
DIRECTOR: Michael Sporn
ANIMATOR: Michael Sporn
NARRATOR: Ryann William, Tucker Bliss
MUSIC: Jerry Dale McFadden
TYPE: Animated
AWARDS: Notable Video, ALA

2001

Click, Clack, Moo
AUTHOR: Doreen Cronin
ILLUSTRATOR: Betsy Lewin
DIRECTOR: Maciek Albrecht
ANIMATOR: Maciek Albrecht &
MaGiK Studio
NARRATOR: Randy Travis
MUSIC: Scotty Huff
TYPE: Animated
AWARDS: Notable Video, ALA;
Silver Remi, WorldFest-Houston
International Film Festival, BAMmie
— Best Animated Short Film,
BAMKids Film Festival; Finalist,
U.S.A. Film Festival

Henry Hikes to Fitchburg
AUTHOR: D. B. Johnson
ILLUSTRATOR: D. B. Johnson
DIRECTOR: Melissa Reilly

NARRATOR: James Naughton
MUSIC: Jon Carroll
TYPE: Iconographic

I, Crocodile
AUTHOR: Fred Marcellino
ILLUSTRATOR: Fred Marcellino
DIRECTOR: Michael Sporn
ANIMATOR: Michael Sporn
NARRATOR: Tim Curry
MUSIC: Raul Malo
TYPE: Animated
AWARDS: Notable Video, ALA;
Bronze Remi, WorldFest-Houston
International Film Festival

I Love You Like Crazy Cakes
AUTHOR: Rose Lewis
ILLUSTRATOR: Jane Dyer
DIRECTOR: Melissa Reilly
NARRATOR: Mia Farrow
MUSIC: Ernest Troost
TYPE: Iconographic
AWARDS: Notable Video, ALA

In the Small, Small Pond
AUTHOR: Denise Fleming
ILLUSTRATOR: Denise Fleming
DIRECTOR: Paul R. Gagne
NARRATOR: Laura Dern
MUSIC: Jerry Dale McFadden
TYPE: Iconographic
AWARDS: Notable Video, ALA

Is Your Mama a Llama?
AUTHOR: Deborah Guarino
ILLUSTRATOR: Steven Kellogg
DIRECTOR: Virginia Wilkos
ANIMATOR: Virginia Wilkos, Ty Varszegi
NARRATOR: Amy Madigan
MUSIC: Ernest Troost
TYPE: Animated
AWARDS: Honorable Mention, Columbus
International Film Festival

Joseph Had a Little Overcoat
AUTHOR: Simms Taback
ILLUSTRATOR: Simms Taback
DIRECTOR: Daniel Ivanick
ANIMATOR: Daniel Ivanick
NARRATOR: Rob Reiner
MUSIC: Joel Goodman, David Bramfitt
TYPE: Animated
AWARDS: Notable Video, ALA; Golden
Eagle, CINE; Silver Screen Award, US
International Film & Video Festival

Possum Magic
AUTHOR: Mem Fox
ILLUSTRATOR: Julie Vivas
DIRECTOR: Leigh Corra, Paul R. Gagne
NARRATOR: Mem Fox
MUSIC: Yothu Yindi
TYPE: Iconographic

Space Case
AUTHOR: Edward Marshall
ILLUSTRATOR: James Marshall
DIRECTOR: Virginia Wilkos, Ty
Varszegi
ANIMATOR: Virginia Wilkos, Ty Varszegi
NARRATOR: Christopher Lloyd
MUSIC: Scotty Huff, Robert Reynolds
TYPE: Animated
AWARDS: Notable Video, ALA; Bronze
Plaque, Columbus International
Film Festival; Finalist, The New
York Festivals

Swamp Angel
AUTHOR: Anne Isaacs
ILLUSTRATOR: Paul O. Zelinsky
DIRECTOR: Paul R. Gagne, Melissa Reilly
TYPE: Iconographic

The Ugly Duckling
AUTHOR: Hans Christian Andersen
ILLUSTRATOR: Jerry Pinkney
DIRECTOR: Paul R. Gagne, Melissa Reilly
NARRATOR: Lynn Whitfield
MUSIC: Ernest Troost
TYPE: Iconographic

Three Cheers for
Catherine the Great!
AUTHOR: Cari Best
ILLUSTRATOR: Giselle Potter
DIRECTOR: Daniel Ivanick
ANIMATOR: Daniel Ivanick
NARRATOR: Ekaterina Gordeeva
MUSIC: Joel Goodman, Dan Rosengard
TYPE: Animated

Trashy Town
AUTHOR: Andrea Zimmerman,
David Clemesha
ILLUSTRATOR: Dan Yaccarino
DIRECTOR: Daniel Ivanick
ANIMATOR: Daniel Ivanick
NARRATOR: Diana Canova, David de Vries
MUSIC: Scotty Huff, Robert Reynolds
TYPE: Animated
AWARDS: Notable Video, ALA; Honorable

Mention, Columbus International
Film Festival

2002

Five Creatures
AUTHOR: Emily Jenkins
ILLUSTRATOR: Tomek Bogacki
DIRECTOR: Melissa Reilly
NARRATOR: Kristen Hahn
MUSIC: Jerry Dale McFadden
TYPE: Iconographic

Goose
AUTHOR: Molly Bang
ILLUSTRATOR: Molly Bang
DIRECTOR: Daniel Ivanick
ANIMATOR: DMI Productions
NARRATOR: Laura Dern
MUSIC: John Jennings
TYPE: Animated
AWARDS: Honorable Mention, Columbus
International Film Festival

How Do Dinosaurs Say
Good Night?
AUTHOR: Jane Yolen
ILLUSTRATOR: Mark Teague
DIRECTOR: Maciek Albrecht &
MaGiK Studio
ANIMATOR: Maciek Albrecht &
MaGiK Studio
NARRATOR: Jane Yolen
MUSIC: Jerry Dale McFadden
TYPE: Animated
AWARDS: Notable Video, ALA

If You Made a Million
AUTHOR: David M. Schwartz
ILLUSTRATOR: Steven Kellogg
DIRECTOR: Ray Messecar
ANIMATOR: Ro Marcenaro
NARRATOR: Bruce Johnson
MUSIC: Bruce Zimmerman
TYPE: Animated
AWARDS: Golden Eagle, CINE; Honorable
Mention, Columbus International
Film Festival

Martin's Big Words
AUTHOR: Doreen Rappaport
ILLUSTRATOR: Bryan Collier
DIRECTOR: Melissa Reilly
NARRATOR: Michael Clarke Duncan
MUSIC: Crystal Taliefero
TYPE: Iconographic

Merry Christmas, Space Case
AUTHOR: James Marshall
ILLUSTRATOR: James Marshall
DIRECTOR: Virginia Wilkos
ANIMATOR: Virginia Wilkos
NARRATOR: Christopher Lloyd
MUSIC: Scotty Huff, Robert Reynolds
TYPE: Animated
AWARDS: Notable Video, ALA; Bronze Plaque, Columbus International Film Festival

So You Want to Be President?
AUTHOR: Judith St. George
ILLUSTRATOR: David Small
DIRECTOR: Gary McGivney
ANIMATOR: Gary McGivney
NARRATOR: Stockard Channing
MUSIC: Scotty Huff, Robert Reynolds
TYPE: Animated
AWARDS: Andrew Carnegie Medal for Excellence in Children's Video; Notable Video, ALA, Golden Eagle, CINE; Gold World Medal, The New York Festivals; 1st Place, Columbus International Film Festival

The Star-Spangled Banner
AUTHOR: Francis Scott Key
ILLUSTRATOR: Peter Spier
DIRECTOR: Gary McGivney
ANIMATOR: Martin Haughey & Emma Collicott of Zippitoons
NARRATOR: Rex Robbins, Aretha Franklin (vocals)
MUSIC: William S. Fischer (arranged), H. B. Barnum (directed)
TYPE: Animated
AWARDS: Gold Remi, WorldFest-Houston International Film Festival

There Was an Old Lady Who Swallowed a Fly
AUTHOR: Simms Taback
ILLUSTRATOR: Simms Taback
DIRECTOR: Konstantin Bronzit
ANIMATOR: "Melinista"
NARRATOR: Cyndi Lauper
MUSIC: Scotty Huff, Robert Reynolds
TYPE: Animated

Too Many Tamales
AUTHOR: Gary Soto
ILLUSTRATOR: Ed Martinez
DIRECTOR: Paul R. Gagne, Leigh Corra
NARRATOR: Blanca Camacho

MUSIC: David Bramfitt, Joel Goodman
TYPE: Iconographic

Waiting for Wings
AUTHOR: Lois Ehlert
ILLUSTRATOR: Lois Ehlert
DIRECTOR: Kris Tercek
ANIMATOR: Cha-Pow!
NARRATOR: Crystal Taliefero
MUSIC: Crystal Taliefero
TYPE: Animated
AWARDS: Notable Video, ALA

Why Don't You Get a Horse, Sam Adams?
AUTHOR: Jean Fritz
ILLUSTRATOR: Trina Schart Hyman
DIRECTOR: Leigh Corra
NARRATOR: David de Vries
MUSIC: David Bramfitt
TYPE: Iconographic

2003

Bark, George
AUTHOR: Jules Feiffer
ILLUSTRATOR: Jules Feiffer
DIRECTOR: Gene Deitch
ANIMATOR: Zdenka Deitchová
NARRATOR: John Lithgow
MUSIC: Lucy Fillerey
TYPE: Animated
AWARDS: Notable Video, ALA; Gold Star, Special Jury Award, WorldFest-Houston International Film Festival; Best Short Animation Classic, International Family Film Festival

Chato and the Party Animals
AUTHOR: Gary Soto
ILLUSTRATOR: Susan Guevara
DIRECTOR: Ed Mironiuk, Kris Tercek
ANIMATOR: Ed Mironiuk, Kris Tercek
NARRATOR: Luis Guzman
MUSIC: Otmaro Ruiz
TYPE: Iconographic
AWARDS: Bronze Remi, WorldFest-Houston International Film Festival; Golden Eagle, CINE

Come On, Rain!
AUTHOR: Karen Hesse
ILLUSTRATOR: Jon J. Muth
DIRECTOR: Leigh Corra
NARRATOR: Leila Ali
MUSIC: Jerry Dale McFadden

TYPE: Iconographic
AWARDS: Notable Video, ALA; Honorable Mention, Columbus International Film Festival

Dem Bones
AUTHOR: Bob Barner
ILLUSTRATOR: Bob Barner
DIRECTOR: Gary McGivney
ANIMATOR: Zippitoons
NARRATOR: Chris Thomas King
MUSIC: Raul Malo
TYPE: Animated
AWARDS: Notable Film, ALA; Silver Remi, WorldFest-Houston International Film Festival; Finalist, International Family Film Festival

Dot the Fire Dog
AUTHOR: Lisa Desimini
ILLUSTRATOR: Lisa Desimini
DIRECTOR: Leigh Corra
NARRATOR: Ruth Berliner
MUSIC: Jon Carroll
TYPE: Iconographic

Ella Fitzgerald: The Tale of a Vocal Virtuosa
AUTHOR: Andrea Davis Pinkney
ILLUSTRATOR: Brian Pinkney
DIRECTOR: Gary McGivney
ANIMATOR: Zippitoons
NARRATOR: Billy Dee Williams
MUSIC: Joel Goodman, Dan Rosengard
TYPE: Animated
AWARDS: Notabable Video, ALA; Golden Eagle, CINE; Bronze Plaque, Columbus International Film Festival

Giggle, Giggle, Quack
AUTHOR: Doreen Cronin
ILLUSTRATOR: Betsy Lewin
DIRECTOR: Maciek Albrecht & MaGiK Studio
ANIMATOR: MaGiK Studio
NARRATOR: Randy Travis
MUSIC: Scotty Huff
TYPE: Animated
AWARDS: Andrew Carnegie Medal for Excellence in Children's Video; Notable Video, ALA; Finalist, The New York Festivals; Honorable Mention, Columbus International Film Festival

Henry Builds a Cabin
AUTHOR: D. B. Johnson

ILLUSTRATOR: D. B. Johnson
DIRECTOR: Melissa Reilly
NARRATOR: James Naughton
MUSIC: Jon Carroll
TYPE: Iconographic

Shrinking Violet
AUTHOR: Cari Best
ILLUSTRATOR: Giselle Potter
DIRECTOR: Gary McGivney
ANIMATOR: Zippitoons
NARRATOR: Calista Flockhart
MUSIC: Ernest Troost
TYPE: Animated
AWARDS: Silver Remi, WorldFest-Houston International Film Festival; Golden Eagle, CINE

Snowflake Bentley
AUTHOR: Jacqueline Briggs Martin
ILLUSTRATOR: Mary Azarian
DIRECTOR: Paul R. Gagne, Sarah Kerruish, Melissa Reilly
NARRATOR: Sean Astin
MUSIC: David J. Reading
TYPE: Iconographic; Live-action
AWARDS: Notable Video, ALA; Bronze Plaque, Columbus International Film Festival

The Teacher from the Black Lagoon
AUTHOR: Mike Thaler
ILLUSTRATOR: Jared Lee
DIRECTOR: Maciek Albrecht & MaGiK Studio
ANIMATOR: MaGiK Studio
NARRATOR: Jonathan Lipnicki, Diana Canova
MUSIC: Scotty Huff
TYPE: Animated
AWARDS: Notable Video, ALA

2004

Diary of a Worm
AUTHOR: Doreen Cronin
ILLUSTRATOR: Harry Bliss
DIRECTOR: Gene Deitch
ANIMATOR: Gene Deitch
NARRATOR: Alesander Gould
MUSIC: Zdenek Zdenek
TYPE: Animated
AWARDS: Notable Video, ALA; Special Jury Award, WorldFest-Houston International Film Festival

Duck for President
AUTHOR: Doreen Cronin
ILLUSTRATOR: Betsy Lewin
DIRECTOR: Maciek Albrecht
ANIMATOR: Maciek Albrecht &
MaGiK Studio
NARRATOR: Randy Travis
MUSIC: Scotty Huff, Robert Reynolds
TYPE: Animated
AWARDS: Notable Video, ALA

I Lost My Bear
AUTHOR: Jules Feiffer
ILLUSTRATOR: Jules Feiffer
DIRECTOR: Gene Deitch
ANIMATOR: Zdenka Deitchová
NARRATOR: Halley Feiffer, Kristen Hahn
(Read-along audio)
MUSIC: Michael Wolff
TYPE: Animated

I Stink!
AUTHOR: Kate McMullan
ILLUSTRATOR: Jim McMullan
DIRECTOR: Maciek Albrecht &
MaGiK Studio
ANIMATOR: MaGiK Studio
NARRATOR: Andy Richter
MUSIC: Joel Goodman
TYPE: Animated
AWARDS: Notable Video, ALA; Honorable
Mention, Columbus International Film
Festival; Bronze Medal, Kalamazoo
Animation Festival International

No Roses for Harry!
AUTHOR: Gene Zion
ILLUSTRATOR: Margaret Bloy Graham
DIRECTOR: Virginia Wilkos
ANIMATOR: Virginia Wilkos
NARRATOR: Bruce Johnson
MUSIC: Ernest Troost
TYPE: Animated
AWARDS: Golden Eagle, CINE

Players in Pigtails
AUTHOR: Shana Corey
ILLUSTRATOR: Rebecca Gibbon
DIRECTOR: Paul R. Gagne, Melissa Reilly
NARRATOR: Zooey Deschanel, Sherry
Goffin Kondor (vocals)
MUSIC: Joel Goodman
TYPE: Iconographic

The Dot
AUTHOR: Peter H. Reynolds

ILLUSTRATOR: Peter H. Reynolds
DIRECTOR: Johnathan Lechner,
Gary Goldberger
ANIMATOR: FableVision Studios
NARRATOR: Thora Birch
MUSIC: Jerry Dale McFadden
TYPE: Animated
AWARDS: Andrew Carnegie Medal for
Excellence in Children's Video; Notable
Video, ALA; 2nd Prize, Chicago
International Children's Film Festival;
Honorable Mention, Columbus
International Film Festival

The Elves and the Shoemaker
AUTHOR: Retold by Jim LaMarche
ILLUSTRATOR: Jim LaMarche
DIRECTOR: Leigh Corra
NARRATOR: Patrick Stewart
MUSIC: John Jennings
TYPE: Iconographic

The Pot That Juan Built
AUTHOR: Nancy Andrews-Goebel
ILLUSTRATOR: David Diaz
DIRECTOR: Leigh Corra
NARRATOR: Alfred Molina
MUSIC: Otmaro Ruiz
TYPE: Iconographic
AWARDS: Notable Video, ALA

The Wheels on the Bus
AUTHOR: Paul O. Zelinsky
ILLUSTRATOR: Paul O. Zelinsky
DIRECTOR: Gary McGivney
ANIMATOR: Zippitoons
MUSIC: The Bacon Brothers (vocals)
TYPE: Animated
AWARDS: Notable Video, ALA; 1st Prize,
Columbus International Film Festival

*This Is the House That
Jack Built*
AUTHOR: Simms Taback
ILLUSTRATOR: Simms Taback
DIRECTOR: Konstantin Bronzit
ANIMATOR: "Melinista"
NARRATOR: Mandy Patinkin
MUSIC: Scotty Huff
TYPE: Animated

Will I Have a Friend?
AUTHOR: Miriam Cohen
ILLUSTRATOR: Lillian Hoban
DIRECTOR: Leigh Corra
NARRATOR: David de Vries

MUSIC: Jon Carroll
TYPE: Iconographic

2005

Arne the Doughnut
AUTHOR: Laurie Keller
ILLUSTRATOR: Laurie Keller
DIRECTOR: Daniel Ivanick
ANIMATOR: Daniel Ivanick
NARRATOR: Michael McKean
MUSIC: Scotty Huff, Robert Reynolds
TYPE: Animated
AWARDS: Certificate of Excellence,
Chicago International Children's Film
Festival; Audie Award Winner; Finalist,
International Family Film Festival

Bear Snores On
AUTHOR: Karma Wilson
ILLUSTRATOR: Jane Chapman
DIRECTOR: Melissa Reilly
NARRATOR: Karma Wilson
MUSIC: John Jennings
TYPE: Iconographic
AWARDS: Gold Award Winner, National
Parenting Publications Awards

Chicka, Chicka 1, 2, 3
AUTHOR: Bill Martin, Jr., Michael
Sampson
ILLUSTRATOR: Lois Ehlert
DIRECTOR: Virginia Wilkos
ANIMATOR: Virginia Wilkos
NARRATOR: Crystal Taliefero
MUSIC: Crystal Taliefero
TYPE: Animated

Ellington Was Not a Street
AUTHOR: Ntozake Shange
ILLUSTRATOR: Kadir Nelson
DIRECTOR: Paul R. Gagne, Melissa Reilly
NARRATOR: Phylicia Rashad
MUSIC: Duke Ellington
TYPE: Iconographic
AWARDS: Notable Video, ALA; The Chris
Award, Columbus International
Film Festival

Getting to Know Simms Taback
DIRECTOR: Leigh Corra
TYPE: Live-action

Hansel and Gretel
AUTHOR: James Marshall
ILLUSTRATOR: James Marshall
DIRECTOR: Virginia Wilkos

ANIMATOR: Virginia Wilkos
NARRATOR: Kathy Bates
MUSIC: Ernest Troost
TYPE: Animated

*How Do Dinosaurs
Get Well Soon?*
AUTHOR: Jane Yolen
ILLUSTRATOR: Mark Teague
DIRECTOR: Maciek Albrecht &
MaGiK Studio
ANIMATOR: Maciek Albrecht &
MaGiK Studio
NARRATOR: Jane Yolen
MUSIC: Jerry Dale McFadden
TYPE: Animated
AWARDS: Gold Award, Parents' Choice;
Bronze Plaque, Columbus International
Film Festival

Ish
AUTHOR: Peter H. Reynolds
ILLUSTRATOR: Peter H. Reynolds
DIRECTOR: FableVision Studios
ANIMATOR: FableVision Studios
NARRATOR: Chester Gregory
MUSIC: Joel Goodman
TYPE: Animated
AWARDS: Notable Video, ALA; 2nd Prize,
Animated Short, Chicago International
Children's Film Festival; Anima Mundi
Finalist; Official Selection, Little Big
Shots International Animation Festival

Planting a Rainbow
AUTHOR: Lois Ehlert
ILLUSTRATOR: Lois Ehlert
DIRECTOR: Ed Mironiuk, Kris Tercek
ANIMATOR: Ed Mironiuk, Kris Tercek
NARRATOR: Crystal Taliefero
MUSIC: Crystal Taliefero
TYPE: Animated

Roberto the Insect Architect
AUTHOR: Nina Laden
ILLUSTRATOR: Nina Laden
DIRECTOR: Galen Fott, Jerry Hunt
ANIMATOR: Galen Fott
NARRATOR: Sean Hayes
MUSIC: Jerry Hunt
TYPE: Animated
AWARDS: Notable Video, ALA; Best Short
Film Award, Kids First!; Audience
Award, Showcomotion Young
People's Film Festival; Semi-Finalist,
Moondance International Film Festival;

Best Children's Film, Weekend Digital Film Festival; Bronze Remi, WorldFest-Houston International Film Festival; Official Selection, Little Big Shots International Film Festival

Stars! Stars! Stars!
AUTHOR: Bob Barner
ILLUSTRATOR: Bob Barner
DIRECTOR: Gary McGivney
ANIMATOR: Gary McGivney
MUSIC: Joel Goodman
TYPE: Animated
AWARDS: Notable Video, ALA

T Is for Terrible
AUTHOR: Peter McCarty
ILLUSTRATOR: Peter McCarty
DIRECTOR: Leigh Corra
NARRATOR: David de Vries
MUSIC: Scotty Huff, Robert Reynolds
TYPE: Iconographic

The Man Who Walked Between the Towers
AUTHOR: Mordicai Gerstein
ILLUSTRATOR: Mordicai Gerstein
DIRECTOR: Michael Sporn
ANIMATOR: Michael Sporn
NARRATOR: Jake Gyllenhaal
MUSIC: Michael Bacon
TYPE: Animated
AWARDS: Andrew Carnegie Medal for Excellence in Children's Video; Notable Video, ALA, Best Short Animation Classic, International Family Film Festival; Crystal Heart Award, Heartland Film Festival; Silver World Medal, The New York Festivals; Academy Award Short List for Best Animated Short Film; Storytelling World Award; 1st Place, Best Animation, ASIFA (The International Animated Film Society); Best Short Children's Film, Ottawa International Animation Festival

Wild About Books
AUTHOR: Judy Sierra
ILLUSTRATOR: Marc Brown
DIRECTOR: Maciek Albrecht & MaGiK Studio
ANIMATOR: Maciek Albrecht & MaGiK Studio
NARRATOR: Catherine O'Hara
MUSIC: Scotty Huff

TYPE: Animated
AWARDS: Notable Video, ALA; Editors' Choice Film, Booklist

Will You Sign Here, John Hancock?
AUTHOR: Jean Fritz
ILLUSTRATOR: Trina Schart Hyman
DIRECTOR: Leigh Corra
NARRATOR: Jeff Brooks
MUSIC: Ernest Troost
TYPE: Iconographic
AWARDS: Editors' Choice Film, Booklist

2006

Bear Wants More
AUTHOR: Karma Wilson
ILLUSTRATOR: Jane Chapman
DIRECTOR: Melissa Reilly
NARRATOR: Karma Wilson
MUSIC: Jo-hn Jennings
TYPE: Iconographic

Cinderella
AUTHOR: James Marshall
ILLUSTRATOR: James Marshall
DIRECTOR: Virginia Wilkos
ANIMATOR: Virginia Wilkos
NARRATOR: Stephanie J. Block
MUSIC: Ernest Troost
TYPE: Animated
AWARDS: Notable Video, ALA; Platinum Remi, WorldFest-Houston International Film Festival

Diary of a Spider
AUTHOR: Doreen Cronin
ILLUSTRATOR: Harry Bliss
DIRECTOR: Gene Deitch
ANIMATOR: Gene Deitch
NARRATOR: Angus T. Jones
MUSIC: Zdenek Zdenek
TYPE: Animated
AWARDS: Best Titles List, Capitol Choices; Best Short Film, London Children's Film Festival

Dinosaur Bones
AUTHOR: Bob Barner
ILLUSTRATOR: Bob Barner
DIRECTOR: Gary McGivney
ANIMATOR: Zippitoons
NARRATOR: Jerry Dixon, Raul Malo
MUSIC: Raul Malo
TYPE: Animated

AWARDS: Notable Video, ALA; Gold Remi, WorldFest-Houston International Film Festival; Finalist, CINE

Emily's First 100 Days of School
AUTHOR: Rosemary Wells
ILLUSTRATOR: Rosemary Wells
DIRECTOR: Gene Deitch
ANIMATOR: Gene Deitch
NARRATOR: Diana Canova
MUSIC: Zdenek Zdenek
TYPE: Animated
AWARDS: Silver Remi, WorldFest-Houston International Film Festival

He's Got the Whole World in His Hands
AUTHOR: Oral tradition
ILLUSTRATOR: Kadir Nelson
DIRECTOR: Melissa Reilly
NARRATOR: Crystal Taliefero
MUSIC: Crystal Taliefero
TYPE: Iconographic

Hondo and Fabian
AUTHOR: Peter McCarty
ILLUSTRATOR: Peter McCarty
DIRECTOR: Leigh Corra
NARRATOR: Jeff Brooks
MUSIC: Joel Goodman, David Bramfitt
TYPE: Iconographic
AWARDS: Notable Video, ALA; Honorable Mention, Columbus International Film Festival

I Could Do That! Esther Morris Gets Women the Vote
AUTHOR: Linda Arms White
ILLUSTRATOR: Nancy Carpenter
DIRECTOR: Leigh Corra
NARRATOR: Joan Allen
MUSIC: David Mansfield
TYPE: Iconographic
AWARDS: Editors' Choice Film, Booklist

Inch by Inch
AUTHOR: Leo Lionni
ILLUSTRATOR: Leo Lionni
DIRECTOR: Gary McGivney
ANIMATOR: Zippitoons
NARRATOR: Ron McLarty
MUSIC: Joel Goodman
TYPE: Animated

Knuffle Bunny
AUTHOR: Mo Willems
ILLUSTRATOR: Mo Willems
DIRECTOR: Maciek Albrecht & MaGiK Studio
ANIMATOR: Maciek Albrecht & MaGiK Studio
NARRATOR: Mo Willems, Trixie Willems, Cheryl Willems
MUSIC: Scotty Huff, Robert Reynolds
TYPE: Animated
AWARDS: Andrew Carnegie Medal for Excellence in Children's Video; Notable Video, ALA; BAMmie Award for Best Animated Short Film, BAMkids Film Festival; Finalist, Kalamazoo Animation Festival International; Offical Selection, San Francisco International Film Festival; Best of the Fest, NY International Children's Film Festival; Short Film Award, Kids First!

Lon Po Po
AUTHOR: Ed Young
ILLUSTRATOR: Ed Young
DIRECTOR: Ed Mironiuk, Kris Tercek
NARRATOR: B. D. Wong
MUSIC: Ernest Troost
TYPE: Iconographic

Open Wide: Tooth School Inside
AUTHOR: Laurie Keller
ILLUSTRATOR: Laurie Keller
DIRECTOR: Daniel Ivanick
ANIMATOR: Daniel Ivanick
NARRATOR: Michael McKean, Stephanie J. Block, & others
MUSIC: Scotty Huff, Robert Reynolds
TYPE: Animated
AWARDS: Honorable Mention, Columbus International Film Festival; Best Titles List, Capitol Choices

Reading to Your Bunny
AUTHOR: Rosemary Wells
ILLUSTRATOR: Rosemary Wells
DIRECTOR: Michael Sporn
ANIMATOR: Michael Sporn
NARRATOR: Diana Canova, Joey Stack, David deVries, Rosemary Wells, & others
MUSIC: John Jennings, Mary Chapin Carpenter (vocals)
TYPE: Animated

That New Animal
AUTHOR: Emily Jenkins
ILLUSTRATOR: Pierre Pratt
DIRECTOR: Paul R. Gagne, Melissa Reilly
NARRATOR: Emily Jenkins
MUSIC: Scotty Huff, Robert Reynolds
TYPE: Iconographic
AWARDS: Notable Video, ALA; Booklist Editor's Choice Film; Bronze Plaque, Columbus International Film Festival

2007

A Very Brave Witch
AUTHOR: Alison McGhee
ILLUSTRATOR: Harry Bliss
DIRECTOR: Virginia Wilkos
ANIMATOR: Virginia Wilkos
NARRATOR: Elle Fanning
MUSIC: David Mansfield
TYPE: Animated
AWARDS: Notable Video, ALA; Platinum Remi, WorldFest-Houston International Film Festival

Dooby Dooby Moo
AUTHOR: Doreen Cronin
ILLUSTRATOR: Betsy Lewin
DIRECTOR: Maciek Albrecht & MaGiK Studio
ANIMATOR: Maciek Albrecht & MaGiK Studio
NARRATOR: Randy Travis
MUSIC: Scotty Huff, Robert Reynolds
TYPE: Animated
AWARDS: Notable Video, ALA

Giraffes Can't Dance
AUTHOR: Giles Andreae
ILLUSTRATOR: Guy Parker-Rees
DIRECTOR: Bryan Cox
ANIMATOR: DMA Animation
NARRATOR: Billy Dee Williams
MUSIC: David Mansfield
TYPE: Animated
AWARDS: Gold Remi, WorldFest-Houston International Film Festival

How Do Dinosaurs Eat Their Food?
AUTHOR: Jane Yolen
ILLUSTRATOR: Mark Teague
DIRECTOR: Maciek Albrecht & MaGiK Studio
ANIMATOR: Maciek Albrecht & MaGiK Studio
NARRATOR: Jane Yolen

MUSIC: Jon Carroll
TYPE: Animated

John, Paul, George, and Ben
AUTHOR: Lane Smith
ILLUSTRATOR: Lane Smith
DIRECTOR: Maciek Albrecht & MaGiK Studio
ANIMATOR: Maciek Albrecht & MaGiK Studio
NARRATOR: James Earl Jones
MUSIC: Scotty Huff, Robert Reynolds
TYPE: Animated
AWARDS: Notable Video, ALA; Short Film Award, Kids First!, Editors' Choice Film, Booklist

Leonardo the Terrible Monster
AUTHOR: Mo Willems
ILLUSTRATOR: Mo Willems
DIRECTOR: Pete List
ANIMATOR: Pete List
NARRATOR: Mo Willems
MUSIC: Joel Goodman
TYPE: Animated
AWARDS: Notable Video, ALA; Short Film Award, Kids First!

Max's Words
AUTHOR: Kate Banks
ILLUSTRATOR: Boris Kulikov
DIRECTOR: Galen Fott, Jerry Hunt
ANIMATOR: Galen Fott
NARRATOR: T. R. Knight
MUSIC: Jerry Hunt
TYPE: Animated
AWARDS: Notable Video, ALA; Platinum Remi, WorldFest-Houston International Film Festival; Short Film Award, Kids First!

My Senator and Me
AUTHOR: Edward M. Kennedy
ILLUSTRATOR: David Diaz
DIRECTOR: Gary McGivney
ANIMATOR: Gary McGivney
NARRATOR: David de Vries, Edward M. Kennedy
MUSIC: Scotty Huff, Robert Reynolds
TYPE : Animated
AWARDS: Bronze Remi, WorldFest-Houston International Film Festival; Short Film Award, Kids First!

Rosa
AUTHOR: Nikki Giovanni
ILLUSTRATOR: Bryan Collier
DIRECTOR: Paul R. Gagne, Melissa Reilly
NARRATOR: Nikki Giovanni
MUSIC: Ernest Troost
TYPE: Iconographic
AWARDS: Notable Video, ALA; Editors' Choice Film, Booklist; Platinum Remi, WorldFest-Houston International Film Festival; Short Film Award, Kids First!

Seven Blind Mice
AUTHOR: Ed Young
ILLUSTRATOR: Ed Young
DIRECTOR: Virginia Wilkos
ANIMATOR: Virginia Wilkos
NARRATOR: B. D. Wong
MUSIC: Ernest Troost
TYPE: Animated
AWARDS: Notable Video, ALA; Silver Remi, WorldFest-Houston International Film Festival

The Fox Went Out on a Chilly Night
AUTHOR: Oral tradition
ILLUSTRATOR: Peter Spier
DIRECTOR: Florence Barrau-Adams
NARRATOR: Alice Peacock (performed)
MUSIC: Alice Peacock (arranged)
TYPE: Iconographic
AWARDS: Honors Award Certificate, American Film Festival

The Journey of the One and Only Declaration of Independence
AUTHOR: Judith St. George
ILLUSTRATOR: Will Hillenbrand
DIRECTOR: Leigh Corra
NARRATOR: Jeff Brooks
MUSIC: Ernest Troost
TYPE: Iconographic
AWARDS: Short Film Award, Kids First!

The Librarian from the Black Lagoon
AUTHOR: Mike Thaler
ILLUSTRATOR: Jared Lee
DIRECTOR: Galen Fott
ANIMATOR: Galen Fott
NARRATOR: Alexander Gould, Diana Canova
MUSIC: Scotty Huff, Robert Reynolds
TYPE: Animated

AWARDS: Silver Remi, WorldFest-Houston International Film Festival; Short Film Award, Kids First!

Wallace's Lists
AUTHOR: Barbara Bottner, Gerald Kruglik
ILLUSTRATOR: Olof Landstrom
DIRECTOR: Alexandr Guriev
ANIMATOR: N. Bobomolova, M. Voskanyants, D. Kupriyanov, V. Magaziner, A. Mazaev, T. Podgorskaya, M. Tiabut, M. Rgova, Vas. Shevtchenko
NARRATOR: Zach Braff
MUSIC: Ernest Troost
TYPE: Animated
AWARDS: Notable Video, ALA; Short Film Award, Kids First!

2008

Art
AUTHOR: Patrick McDonnell
ILLUSTRATOR: Patrick McDonnell
DIRECTOR: Fyodor Dmitriev
ANIMATOR: Darina Shmidt
NARRATOR: Bobby McFerrin
MUSIC: Bobby McFerrin
TYPE: Animated
AWARDS: Notable Video, ALA

Bugs! Bugs! Bugs!
AUTHOR: Bob Barner
ILLUSTRATOR: Bob Barner
DIRECTOR: Gary McGivney
ANIMATOR: Zippitoons
NARRATOR: Crystal Taliefero
MUSIC: Crystal Taliefero
TYPE: Animated
AWARDS: Notable Video, ALA

Diary of a Fly
AUTHOR: Doreen Cronin
ILLUSTRATOR: Harry Bliss
DIRECTOR: Gene Deitch
ANIMATOR: Gene Deitch
NARRATOR: Abigail Breslin
MUSIC: Zdenek Zdenek
TYPE: Animated
AWARDS: Notable Video, ALA

Do Unto Otters
AUTHOR: Laurie Keller
ILLUSTRATOR: Laurie Keller
DIRECTOR: Galen Fott
ANIMATOR: Galen Fott

NARRATOR: Jack Sundrud, David de Vries, Rusty Young, Diana Canova, Galen Fott
MUSIC: Jack Sundrud, Rusty Young
TYPE: Animated
AWARDS: Notable Video, ALA; Short Film Award, Kids First!

Grandfather's Journey
AUTHOR: Allen Say
ILLUSTRATOR: Allen Say
DIRECTOR: Steve Syarto
NARRATOR: B. D. Wong
MUSIC: Ernest Troost
TYPE: Iconographic
AWARDS: Notable Film, ALA

Great Joy
AUTHOR: Kate di Camillo
ILLUSTRATOR: Bagram Ibatoulline
DIRECTOR: Paul R. Gagne, Melissa Reilly
NARRATOR: Jane Curtin
MUSIC: Ernest Troost
TYPE: Iconographic

I'm Dirty!
AUTHOR: Kate McMullan
ILLUSTRATOR: Jim McMullan
DIRECTOR: Galen Fott
ANIMATOR: Galen Fott
NARRATOR: Steve Buscemi
MUSIC: David Mansfield
TYPE: Animated
AWARDS: Notable Video, ALA

Madam President
AUTHOR: Lane Smith
ILLUSTRATOR: Lane Smith
DIRECTOR: Pete List
ANIMATOR: Pete List
NARRATOR: Anna Chiodo
MUSIC: Scotty Huff, Robert Reynolds
TYPE: Animated
AWARDS: Notable Video, ALA

March On! The Day My Brother Martin Changed the World
AUTHOR: Christine King Farris
ILLUSTRATOR: London Ladd
DIRECTOR: Paul R. Gagne, Melissa Reilly
NARRATOR: Lynn Whitfield
MUSIC: Michael Bacon
TYPE: Iconographic
AWARDS: Andrew Carnegie Medal for Excellence in Children's Video; Notable Video, ALA

Otto Runs for President
AUTHOR: Rosemary Wells
ILLUSTRATOR: Rosemary Wells
DIRECTOR: Virginia Wilkos
ANIMATOR: Virginia Wilkos
NARRATOR: Diana Canova
MUSIC: Ernest Troost
TYPE: Animated

The Boy Who Cried Wolf
AUTHOR: B. G. Hennessy
ILLUSTRATOR: Boris Kulikov
DIRECTOR: Konstantin Bronzit
ANIMATOR: Darina Shmidt
NARRATOR: Peter Scolari
MUSIC: John Jennings
TYPE: Animated
AWARDS: Notable Video, ALA

The True Story of the Three Little Pigs
AUTHOR: Jon Scieszka
ILLUSTRATOR: Lane Smith
DIRECTOR: Konstantin Bronzit
ANIMATOR: Alexey Pichuzin
NARRATOR: Paul Giamatti
MUSIC: Chris Thomas King
TYPE: Animated
AWARDS: Notable Video, ALA; Short Film Award, Kids First!

Voyage to the Bunny Planet
AUTHOR: Rosemary Wells
ILLUSTRATOR: Rosemary Wells
DIRECTOR: Gene Deitch
ANIMATOR: Gene Deitch
NARRATOR: Maggie Gyllenhaal
MUSIC: Zdenek Merta
TYPE: Animated

What Do You Do with a Tail Like This?
AUTHOR: Robin Page
ILLUSTRATOR: Steve Jenkins
DIRECTOR: Ed Mironiuk, Kris Tercek
ANIMATOR: Ed Mironiuk, Kris Tercek
NARRATOR: James Naughton
MUSIC: David Mansfield
TYPE: Animated
AWARDS: Notable Video, ALA

2009

Crazy Hair Day
AUTHOR: Barney Saltzberg
ILLUSTRATOR: Barney Saltzberg

DIRECTOR: Virginia Wilkos
ANIMATOR: Virginia Wilkos
NARRATOR: Zach Braff
MUSIC: Barney Saltzberg, Eric Eckstein
TYPE: Animated

Don't Let the Pigeon Drive the Bus!
AUTHOR: Mo Willems
ILLUSTRATOR: Mo Willems
DIRECTOR: Pete List
ANIMATOR: Pete List
NARRATOR: Mo Willems, Jon Scieszka
MUSIC: Pete List
TYPE: Animated

First the Egg
AUTHOR: Laura Vaccaro Seeger
ILLUSTRATOR: Laura Vaccaro Seeger
DIRECTOR: Ed Mironiuk, Kris Tercek
ANIMATOR: Ed Mironiuk, Kris Tercek
NARRATOR: Elle Fanning
MUSIC: Jack Sundrud, Rusty Young
TYPE: Animated

Fletcher and the Falling Leaves
AUTHOR: Julia Rawlinson
ILLUSTRATOR: Tiphanie Beeke
DIRECTOR: Ed Mironiuk, Kris Tercek
ANIMATOR: Ed Mironiuk, Kris Tercek
NARRATOR: Katherine Kellgren
MUSIC: John Jennings
TYPE: Animated

Getting to Know Mo Willems
DIRECTOR: Paul R. Gagne, Melissa Reilly
TYPE: Live-action

Henry's Freedom Box
AUTHOR: Ellen Levine
ILLUSTRATOR: Kadir Nelson
DIRECTOR: Paul R. Gagne, Melissa Reilly
NARRATOR: Jerry Dixon
MUSIC: David Mansfield
TYPE: Iconographic

Knuffle Bunny Too
AUTHOR: Mo Willems
ILLUSTRATOR: Mo Willems
DIRECTOR: Karen Villarreal
ANIMATOR: Karen Villarreal
NARRATOR: Mo Willems, Trixie Willems
MUSIC: Scotty Huff, Robert Reynolds
TYPE: Animated

Lincoln and Douglass
AUTHOR: Nikki Giovanni

ILLUSTRATOR: Bryan Collier
DIRECTOR: Paul R. Gagne, Melissa Reilly
NARRATOR: Danny Glover
MUSIC: Ernest Troost
TYPE: Iconographic

Los Gatos Black on Halloween
AUTHOR: Marisa Montes
ILLUSTRATOR: Yuyi Morales
DIRECTOR: Ed Mironiuk, Kris Tercek
ANIMATOR: Ed Mironiuk, Kris Tercek
NARRATOR: Maria Conchita Alonso
MUSIC: Raul Malo
TYPE: Animated

Math Curse
AUTHOR: Jon Scieszka
ILLUSTRATOR: Lane Smith
DIRECTOR: Daniel Ivanick
ANIMATOR: Daniel Ivanick
NARRATOR: Nancy Wu
MUSIC: Scotty Huff, Robert Reynolds
TYPE: Animated

That Book Woman
AUTHOR: Heather Henson
ILLUSTRATOR: David Small
DIRECTOR: Paul R. Gagne, Melissa Reilly
NARRATOR: not yet assigned
MUSIC: Jack Sundrud, Rusty Young
TYPE: Iconographic

The Dinosaurs of Waterhouse Hawkins
AUTHOR: Barbara Kerley
ILLUSTRATOR: Brian Selznick
DIRECTOR: Paul R. Gagne
NARRATOR: Jonathan Pryce
MUSIC: not yet assigned
TYPE: Iconographic

The Scrambled States of America Talent Show
AUTHOR: Laurie Keller
ILLUSTRATOR: Laurie Keller
DIRECTOR: Galen Fott
ANIMATOR: Galen Fott
NARRATOR: Jon Carroll, Diana Canova, David de Vries, Galen Fott, & others
MUSIC: Scotty Huff, Robert Reynolds
TYPE: Animated

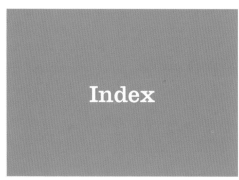

Index

T. UNGERER

Tomi Ungerer's proposed design for a Weston
Woods logo, ca. late 1970s, early 1980s.